Land Use Conflicts

Herman L. Boschken

Land Use Conflicts

Organizational Design and Resource Management

University of Illinois Press

Urbana Chicago London

This book is printed on acid-free paper.

Library of Congress Cataloging in Publication Data

Boschken, Herman L.
   Land Use Conflicts

   Bibliography: p.
   Includes index.
   1. Land use — Government policy — United States.
2. Natural resources — Government policy — United
States.   3. Regional planning — Government policy —
United States. I. Title.
HD205 1982.B67   333.7′15′0973   81-7443
ISBN 0-252-00901-0   AACR2

To my parents, Herman and Lutha

Acknowledgments

The idea for this study occurred to me in 1975. For some time I had been interested in how administrative structure affected the behavior of managers in both public and private organizations. At that point I had just completed a book on corporate power in urban development, which examined a large-scale corporation and the consequences of monopolistic behavior on policy and customers. Teaching management classes in a school of business always made the issues of monopoly behavior and competitive markets fertile topics of discussion. It seemed to me, however, that public organizations were subject to similar kinds of issues. So the conception of this book has at its roots a focus on the public sector with the intent of examining similar behavior patterns. A central theme is that public organizations are part of the allocation process and therefore affect markets and the production of goods and services. Land use is of particular relevance here because of the seminal relationship of land use control to the utilization of natural resources.

Carrying out such a study was a complex task involving the cooperation, patience, and hard work of a number of people. In the gathering of data, I am indebted to the research assistance of Janel Egman, Nancy Wilson, and Patricia Vance. In acquiring access to data, I am indebted to numerous people in the Forest Service, Park Service, California Coastal Zone Conservation Commission, San Diego Gas and Electric, Rand Corporation, Harstad and Associates of Seattle, Boise Cascade, and Kitsap County. Special gratitude is expressed to Irene Boschken and Artimese Porter for manuscript typing, and to James O'Malley for graphics and art work. Partial funding of the study by the Washington Sea Grant Program and the San Diego State Foundation is also acknowledged.

Finally, I am especially indebted to my colleagues, who have taken valuable time in reviewing the original draft: Robert Bish at the University of Victoria, Lawrence Susskind at MIT, Elinor Ostrom at Indiana,

Lowdon Wingo at the University of Southern California, Grant Mc-Connell at the University of California in Santa Cruz, Jens Sorensen at the University of California in San Diego, Elmer Keen at San Diego State, and Robert Warren at the University of Delaware. Their insights and suggestions are greatly appreciated.

Contents

Illustrations

Part I | Introduction

CHAPTER 1

Political Spheres and the Competition for Land

THE LAST thirty years have seen much urban expansion and substantial change in the complexity of metropolitan processes. This is visible in many ways, but especially in land price increases, greater competition among uses, and renewed emphasis on land use planning. Although land allocation problems exist in all areas, this condition is particularly acute in the urban periphery where competition includes not only urban industrial and development interests but pastoral, recreational, and natural resource interests as well. The competition does not revolve merely around traditional property rights and economic considerations. Instead, a "new land ethic" of environmental interest suggests "that there is an element of livability in the development of land . . . and that this livability element can, if need be, overrule the economic element" (Younger, 1973). As a result, land use control has emerged as a central political issue in many areas of the United States.

The process of land allocation involves a system of multiple mechanisms, engaging both market forces and the political and administrative actions of government. The market, of course, has been the central element in the process, and the configuration of land use occurs principally through the aggregation of individual locational choices (Bish and Nourse, 1975; Edel and Rothenberg, 1972; Barlowe, 1972; Hoover, 1948). The criterion for choice results from prioritizing land use according to utilitarian value. "Land resources are at their highest and best use when they are used in such a manner as to provide the optimum return to their operators or to society" (Barlowe, 1972, pp. 14-15). This "highest and best use" doctrine is important economically, but it is also reinforced culturally by Jeffersonian thought (Jefferson,

This chapter appeared in a slightly different version under the title "Public Control of Land Use: Are Existing Administrative Structures Appropriate?" *Public Administration Review* 37, no. 5 (1977): 495-504.

1964) and the pre-industrial circumstance of the frontier (Weinberg, 1935, ch. 3). Consequently, the market is relied upon heavily as both the most efficient and most legitimate mechanism.

Nevertheless, the market is not without its dysfunctions, and a public decision-making role has been used to direct, alter, and sometimes supersede the price mechanism. Although state and federal governments own about a third of all land in America (mostly nonurban parks and forests), authority and control over general land use (public and private) traditionally have been vested in local governments: towns, cities, and counties. These public agencies have shaped the character of urban growth through zoning ordinances, use permits, general land use plans, and project evaluations (Mandelker, 1971; Babcock, 1966). Such methods have sought to follow a flat-plane grid system that separates a limited number of land use categories so as to provide a well-ordered, comprehensive physical pattern. Outside the management of parks and forests, the role of state and national government until recently has been to improve the capacity of local authorities by providing fiscal incentives and technical assistance.

These instruments for public control of land, especially zoning ordinances, are not of recent origin and are certainly not unique to American society (Beuscher, 1954, ch. 1). The comprehensive structure of methods employed presently, however, stems from the Progressive era and the desire to eliminate corruption in government and promote orderly professional administration of the public interest (Scott, 1969, ch. 1). State enabling legislation, giving local government authority over land use, became widespread during the 1920s and was especially aided by the federal government. Under the direction of Commerce Secretary Herbert Hoover, the Federal Standard State Zoning Enabling Act was issued in 1924, a model upon which most state land use control instruments are still based (National Commission on Urban Problems, 1968, p. 201). The essential purpose of public land use control has been threefold: to maintain orderly development by separating uses physically; to protect property values by restricting obnoxious activities; and to provide public land for such private development as urban renewal, resource extraction, and recreational concessions (Reilly, 1973; Delafons, 1969; Altshuler, 1965; Barlowe, 1972, ch. 17).

As illustrated by legislative activity and much judicial controversy, renewed interest in control processes has centered around zoning administration and environmental management. Such heavy reliance on strengthening existing controls has precipitated a number of constitutional issues ranging from down zoning and the "taking" issue (Bosselman, Callies, and Banta, 1973; Winters, 1973); to no-growth zoning like the Petaluma Plan and its implications for the right to "travel" (*Construction Industry Association of Sonoma County v. City of Petaluma*, 1975); to environmentally sensitive zoning and legal "standing" (Stone, 1974). In addition, a number of unique organizational and procedural experiments have arisen (Bosselman and Callies, 1971; Healy, 1976; Prisbylla, 1977). Some of these relate to a debate started by the American Law Institute's Revised Model State Land Use Code (1974), which centers on appropriate levels of government control. Renewed public interest has also helped allocate a more direct role to the federal government in the form of long-term agency involvement, some incremental attempts at land use planning, and the National Environmental Policy Act of 1969 (Anderson, 1973; Reilly, 1973). However, with this trend toward more complex zoning administration and a consolidation of power in larger bureaucracies, a number of questions have emerged. If past zoning measures have proven insufficient for present circumstances, will more zoning procedures mitigate the problem? Do the traditional purposes of zoning correspond to the emerging land use issues? Do the size and structure of government affect the outcome of public land use decisions? What role do values play in the public control of land use allocation?

Stages of Urban Growth

Before one can address these general concerns, some understanding of the nature and complexity of existing urban forces should be outlined. Of central importance is the configuration of urban growth and its relationship to population characteristics and natural resources. The past assumption has been that "with increasing population growth and the increasing material requirements of modern life, the area needs of almost every type of land use are bound to increase" (Barlowe, 1972, p. 85). The compounding problem in such an assertion, however, is that the context of these dynamics has become highly uncertain and the relationship between diverse interests and land resources ambiguous.

This is particularly evidenced in the fact that land use issues do not stem from land scarcity *per se*. About 90 percent of the population lives in metropolitan areas (SMSAs) that constitute only about 35 percent of the land. Nor can the essential issues be explained in terms of territorial propinquity either. Those issues that deal with air and water quality, resource extraction, energy use, transportation, industrial production, and leisure activities have in the past been associated with migration toward and concentration of territorially bounded and finite urban cores. This association has diminished. For example, figures for urban growth indicate that absolute increases in population density have decreased measurably since the pre–World War II years. Derived from U.S. Census data, the average decade rate of increase in population density was 22 percent between 1880 and 1940 but only 13.5 percent between 1940 and 1970. Likewise, the "percent urban" population changed at an average decade rate of 14 percent between 1880 and 1940, and then dropped off to 4.25 percent from 1940 to 1970 (U.S. Department of Commerce, 1970). What these figures suggest is that while land use issues in the postwar period have reached their greatest visibility since the 1920s, the frequently attributed causes of conflict among competing demands have diminished significantly from prewar years.

This anomalous condition raises the possibility that urbanization has changed from the prewar territorial image to something that defies physical boundedness and conventional behavioral assumptions. To see this, one may distinguish two stages of growth, with the Depression and the start of World War II marking the transition. The first stage is the period of rural to urban migration, while the second is the postwar period involving the spillover of urban culture into an enlarged regional setting.

Shaped primarily by technologies of the American Industrial Revolution and European migration, the first stage subsumes both the Populist and the Progressive eras in America. The character of city life reflected a dualistic perspective with the provincial purity of rural life at one extreme, and rational cosmopolitan existence matched with ethnic territories at the other. Social thought was replete with cultural and physical boundaries between "just plain folk" and the "gatekeepers of mass society" (Vidich and Bensman, 1968). This dualism was further linked to governmental reform, which stated that the dichotomy "should be clearly expressed in the physical and spatial form of the city, that orderliness depends upon boundedness, and that boundaries are in some way barriers" (Webber, 1963, p. 34).

From this emerged the territorial model of urban activity and goverance. The referent assumptions of the model were that people behaved with respect to physical identity and cost gradients; therefore, municipalities of any size existed in finite space. Virtually all of the urbanized population resided within the city limits, with the hinterland beyond. Limited by walking distance or early forms of mass transit, most people's interests, including jobs, businesses, social and religious associations, and recreation, were geographically ascribed and contiguous. Even those who moved out of the urban center were limited to a contiguous suburban ring and were either consolidated into the core city or incorporated into suburban municipalities (Timms, 1971; Glaab and Brown, 1967; Bish and Nourse, 1975, ch. 2). Unwanted actors or messages from the "outside" were excluded on the basis of legal residency and through censorship. The governance process, including jurisdictions and administrative methods, mirrored territorial interests, so that most large cities could be accurately described as "territorial-bounded governmental systems" (Warren and Weschler, 1972, p. 11). In short, people behaved as if they lived in "island communities" that were socially and politically protected by impermeable walls.

The first stage of urban growth, then, is perhaps best analyzed as a period of intensive expansion within well-defined boundaries. Although much annexation took place incrementally, expansion occurred around a center-peripheral dependency as seen in the development of cities like Boston, New York, Chicago, and San Francisco. By contrast, this confinement gave way in the late 1930s to the emergence of urban forces flowing throughout an extended metropolitan area and causing a shift in complexity to a regionwide interdependence among interests, problems, and activities. Suburbanization, which started for most cities at various times prior to World War II, became widespread in unincorporated rural areas and was simultaneously less dependent on any single urban center. Moreover, with an increasing dispersion of persons and activities, the distinction between urban and rural was reduced.

Under these circumstances, a regional core is not filled with activity before peripheral areas are influenced by urban processes. Instead, regionwide land use may occur from many vector influences, and activity in peripheral areas will result from multiple demands of the amorphous region as a whole. As seen in price differentials occurring from conversion of rural farm lands to urban industrial/residential uses (Economic Research Service, 1971), the traditional relationships between contiguous land and human activity are greatly diminished. Suspension of clear center-periphery relationships blurs the conical image of economic values historically involving intense activity at the region's center with rapid tapering off toward the periphery.

The forces attributable to dispersion may be explained in the context of higher resource availability and lower mobility and communication costs. For most households, resources in the form of higher family incomes, spreading educational opportunities, and more leisure time advanced much more rapidly in the 1950s, 1960s, and 1970s than before. Declining activity costs (except for energy) also contributed to the enlarged regional interests. For corporations previously limited by the cost advantages of proximity, this new mobility factor provided the means to produce and distribute goods and work out management and product plans on an extra-regional scale. For individuals, innovations in communications provided the ability to maintain close relationships with those separated by distance. Furthermore, penetration of national and regional network media, especially television, enlarged the knowledge of distant and diverse opportunities for greater numbers at low cost. Reinforcing all of this is the continued impact of transportation technology, especially the urban and interurban freeway system. Among other things, the high-speed network augments an unprecedented degree of freedom in moving among widely separated establishments in conducting affairs.

Some might argue that more current forces may mitigate all this. Since 1975 some population trends have changed, growth patterns have shifted somewhat, central city revitalization looks like a possibility, energy costs may have some long-term impact on growth patterns, and housing costs have skyrocketed. Many of these, however, have a smaller effect on where to live and what interests to pursue than on what form of housing and what car to buy. For example, the "energy crisis" of the 1970s did not seem to slow second-stage trends except during the few months when people were stunned by the unavailability of gas. Even with gas prices quadrupling, demand remains essentially inelastic and people continue to egress from metropolitan areas. Beyond this, adaptation to smaller cars and use of more efficient engines will probably tend to partially mitigate rising fuel costs in the future. Likewise, mass transit probably won't have much *reversal* effect because new modes will need to be created around the already set regional patterns.

With greater resources and lower costs, individuals have the ability to substitute mobility for propinquity and have used this opportunity to develop interests beyond their immediate geographical associations.[1] As a result, individuals are less likely to identify with the fate of geographical communities *per se* and more with activities that are closest to their interests: ". . . the network of interdependence among various groups [is] becoming functionally intricate and spatially widespread" (Webber, 1963, p. 24). Such a community, then, may be composed of different sorts of people who are distributed among distinct settlements but who develop bonds around shared and specific interests.

Furthermore, while order and boundedness may be less visible in terms of spatial propinquity and physical demarcations, the patterns of human activities may be seen in a psychic context where diverse and dispersed locations are linked together in a network of interests (Orleans, 1973; Warren and Weschler, 1972). People choose different places for multiple reasons and not because of density gradients and work commutes alone. This is at least partially evidenced in the behavior of such groups as environmentalists and civil rights activists. Environmentalists, who have acute interests in the urban periphery,

---

[1]On the surface, this frequently appears as the consummation of mass society and homogeneous interests. In fact, the loss of geographical distinctions and the amalgamation of rural and urban societies have been associated with a movement toward faceless, "other directed" urban sprawl and subsequent cultural decline (Wurster, 1963; Jacobs, 1961). Such views, however, have their origin in the sanctity of boundedness and discrete physical order. If this criterion is relaxed, mobility and a broader awareness of opportunities promise not conformity but the possibility of more diverse activities and a wider scope of interests. Therefore, an equally plausible perspective on urban dispersion is that it represents a maze or mosaic of diverse subcultures (Webber, 1963; Friedmann and Miller, 1965). The fact that this is not visible in bounded territory does not necessarily yield a faceless mass society except perhaps to those viewing it at its most aggregate level. On the contrary, the associations to which individuals belong may no longer be communities of place but communities of varied interest.

tend to define a "mental space" concerning the quality of life on an ecological significance scale. Consequently, the efforts to preserve a wilderness area from resort development, save fishing by blocking dam construction, and stall an atomic reactor utility plant along an isolated seacost may all be within the operating scope of a community of individuals, even though the activities and actors are spatially separated.

This second stage of urban growth raises the problem of how to conceptualize and deal with complex forces and relationships. The blurring territorial model appears to be outmoded for administrative purposes because it does not adequately account for the patterns, modes, and connecting flows of people, information, and commodities that transcend boundaries and territorial subsystems. Most proposals of new models such as the "urban field" concept (Friedmann and Miller, 1965) are too ambiguous to have much empirical or practical value. Activity or transaction analysis holds some interesting possibilities but is incomplete as a model of urban processes. What we are left with is the unsettling notion that a set of processes and behaviors exists as a dynamic system of overlapping activity modes constructed at a micro level by people living in certain places and having many interests for many different reasons. Some of these modes may have a high degree of propinquity for some lifestyles or issues, while others may appear as physically disassociated parts connected only by transportation routes or communication networks. Their numerous points of overlap, however, generate degrees of complexity and conflict not usually recognized in conventional city terms of density and commuting times.

A Problem of Governance and Administration

The above discussion does not do away with the study of cities, but it does raise some concern about existing forms of governance and administration, especially with regard to the questions of adequate zoning, administrative structure, and values. By transcending territorial boundaries and forming amorphous patterns and impacts, the ingredients of the second stage have had the effect of placing political processes on a plane that is out of reach of conventional constructs. This alludes to a significant mismatch between physical and political boundaries, as well as great differences between the cognition and expectations of citizens and their professional civil servants. In the competition for land, overlapping political infrastructures and transterritorial actors consequently become more problematic. More people have a stake in the facilities, services, and land use profile of areas they regularly visit but have no primary residence in. Technical information about public needs, sources and impacts of pollution, and environmental carrying capacity is more difficult to gather and comprehend. In short, with territorially based governmental structures, public administrators and planners are not well equipped to handle complex physical influences and "constituents" from outside their jurisdictions.

To overcome the threat of public decisions "without representation," many affected parties have insisted on the same rights as legal residents in jurisdictions where they have no residential standing. The experience is especially common in periphery areas where small nonmetropolitan communities have had their political systems "swamped" by external actors who demand or induce certain outcomes. For example, urban-based environmental groups, who operate in a political space that has little to do with formal municipal boundaries, have become active and skilled in overturning public decisions of hinterland towns that would foster economic development. Intrusion of urban migrants into rural towns that do *not* want growth happens as well. In large cities public authorities have been required to negotiate land use changes with nonresident regional and national alliances such as construction unions, environmentalists, and minority groups. The new order of *interdependent* relationships has precipitated this different basis for political involvement, conflict, and legal standing that territorially oriented government had difficulty relating to. The discontinuity lies in the fact that while metropolitan jurisdictions view processes through spatial form (i.e., size, shape, and density), many political forces act without association to spatial consistency. Thus solutions tend to ignore discontinuity and advocate larger-scale governmental forms when large-scale impacts are involved (National Commission on Urban Problems, 1968, pp. 24, 223, 326; Reilly, 1973; Heller, 1971; Office of Planning and Research, 1977).

Since most land use jurisdictions exist at the local level, the target of concern has been the ability of local government to deal with issues and actors that permeate its boundaries. "At the heart of this ferment is recognition that states must have the responsibility to control land-use decisions that affect the interests of people beyond local boundaries if critical environmental lands are to be protected and if development needed by a regional population is not to be blocked by local governments" (Reilly, 1973, p. 15).

The sanctity of local discretion is based on the assumptions of abundant land, low regional interdependence, and local segmented demands for land. Where these assumptions are reversed and an amorphous urban setting is apparent, three central concerns exist. First, local government is seen as too small to efficiently respond to or gain compliance from a variety of processes and institutions that are organized on a regional or national scale. This is reinforced by the emergence of environmental quality as a national issue and the belief that local government by itself cannot make decisions that internalize the ecological base of an interdependent region.

A second concern is with parochial local interests versus regional development needs. With unilateral control by local governments in an interdependent region, the coordination of development and change on a regional scale may be partially frustrated. This is the major concern, for example, with such concepts as the Petaluma and Ramapoo plans, which unilaterally limit growth within a local jurisdiction. Without a regional scope, accommodation of complex overlapping demands is potentially jeopardized.

The third concern is with the inability of local government to adequately evaluate impacts and effectively represent interests when dealing with large corporations that operate on an extra-regional scale. Such firms usually have the financial capacity to construct a variety of projects simultaneously and have the flexibility to overshadow the local review process.

The most often cited solutions to these inadequacies spring from the traditional reform movement and involve the consolidation and shifting upward of authorities usually into a *single* "streamlined" bureaucracy or commission at the state or national level (Reilly, 1973; Heller, 1971; Committee for Economic Development, 1966). Some states like Hawaii and Oregon already have centralized land use control at the statewide level. With the unitary professional bureaucracy or commission, the assumption is that the public interest is best achieved for large impacts with comprehensive and consolidated authority. The problems of home rule are viewed as mitigated by scale in that "increased scale brings significantly greater opportunity to create quality, as well as some incentive to do so" (Reilly, 1973, p. 254). The shifting of control to larger units provides the boundary of authority suitable for gaining compliance among various influences and for making more inclusive plans. Likewise, the greater autonomy of a single authority provides a more conducive atmosphere for a coordination of experts to more rationally plan for growth and deal with giant corporations.

The bureaucratic solution, however, is tantamount to saying that efficiency and effectiveness are a function of monopoly, in contrast to much of what is known about market economics. Moreover, in virtually every land use issue some value choices transcend objective analysis and professional judgment made by a single hierarchy. Bureaucratic values, formed from professional norms and ideological heritage, are seldom made explicit in the decision-making process. Affected parties, overwhelmed by the power and technical language of bureaucratic professionals, frequently are incapable of relating their legitimate interests and of testing unstated values. Thus, with practically no limit to the number of factors pertinent to land use decision making nor guides to rank importance, the weakness in the approach is that maximum discretion rests upon the single comprehensive bureaucracy or commission.

As a result, critics contend that the professional bureaucracy only works satisfactorily under conditions where proposals of change carry a high degree of consensus among affected interests and where primarily routine decisions are required. Where unique decisions are necessary or where the scale of a proposal affects multiple interests arrayed over a geographically discontinuous area, the unitary bureaucracy may not have the means to appropriately perceive and internalize constituent needs and desires. This is especially acute in land use control, where the roles of planning and zoning activities are largely those of anticipating land use development and making adequate provision for all acceptable uses. The overlapping flows and subsequent conflicts of regionwide interdependencies are not conducive to stable and predictable patterns of low uncertainty needed for standardized bureaucratic mechanisms to work properly (National Commission on Urban Problems, 1968, p. 224; Bolan, 1967, p. 234). The unitary authority consequently carries a higher risk of neglecting pertinent technical considerations and of underrepresenting constituents within its broad jurisdiction.

An alternative to bureaucratic control of land use is an intergovernmental structure of specialized jursidictions. Although historically quite old, this pattern has been less visible than the reform bureaucracy. It has sometimes been identified as a more open system of "concurrent government," but it does not exclude bureaucracies or regulatory commissions as part of the configuration (Ostrom, 1973; Boschken, 1976, 1982). In matching governmental jurisdiction to a societal setting, it utilizes an interdependent but nonhierarchical network of interest- and knowledge-specific agencies, local government, and partisan inputs. Not to be confused with the center-periphery model represented as a hierarchy of governmental levels, this policentric system is a coordination of overlapping jurisdictions based on individual agencies having specialized expertise and certification authority. Mixes of these agencies are consequently drawn together around specific land use proposals or issues as interdependent decision-making units. The overall decision process emphasizes "mutual adjustment" where agencies negotiate according to their mandates for benefits and accept the costs of accommodation. Such trade-off processes tend to mitigate error and monopoly behavior, since reducing adverse effects on parties is the basis for consensus among diverse interests.

This nonhierarchical approach incurs a different set of costs from the unitary hierarchy. Where the latter runs the risk of underrepresentation, judgmental error, and oversight, concurrent government has the problem of more costly forms of integrating different agency perspectives and mandates. Nevertheless, the incentive for such a system to coordinate and operate efficiently and effectively stems from the interdepency of jurisdictions and the power of reciprocal review among participating agencies. With incomplete authority over any proposal or issue, individual agencies have a need for on-going and predictable intergovernmental relations in order to carry out their individual statutory responsibilities. To ignore or circumvent other network jurisdictions creates administrative dysfunctions detrimental to all in the long run and usually provides some motivation to cooperate. Speaking of the "consequences of conjoint action," Dewey says, "Individuals still do the thinking, desiring and purposing, but *what* they think of is the consequences of their behavior upon that of others and that of others upon themselves" (1927, p. 24). Cases of this nonhierarchical approach in land use are becoming more widespread as the need forces agencies into a more cooperative open system (Bosselman and Callies, 1971; Healy, 1976; Bish *et al.*, 1975; Scott, 1975).

The Analytical Frame

The above impressions point to the reality that any discussion of land use control revolves around competing administrative paradigms. It is by now also evident that zoning and environmental management are problems partially subsumed under the overall question of appropriate patterns of governmental structure and levels of authority. The thesis drawn here is that no single set of strategies or structure can guarantee appropriate policies or decisions for all values that are affected by land use policy. Because of the broad spectrum of interests involved in any major land use issue, there are also no *cost-free* alternatives. The problem, therefore, is not to seek out a "one best way" but, instead, to devise decision processes that are both efficient in providing desired public output and effective in achieving fair outcomes for affected parties.

The fairness question is especially crucial because all affected interests are not satisfied by maximizing social welfare at large. Moreover, different patterns of jurisdictional power will affect both political access and who is included in the majority and minority on different issues, thus conditioning the distribution of costs and benefits. Consequently, the function and role of the political process should have less to do with allocating and separating land uses (this is the market function), and more to do with handling market allocation inadequacies. Because of the variety of potential impacts external to the market, this may require not only the use of bureaucratic rules and procedures but also an enlarged role for intergovernmental deliberation and negotiation.

In real life the administrative alternatives and their associated problems appear to revolve around how the administrative patterns emerge to meet land use situations confronted by government. Some types of organizational arrangements seem to work better than others, but the variability of successful outcomes greatly obscures gross generalizations. Nevertheless, if the land use setting is assumed to be predictable or "known," the tendency is to advocate a consolidated hierarchy where public participation may be the primary means of reality testing. On the other hand, if circumstances appear clouded by uncertainty and competing views, the tendency is to advocate a more policentric administrative structure of deliberation.

The bulk of this chapter has contended that land use control is characterized predominantly by a situation of diverse actors, interests, and resources and high levels of information uncertainty. Moreover, the larger and more far-reaching the issues are for any case, the more complex the decisional task is likely to be. Hence the administrative problems in land use are probably not ones of scale *per se*, but ones of interdependence among political access, decisional process, and representation, where administrative structure becomes a critical determinant of outcomes.

By administrative structure, the intention is not to leave out the roles of legislatures and courts. Courts in particular have been instrumental in land use control over the last twenty years through their federalist role of judicial review. Although most would argue that courts were not meant to be a primary source of administrative concurrence, judicial scrutiny is supposed to provide a check on the *primary* actors of administrative decision making (Vose, 1966). Both because of the political implications (Cramton and Boyer, 1972) and because of the impairment of the court's "ability to perform more traditional judicial functions" (*Yale Law Journal*, 1960, p. 910), many have urged caution against too ready acceptance of the courts as an alternative to the agencies. Moreover, a fundamental issue exists as to whether the courts have the necessary expertise to engage in the review of highly complex considerations. According to some, the judiciary does not have "the technical competency or institutional capacity to deal with broad, relatively undefined environmental problems" (Cramton and Boyer, 1972, p. 413). Many suggest the courts should therefore maintain their more limited role of reviewing the *legality* of administrative procedures. In that role the judiciary becomes a coercive incentive which encourages agencies to seek decisions that accommodate divergent interests. "Bargaining for agreement with active opponents is often perceived as less costly than judicial proceedings and the chance of losing a [winner-take-all] case" (Bish *et al.*, 1975, p. 103).

One of the primary reasons for increased legal activity in land use and natural resource administration is the passage in 1969 of the National Environmental Policy Act (NEPA). Among other mandates, the act requires the use of environmental impact statements, an instrument that many states have adopted as well. Although NEPA and its state counter-parts change some agency procedural requirements, they neither imply impartiality nor require concurrent authority in making decisions. In one of the first tests of NEPA the federal court said of the EIS that "although obviously not as fair and impartial and objective as if it had been compiled by a disinterested third person, it meets the full disclosure requirements of NEPA ..." (*EDF v. Corps of Engineers*, 1972). As a result, some have suggested that instead of opening up the deliberation process, NEPA may reinforce existing autonomy of agen-cies (Ferguson and Bryson, 1972, pp. 511-12; Dolgin and Guilbert, 1974, pp. 246-47). The ultimate impact, therefore, could be negative in that the EIS is a nonhearing substitute for public participation which may also discourage recriprocal review among agencies and place more direct reliance on the judicial review process (Winters, 1973; Anderson, 1973). Disagreement exists over this conclusion (Andrews, 1976), thus making NEPA's impact an important variable to deal with in assessing administrative patterns in land use control.

A way of examining the above administrative alternatives and their consequences is to view them in the context of three categories of analyt-ical issues. The first is an aggregate frame where the *fit* between admin-istrative *structure* and the land use *setting* may be related. Settings may range widely in complexity, consisting of both simple predictable variables and highly interdependent factors of uncertain consistency. In this study, where large-scale land use changes are concerned, the design of administrative structure is a key determinant of organizational pro-cess and its consequences. Given similar settings, consequences in one case will vary from another when administrative patterns are different. Hence structure may connote policy makers' cognitions of what consti-tutes their tasks, the process by which public interests are pursued, assumptions about administrative politics, and how power is distrib-uted intra- and interorganizationally. To frame the analysis of this ag-gregate set of relationships, the following questions are posed:

1. What are the variable characteristics in the land use setting and what levels of complexity do they create for policy formulation and con-trol?

2. Does the pattern of administrative control in particular land use controversies correspond to the degree of complexity and uncertainty of the setting? How?

3. What are the consequences of using different mechanisms of inter-governmental coordination? Do the courts have a coordination role for intergovernmental relations?

4. What role does public participation have in supplementing ad-ministrative structure?

5. In assessing the fit between setting and structure, what trade-offs

are made regarding efficiency and administrative ease on the one hand
and consideration of adverse effects on the other?

A second and more micro level of analysis deals with the impact of administrative behavior on the representation of interests. Suggesting that
behavior is related to organization structure, the focus is on how societal
interests and values become translated into public policy. In this process, decision rules act as visible indicators of how structure affects behavior. They determine how the "publics" are identified, and they impart procedural strategies related to legal, political, and cultural
norms. Hence, in guiding the deliberation process, decision rules will
affect who is represented in policy making and how costs and benefits
are allocated. To frame the analysis in this set of considerations, the
following questions are posed:

1. What specific decision rules can be observed in land use control
cases?

2. Regarding consequences, what relationship exists between decision rules and whose values are accommodated?

3. What are the relationships between decision rules and the policy
process? Does focus on an at-large "public interest" or inputs by affected
parties provide clearer and more appropriate perceptions of public need
in situations of conflict? Do different decision rules promote different
strategies in the representation of public issues?

4. How important are organizational values relative to public needs
in making professional judgments? Under what conditions does system
maintenance override due process and proper representation of interests?

5. In terms of public accountability, who knows best in making policy judgments where value conflicts are at issue? What role do NEPA
and the courts play in making representative public policy?

The third category of issues is also at a micro level, but deals more
with the nature and impacts of expertise. Values play an essential role
here, but focus is on how they affect inquiry and the search for and use
of information. Factors here include the role of interest groups in providing information, how factual data are treated by administrative experts, and how information is translated into the deliberation over
alternatives. Of real concern is the usefulness of experts in perceiving
and mitigating potential external effects in land use allocation. Innovative solutions in design and problem mitigation may be partly a function
of what role experts play in public policy analysis and the kind of authority granted them in deliberations. To frame the analysis in this set of
considerations, the following questions are posed:

1. What administrative and other factors tend to cause differences in
the gathering and use of information by public organizations? Is the in-

centive to seek accurate and appropriate information related to the structure of administration?

2. What sorts of deliberation procedures, sources of information, and levels of expertise are necessary in identifying environmental impacts, perceiving errors, and mitigating oversight?

3. What administrative characteristics tend to promote innovation? Are the alternative patterns of administration equally capable of perceptive thinking, reflective learning, and adjustment?

In addition to these categories of questions, a number of lesser or subsidiary issues may also be relevant in individual cases.

As these sets of questions suggest, the central focus of the study is not on controversy *per se* but on the organizational context and administrative politics of large-scale government. To the extent that administrative structure poses certain imperatives on the organizational process and behavior, the study suggests a causal chain that starts with structural arrangements and ends with the consequences of policy action in the land use setting. A central theme is that the large bureaucratic decision structures coupled with a welfare-at-large ideology have reinforced a myopia that de-emphasizes environmental dynamics and the need for broader representation. A second theme is that a policentric or nonhierarchical network may produce results that have a lower *net cost* to society in the long run than the unitary bureaucracy. To examine these contentions, this book develops and analyzes three major cases of consequence to land use control. While the cases are organized around particular controversies, the focus is on public agencies' behaviors. Moreover, each case contains elements reflective of both the bureaucratic pattern of authority and the more policentric network structure.

All the controversies reached a national level of attention at their peaks, but perhaps the most widely known one is Mineral King in Sequoia National Forest. The case concerned proposals to develop the world's largest ski resort facility in a small valley recognized for its pristine wilderness. While several state and federal agencies and the judiciary were involved, nearly exclusive authority was exercised by the U.S. Forest Service. As one of the best examples of unitary bureaucracy, the agency traces its origin to Gifford Pinchot and the Progressive movement. Managing vast forestlands for multiple use, it is America's largest land use agency. Its relevance here stems from the historical persistence of bureaucratic style and the problems associated with exclusive and unitary authority.

In many ways the Forest Service was to find the second stage of urban growth to be both a boon to its prestige and the source of administrative catastrophes. To the growing demands on forestlands and the conflicts that ensued, the service's responses frequently reflected a narrowed vision of what physical and societal forces were involved. No case in this regard is more central than the Mineral King controversy, which spans the period between 1945 and 1978.

A second case of consequence is the San Onofre nuclear reactor controversy, which occurred in the early 1970s over the siting of facilities along an isolated stretch of California seacoast in north San Diego County. It involved a proposal to construct additional reactors that would make the site the world's largest nuclear generating facility. The expansion would provide sufficient capacity to serve several million customers in two population centers a short distance away. While numerous local, state, and federal agencies were involved, the analytical focus centers on the struggle between the Atomic Energy Commission (now the Nuclear Regulatory Commission) and the California Coastal Zone Conservation Commission. Attempts by the state to assure public health and safety, and preserve environmentally significant lands and marine life, were confounded by the AEC's desire to maintain exclusive jurisdiction over nuclear development. Analytical relevance here revolves around the struggle as an example of how different administrative paradigms relate to questions of representation and expertise. The case is a clear example neither of unitary bureaucracy nor of the policentric pattern. The struggle between the two administrative worlds produces some interesting behaviors and results that are recurring themes in American administrative history.

The third case is the Nettleton Lakes recreation community controversy, which occurred over use of a remote area of Kitsap County in the Puget Sound area of Washington. Located on private land used for timber growth and known for its rural and pastoral setting, the area was proposed for conversion by a large corporation to a restricted-access community of 6,000 lots with numerous urban-type recreational amenities. The developer, however, intended not to provide environmental safeguards such as sewers, a water supply, and proper erosion control. In addition, the size and urban character of the project would have constituted a significant change-of-use from the remote and esthetic surroundings. The conflict that emerged centered on highly incompatible uses for a valuable land resource. Again, many levels of public agencies were involved, but the controversy focused on county government acting as one element in a policentric network of local, state, and federal agencies. Relevance of this case centers on agency response, intergovernmental behavior, and outcomes in a nonhierarchical administrative pattern. The role of local government is an especially interesting aspect, since collaboration with other agencies seemed to be a more powerful motive than parochialism.

While all three cases are fairly recent, much new environmental legislation (especially in air and water quality) has passed since the controversies were resolved. Some might contend, then, that the newer laws would prevent such controversies from happening today. Perhaps in some ways this is true, but this factor is not very relevant here. The essential focus of this book is on organizational behavior, administrative structure, and the quality of decision making, not the mechanics of planning and regulation. The newer laws may in fact have prevented a Nettleton Lakes or a Mineral King, but they do not, for the most part, change institutional behaviors in complex organizations. If changes in laws were major barriers to the study of political economy and administration, then many landmark cases in administrative structure and behavior would have little relevance for today. To see the fallacy, one need only reflect upon the great value still to be gained from works like *TVA* (Selznick, 1949), *The Forest Ranger* (Kaufman, 1967), and Chandler's studies of large corporations (1962).

Methodology and Organization

The focus of this book is on what difference organizational processes and structure make in complex land use control decisions. While descriptions of land use instruments and planning techniques are developed where needed, they are not of central interest *per se* in understanding problematic areas. Hence the essential thrust is to examine the issues raised by the above sets of questions in the context of three cases. In so doing, the organization of the book follows a methodological sequence which includes, first, the development of comparative administrative frames (Part I, Chapter 2); next, the development of three land use cases illustrative of complex land use and environmental settings (Part II); and, finally, a comparative analysis of the central questions as revealed in the cases (Part III).

Chapter 2 provides the framework for analyzing the cases which follow. The first component of the chapter is a preliminary discussion which solidifies some issues of the administrative process raised here in Chapter 1. The second component sets out three alternative administrative structures as patterns evident in land use control.

Part II contains the cases and provides a stage-setting descriptive analysis of the issues, physical circumstances, actors, actions, and governmental structures involved. As such, the cases draw out the maneuvers (active and passive) and nuances of action by emphasizing assumptions, aims, value systems, temperaments, constituencies, codes of rhetoric, behavior, definitions of responsibility, and perceptions of empowerment to act by a variety of actors. The attempt is to impart dynamics to an otherwise colorless investigation. Unavoidably, though, it emphasizes conflict at the expense of consensus. The cases deal critically with actions of people who could not possibly have acted so as to forestall all possible criticism.

Selection of the cases reflected three factors. First, since land use deals not only with the impact of urbanization but also with extraction and utilization of natural resources, all cases contain these components as major features of controversy. Although important, redevelopment of core cities was omitted in favor of situations where natural resource allocation was *directly and visibly* at stake. Second, each case reflects a different *mix* of the patterns of political economy as defined in Chapter 2. Situations that failed to involve more than purely local government are not included because their level of significance was seen as less important to land use control in the larger societal arena. Third, owing to the desire for more complete information and the obstacles to data collection in cases of lesser visibility, the cases included in this study are widely known. Moreover, they are about complex and widespread impacts on society and therefore represent the land use conditions outlined in this chapter. The cases include for the most part the three levels and branches of the federalist system and highlight intergovernmental relations and involvement of numerous agencies.

Part III provides the comparative analysis and generalizations. It contains four chapters, one each for the three categories of questions raised above and one for generalization and reconstruction. As an examination of rival patterns, the analysis provides a systematic comparative assessment of plausibility between alternative frames. Data sources supporting the comparative analysis were identical for all cases and included intra- and interagency memos, correspondence among agencies and the public, transcribed testimony from public hearings, reports and research studies done in conjuction with the controversies, interviews with actors, and numerous newspaper and journal articles. The analysis is meant to show tendencies of behavior through a weight of evidence *as a whole.* To avoid arbitrary use of fragmentary data, a single statement or characterization of action by any single actor should not be taken alone as indicative or definitive. A more valid picture of the variables is drawn from viewing the fragments as they converge around certain tendencies and reinforce the whole.

The book should provide the reader with a clearer understanding of the elements of land use administration as they pertain to use of information, organizational learning capabilities, public access and representation, decision costs, and resource allocation. The reader should further discover that governmental actions in land use affecting region-wide issues are more adequately interpreted through a frame of overlapping patterns of analysis than by a single unified framework of explanation.

CHAPTER 2

Administrative Patterns and Historical Origins

" . . . it is getting harder to *run* a constitution
than to frame one."

Woodrow Wilson

PUBLIC PROBLEMS in land use are in many ways
common to those of an institutionalized society in general. Different
people face different incentive systems and have different objectives in
life. In situations where the discretion to decide is removed from individuals, conflicts arise over representation. Moreover, institutionalized
decision making causes a variety of intended and unintended consequences for people. Hence, as institutional growth and organizational
imperatives consume more of the discretion over our political economy,
problems increasingly become characterized as political/administra-
tive. Rightly or wrongly, society is probably too interdependent and
complex to completely reverse this condition. Indeed, much of what
was developed in Chapter 1 connotes a *need* for better public policies
and administrative arrangements in land use.

A Summary of Concerns

In discussions of interests, institutional frames, and consequences,
the public problems that emerge usually result from the interdependence of several administrative variables. A way of distilling them from
Chapter 1 is to perceive them as the following four problems of administration:

1. The Individualistic Public: how to develop a peaceful and secure
state around individuals expressing anticollectivist tendencies and
behaving with self-interested motives.

2. Human Fallibility: how to structure interrelationships and the
search for information to mitigate error and oversight.

3. Diversity: how to deal with complex technical matters and uncertain societal contexts.

4. Scale of Problems: how to organize institutional decision making to handle problems having different scales of impact.

As noted in Chapter 1, the nature of modern society enlarges the complexity of these problems by obscuring their relationships to clear territorial boundaries and political jurisdictions.

To the extent that problems in land use control are part of these larger issues of governance, central attention concerns appropriate decision-making processes and organizational forms. The debate surrounding the American Law Institute's Revised Model State Land Use Code (1974) thus has a context larger than land use alone. Most areas of government are struggling with questions of planning and control, where administrative structure and levels of authority are at issue. In the field of land use at least a dozen books and numerous articles have been written in the context of ALI's debate. Focusing primarily on state government, most have been descriptions of new programs that have moved authority away from local and toward regional or statewide agencies. The review of state land use laws by Bosselman and Callies (1971) and the analysis of "collaborative planning" efforts in coastal zone management by Sorensen (1978) are examples of the subnational land use possibilities. In addition, such works as those by Haskell and Price (1973), Haefele (1973), and McAllister (1973) analyze the integral relationship of environmental management and land use control. In each of these works a central theme is how to arrange government to deal with the four problems.

Beyond the question of governmental level, these studies recognize the economic and social value contributed in a variety of ways by government participating in the transactional processes. Rightly understood, public sector involvement is an essential contribution to competitive markets that corrects or compensates for dysfunctions and inadequacies. Land use control fits this idea in that it consists of an interrelationship between public regulatory arenas and a system for producing and exchanging land resources. The overlap and inseparability of issues are an important feature in the political economy of land use but can easily lead to misconceptions.

Probably one of the most significant of these misconceptions stems from associating inappropriate organizational structure with specific institutional tasks in the allocation process. A current case in point is the centralization versus decentralization debate, the issue most commonly raised in land use control when speaking of appropriate levels of authority. The centralization versus decentralization issue greatly oversimplifies the relationships to allocation because it concerns intraorganizational criteria such as position, authority, and work flow without taking into account external diversity and public purpose. Both centralization and decentralization thus have been advocated as "one best way" solutions to all problems (Porter and Olsen, 1976).

Besides promoting unitary solutions, the dichotomy is also wrongly applied. Decentralization implies that authority can only be dispersed if it is delegated by a central authority: "effective centralization must precede effective decentralization" (Golembiewski, 1977, p. 1489). In reality, such a structure may be present as part of the allocation system, but appropriate performance of a system of institutions is not dependent on a central authority. To the extent that the United States is a federalist and competitive political economy, *noncentralized* processes exist as separately derived authorities that provide for the satisfaction of different societal interests (Elazar, 1971).

Consequences of the Administrative Process

We are still left with the need to understand land use control on terms other than those oversimplified by the centralization/decentralization debate. Moreover, in the analysis of alternative patterns of administration, there exists a set of issues much broader and more articulated than the single dichotomy connotes. Addressing those four problems of administration raised above, these issues include the measurement of institutional performance, the costs of external effects, the processes of planning, and the use of decision rules.

Performance

How well an organization performs its task depends on its level of "efficiency." The term deals with implementation of appropriate means to achieve policy ends. As a measure of the quality or condition of methods, the "criterion of efficiency dictates that choice of alternatives which produces the largest result for the given application of resources" (Simon, 1957, p. 179). Although its meaning has been obscured by modern application, "efficiency" describes a relationship between cost and benefit as measured in terms of peoples' values. It is primarily associated with how much people like the outputs they receive given the cost they incur. The term implies individual expectations about the cost/benefit relationship as well as the availability of choice among alternatives. It therefore has little meaning if cost is the only component or if no alternatives exist.

To minimize ambiguity, "efficiency" as defined needs to be subdivided into economic *efficiency* and welfare *effectiveness*, which refer to different aspects of performance in the relationship of means to ends (Boschken, 1976; Simon, 1957, p. 180; Buchanan and Tullock, 1965, p. 99). Efficiency, in this narrowed context, refers to the minimization of administrative or overhead costs and economic costs of production. The term thus implies an association among control, the utilization of technology, and economies of scale. Effectiveness, on the other hand, deals with the relative ability to satisfy public needs or represent constituent interests, and is associated with *qualitative* impacts and minimization of social costs. Adequacy of administrative performance with regard to a satisfied polity of interests is measured by both categories simultaneously.

Problems arise when both are not adequately achieved. An administrative unit may be efficient in a cost-per-unit sense but not effective in providing useful value to people or society. Examples of this might include those welfare programs which perpetuate conditions that welfare laws and policies intended to eradicate. At the same time, these programs may be very efficiently administered in a cost-per-unit sense. In forest management, effective implementation of the Multiple Use Act has often not been achieved because some highly efficient timber-cutting practices and recreational uses have degraded the resource for other uses. The reverse may also be true in that some activities, like NASA's moon program in the 1960s, were effective but "cost was no object."

Recognition of this dual performance function of good government was made as far back as the *Federalist*. According to Madison, "A good government implies two things: first, fidelity to the object of government, which is the happiness of the people; secondly, a knowledge of the means by which that object can be best attained" (Hamilton, Madison, and Jay, 1961, p. 380). Yet performance remains an issue in the administrative process because of the intangible nature of measuring efficiency and effectiveness. From the *Federalist* forward, qualitative judgments have made performance and accountability highly politicized matters, especially in regulatory arenas. In land use control the controversies over "jurisdictional overlap," "holding up approvals," and "the costs of delay" connote the political nature of these intangible measures.

External Effects

Land use control and natural resource utilization often may be construed as special problems associated with "the tragedy of the Commons" (Hardin and Baden, 1977). Few "goods" in the development of land resources are so finite or perfectly packageable that they preclude impacts on individuals who are not parties to private contractual arrangements. For example, building and selling lots in a recreation community on land known for its public access and multiple uses have consequences that extend beyond the parties directly engaged in the market transactions. This becomes doubly visible when public lands are involved such as parks, forests, and seashores. Under these conditions individuals outside the transactions may be adversely affected by the loss of access, destruction of the resource for existing uses, or spillover of the changed character onto adjacent lands.

While external effects may have positive consequences (as when a shopping center or golf course enhances surrounding land values), use of the term in land use control relates primarily to the regulation of negative impacts. Notwithstanding, the term remains somewhat ambiguous and is frequently used out of context in many works. For land use, external effects are an issue of the administrative process because their presence in public deliberation and actions may significantly affect use of the "commons," ecological balance, or existing patterns of resource allocation. Misallocation where environmental as well as commercial and industrial interests are at stake is a troublesome case in point. Many land use controversies occur when developments cause an allocation of the existing environment to other uses such as commercial recreation or industrial production. If the *full costs* of such uses are not accounted for, the ultimate consumers have insufficient market information to compare and evaluate the cost and benefit trade-offs for environmental, commercial, and industrial needs. Under conditions of scarcity an overallocation of commercial or industrial activities will occur and environmental needs in land use will not get their economically justifiable allocation. A similar example for urban core areas is the misallocation that occurs when redevelopment projects ignore uprooting and relocation impacts of displacing indigenous minorities.

The costs of external effects are also an essential consideration in land use control because nonpackageable impacts must be dealt with in conjunction with political arenas and not through the market sector alone. Although the presence of external effects *per se* is neither necessary nor sufficient for public intervention (Coase, 1960, p. 18; Buchanan and Tullock, 1965, p. 60; Buchanan and Stubblebine, 1962, p. 381), most goods and services produced by business and government display some degree of "publicness." Suggesting that public decisions to act against external effects is determined politically, Dewey contends that " . . . the line between private and public is to be drawn on the basis of the extent and scope of the consequences of acts which are so important as to need control whether by inhibition or by promotion" (1927, p. 15). Public control becomes necessary when magnitude precipitates political concern and where "producers and consumers are unable or unwilling to internalize [costs] for themselves . . ." (Ostrom, Tiebout, and Warren, 1961, pp. 832-33). Hence effective performance of public organizations is at least partly concerned with how well implementation of public policy mitigates the potential for external effects. For regulatory agencies like those in land use control, it may be a primary function.

Planning

The planning process is an essential aspect of land use control because it provides a means for systematic collection of information, analysis of impacts, and arrangement of development alternatives. In short, it is a method for policy formation and the determination of external effects. The argument for land use planning revolves around government's role to augment certain freedoms by anticipating the future. Land use control may be construed as an impingement on some freedoms, but "freedom involves more than the absence of restraint. . . . It also involves the provision of opportunities — a kind of 'freedom to' without which 'freedom from' has only minor benefits" (Meyerson, 1954, p. 201). Consequently the freedoms protected by land use control are not only those of developers but those with alternative interests that would suffer unfairly at the benefit of those creating adverse external impacts. Whether or not such freedoms are promoted by planning depends in part on the *kind* of planning that is done and on the set of decision *rules* followed. The issue, then, is not with planning *per se* but with planning administration. The essential contrast that will recur in this study's cases is over whether planning can be done synoptically at a single point in time or whether the vagaries of impact and changing societal interests require an incremental approach.

Synoptic or comprehensive planning is the attempt to lock future decision making into a single internally consistent strategy. Usually associated with centralized control, it is often viewed as a coercive instrument used by unitary bureaucracies to eliminate conflicting public interests. Although synoptic planning envisions a betterment of society, two major dysfunctions arise. First, such planning limits the range of individual choice by minimizing public access and imposing centrally made decisions (Altshuler, 1965, pp. 311-19). Second, planning requires "vastly more accurate knowledge about a huge variety of factors than can be obtained" by such a method (Meyerson, 1954, p. 201).

To account for these problems of public access and dynamic equilibrium, incremental planning is based on the continuance of planning without the expectation of "once and for all" final strategies. In lieu of comprehensive final decisions, incremental planning deals with policy formation at a more manageable level of specific issues over time. The advantages of such an approach are that it (1) concentrates on raising policy questions instead of prioritizing a unitary solution, and (2) helps define planning issues in more discrete terms of immediate consequence to affected parties rather than solely to the public at large. Incremental planning provides for the systematic assessment of demands, without locking solutions to a static strategy. The openness of the process therefore enhances more direct linkage between public policy deliberation and the interests of affected parties.

Decision Rules

Public welfare is the main symbol of concern for public organizations engaged in or regulating allocation. Theoretical discussions of welfare are found in economics dealing with allocation policies under conditions of scarcity (Baumol, 1965, p. 355). The origin of welfare theory lies in the concept of Pareto optimality (Baumol, 1965; Buchanan, 1959). With its focus on individualistic consequences, the term suggests that allocation decisions have reached their optimality when any further change in allocation patterns leads to bettering some individual's condition by simultaneously diminishing the condition of others. Up to the point of optimality, this connotes a decision rule which provides that ". . . any social change is desirable which results in (1) everyone being better off or (2) someone being better off and no one being worse off than before the change" (Buchanan, 1959, p. 125).

In applied form the test of a Pareto improvement toward the optimum condition is consensus among all affected members of society. Since it is based on a contractual premise where all parties agree to the decision, it has been most appropriately used in examining the competitive market process. Although some have tried to apply the Pareto criterion to public decision making where majority rule is used, it has little practical value. Government operates collectively on the basis of constitutionally legitimized coercion and not on contractual agreement among people over specific issues. Therefore, when unanimity of agreement is relaxed, a number of prohibitive problems of representation arise.

The most central of these is identified as the "impossibility theorem" (Arrow, 1963). In the absence of unanimity some percentage of the citizenry is excluded from the contract of agreement (i.e., under majority rule). Under these conditions, where some preferences are unknown, the Pareto criterion would require public agencies to assume the position of an omniscient observer able to "read" and compare individuals' preferences (Buchanan, 1959, p. 126). Under majority rule a Pareto optimal welfare function cannot be determined from individual preferences because the public decision maker has no way of making comparisons between the values and preferences of *all* affected people (Arrow, 1963; Baumol, 1965, p. 376; Wildavsky, 1967). Except in the rare case where a public decision harms no one, such distinctions are crucial to policy choices and implementation. The question of *whose* welfare or utility is to prevail is essential to evaluation because, without unanimity, the rule becomes a subjective measure which potentially releases public decision makers from scrutiny and accountability.

The concept's limitations notwithstanding, the *intent* of Pareto optimality has been used by two different schools which have adapted the welfare logic to practical necessity under majority rule. The first and most prevalent of these holds that the *welfare of society at large* is more important than considerations of individual preference or utility. In its simplest form the at-large rule requires that decisions be made such that the summation of costs to whomever may incur them should be less than the summation of benefits to whoever may receive them. From the standpoint of individuals, such a summation leaves open the question of sufficient overlap in the distribution of costs and benefits. The result is that the costs of any public decision may be proportioned over society differently from the benefits. External effects may be imposed on some for the benefit of others. Hence, even with a net positive summation for society at large, the decision rule does not necessarily mean that a society of partisan interests has been satisfied.

The other school of thought holds to a doctrine of *institutional fairness*. The central tenet here is that appropriate decision rules are not universal and that knowing whether fairness has been achieved is dependent upon *processes* of the specific society. What is fair for one nation, region, or locality may be unacceptable for citizens of another. Hence due process is the main criterion instead of the symbolic determinant of an at-large "majority." Due process is specified by cultural norms and constitutional rules but, in general, stipulates that fair outcomes emerge from negotiated agreements where the potential for mutual gains exists. As a decision rule, fairness conditions the process such that widespread gains can be achieved without disproportional costs. Costs and benefits are incurred proportionately by all affected parties, as in a "positive sum game."

The rule also encourages the seeking out of interests to associate a broad base of citizen preferences with policy formation and implementation. This raises three problems, however. First, in order to get a fair (i.e., proportional or symmetrical) representation of interests, affected parties must possess sufficient resources and constitutionally guaranteed rights to participate. This is not always the case, raising the possibility of a skewed distribution of costs and benefits in favor of the more powerful or more organized.

Second, in the absence of unanimity rule, the process of comparing and infusing individuals' preferences in deliberations is not characterized by the clarity of pure contractual arrangements among consenting parties. Thus sources of concern over fairness are related to questions of coercion, voluntary action, and how well associations can represent the interests of members. Adequate representation of interests is dependent upon how precisely preferences can be reflected through factional associations and public agencies (Olson, 1968). Although twentieth-century pluralists like Bentley and Truman argued that interest groups arise when needs are underrepresented, no government can guarantee a voice for *all*. Some latent interests don't always get represented.

Third, broad inclusion of diverse interests can lead to a condition of "overregulation." The problem here is in deciding what magnitude of impact on affected parties is necessary to invoke public intervention in the allocation process. The question is: does everyone have to be accommodated no matter how little one is impacted by the change in allocation? In the end, only politics can determine this, and the degree of fairness is relative to political and economic parity in the process.

Thus decision rules are an issue of the administrative process because use of one type over another greatly conditions outcomes and consequences for people affected. Neither the at-large nor the fairness rule escapes entirely the problems of status quo, omniscience, comparisons of citizen preferences, and prioritizing interests. By having different emphases, the welfare-at-large function is believed to minimize the status quo issue by lowering administrative decision costs and streamlining deliberations. The fairness doctrine is believed to be more effective in avoiding administrative omniscience, securing outcomes with broader base appeal, and minimizing the potential for external effects.

Patterns of Control: Historical Origins

The consequences of these four issues tend to be evident in nearly all public decision making, but their impacts may vary according to how public organizations are structured. In land use control, three major organizational patterns are evident: the unitary bureaucracy, the task-specific commission, and concurrent government. Each alternative has a particular historical origin, but in modern practice they are usually found in "mixed" forms where overlap obscures clear demarcation of patterns. No matter how dominant one pattern may be at any given time, the others are seldom completely obliterated. Moreover, clear distinctions cannot always be made between types. At times a unitary bureaucracy or commission may appear as part of a larger network of concurrent government.[1]

Since clarity of pattern is important in the examination of alternative arrangements in land use control, this section brings together the rich intellectual history of each. As artifacts of historical development the patterns remain incomplete, but each has a core of ideas and assumptions that have remained viable over time and thus contribute to the understanding of behavior in the cases. Heuristically, the three patterns will appear as ideal types, but realistically, each has internal discontinuities and problems in logic that may well appear in the cases.

---

[1] If the unitary bureaucracy is so dominant as to arrange other agencies on a hierarchical basis, this will be defined as the center-periphery model of intergovernmental relations and not a true policentric network of concurrent government (Bish, 1975).

Unitary Bureaucracy

The predominant form of administration in land use control is the large, general-purpose bureaucracy utilizing the welfare-at-large decision rule. The intellectual origins of this pattern cannot be attributed exclusively to any single period, but a wellspring of thought seems to come from the Progressive era. Unlike most paradigms, Progressivism never lost momentum. Acting first as a font of idealism for bureaucratic liberalism, it then evolved into much of the New Deal logic and eventually came to provide a justification for bureaucracy in the 1950s' "end of ideology" politics (Bell, 1965; McConnell, 1966, pt. I; Rule, 1978, chs. 1 and 4). Some of the ideals changed over time, but the core assumptions favoring a single "public interest" and the autonomy of large-scale bureaucracies transcended the metamorphosis. The triumph of Progressivism came in the 1950s with the attribution of spreading affluence to giant bureaucracy. As a result, Hartz asserted, "we still live in the shadow of the Progressive era" (1955, p. 27). In the 1960s and 1970s the logic of progress and the quest for bigness-as-best came under increasing criticism. This notwithstanding, the paradigm remains a powerful influence in issues of administrative organization and reform.

As an administrative paradigm Progressivism was a loose aggregation of beliefs (Hofstadter, 1955; Wiebe, 1967; Steffens, 1931). According to Waldo, it was composed of "a sheaf of ideas, old and new, and at times incompatible, held together by a buoyant faith in Progress" (1948, p. 16). Most of those who were associated with the paradigm were upper-middle-class reformers, "dreaming of an urban world that they would control for the benefit of all, a paradise of new middle-class rationality" (Wiebe, 1967, p. 170). Despite preachments against waste and corruption, they did not believe in the Malthusian doom. Instead, they were prophets of technology and the transformation of land and natural resources. "They were highly optimistic about the future . . . and they had found the key in science, technology and efficiency" (Hays, 1970, p. 614).

Those instrumental in general "good government" reform were Woodrow Wilson (1887, 1956), Herbert Croly (1909), and Frank Goodnow (1900). The extension to metropolitan reform was made by Chester Maxey (1929), William Anderson (1925), Chester Hanford (1926), and Joseph Wright (1925). Its connection to land use control and city planning was probably first made in Britain by Ebenezer Howard (1902), and later applied in America through the City Beautiful movement (Scott, 1969). Its major application in natural resource administration was accomplished first by Gifford Pinchot (1910, 1947).

The role of the Progressive reformer was to return government to the people. Viewing multiple jurisdictions as "chaotic," most argued that government "finds itself obliged to struggle for civic achievement amid conflicts, dissensions and divergencies of its several component political jurisdictions" (Maxey, 1922, p. 229). The central thrust of this argument lay in the science of administration, "which shall seek to straighten the paths of government, to make its business less unbusinesslike, to strengthen and purify its organization, and to crown its duties with dutifulness" (Wilson, 1941, p. 485). To this end, Progressive bureaucracy was to carry out the public edict based on two assumptions.

First, *bureaucratic efficiency* and the achievement of *welfare at large* were seen as the means-to-ends decision rules. For administrative ease, bureaucratic efficiency requires activities to operate "at the least possible cost either of money or of energy" (Wilson, 1941, p. 481). Measurements of this rule are made in the form of spending per capita or cost per client and do not easily reflect effective output or recipient satisfaction. Its association with welfare at large follows from the belief that least-cost methods are supposed to benefit the polity as a whole. Following this indicator, a public agency will not normally calculate the value of an individual client's time and inconvenience as part of bureaucratic efficiency (Warren, 1970; Kafoglis, 1968). Only those aspects of technical need or bureaucratic routine are of consequence to the calculus. The question of effectiveness is minimized except as it may be symbolically assessed in achieving the at-large public interest. Hence the susbtance of this association has meant a promise of rapid attainment of materialistic security for the "majority."

Second, the strength of at-large rules lies in the *assumption* of society as basically homogeneous, where differences are usually the result of either class or "deviancy." The mass consensus image correlates with the at-large identity because the "melting pot" factor is believed to have washed out significant distinctions between people (Veblen, 1899; Nisbet, 1966, ch. 3). "The Public Interest" is more easily determined over a wide range of issues by identifying only dominant interests as perceived in aggregate trends and periodic majority voting. Persistent partisan interests can be set aside as deviants from the mass. Tocqueville noticed this tendency in nineteenth-century America and attributed it to a monocratic drift: ". . . the idea of intermediate powers is weakened and obliterated; . . . the idea of the omnipotence and sole authority of society at large rises to fill its place" (Tocqueville, 1956, p. 292).

The organizational structure which provides the "least cost" achievement of welfare at large is the large-scale, general-authority bureaucracy. According to advocates of "good government," one form of organization was best for all activities. There was "but one rule of good administration for all governments alike. So far as administrative functions are concerned, all governments have a strong structural likeness; more than that, if they are to be uniformly useful and efficient, they *must* have a strong structural likeness" (Wilson, 1941, p. 502). The kind of structural likeness envisioned was "a strong right arm for the State in the form of an efficient bureaucracy" (Waldo, 1948, p. 17).

The bureaucratic pattern is also justified in Progressive logic by its desire to eliminate competition within government by segmenting political and administrative responsibilities on the basis of "fact" and "value" (Goodnow, 1900; Wilson, 1887, 1956; Willoughby, 1919; Pfiffner, 1935). "The field of administration is a field of business. It is removed from the hurry and strife of politics . . ." (Wilson, 1941, p. 493). Discretion over factual matters is most appropriately administered through the organization and application of systematic knowledge, while the expression of values is reserved for the arena of politics where the "other sovereign, the people, will have a score of differing opinions" (Wilson, 1941, p. 491).

The bureaucratic pattern thus limits public access and control to questions of opinion and grants administrative autonomy in determining fact and carrying out the public interest. "Administrative questions are not political questions" (Wilson, 1941, p. 494). Since politics deals with differing private interests, its dysfunctional nature must be isolated from the process of "good government": ". . . politics should stick to its policy-determining sphere and leave administration to apply its own technical processes free from the blight of political meddling" (Pfiffner, 1935, p. 9).

Although separation of the two functions is ambiguous at best (Simon, 1957, pp. 53-56), the degree of autonomy implied in administration raises a question of accountability to society at large. The Progressives realized that no matter how conscious and deliberate the attempts at separation, some policy discretion is always mixed in with the function of implementation. To assure accountability, such discretion was legitimized by having a responsible unitary command which includes a hierarchically ordered structure and a system of central authority which tapers to a single executive in charge. "Large powers and unhampered discretion seem to me the indispensable conditions of responsibility. . . . There is no danger in power, if only it be not irresponsible. If it be divided, dealt out in shares to many, it is obscured . . . irresponsible" (Wilson, 1941, pp. 497-98). Hence, in place of political competition, "there is always a centre of power" (Wilson, 1956, p. 30). In pursuit of the general welfare that central authority is coordinated into "symmetrical divisions of territory and . . . orderly gradations of office" (Wilson, 1941, pp. 488-89).

While Wilson and the others did not explicitly refer to what is now called the center-periphery model of intergovernmental relations, the Progressive ideals were to eliminate the overlap of checks and balances.

Consequently, along with the establishment of unitary bureaucracies, intergovernmental relations were expected to follow a similar revamping. To assure accountability from government as a whole, the divided agency authorities and levels of government in the older *Federalist* network should be rearranged with a three-level hierarchical structure. Government at all levels should be divisions and levels of one unified bureaucracy, and intergovernmental relations must correspond to vertical authority. As such, the bureaucratic pattern represents a general denial of the *Federalist* interpretation of democracy and its "paper pictures" of an intergovernmental structure that augments checks and balances. Indeed, to the extent that centralized administration brings government into congruity with a homogeneous community of interests, the Progressive reformer argues that ". . . government can be better conducted by one agency than by fourscore of unrelated agencies, and . . . the immediate effect will be greater efficiency . . ." (Reed, 1921, p. 103).

A corollary to the single comprehensive authority is a contention that public organizations should be large and that efficiencies of scale may be infinite for public administration. This idea assumes that information gathering, planning capacities, and representation of the public interest will become continually more efficient with increases in organizational scale. As a result, no limits to size or diminishing scales of return are observed, and further consolidation of governmental units is the basic method for improving bureaucracy. Moreover, with scale advantages, the large structure of central authority provides the capacity and resources of a professionally trained cadre of experts. These experts revolve around a rational and systematic application of knowledge to public problems. Waldo has paraphrased the Progressive logic: "Science has its experts: so we must have 'experts in government.' Science relies upon exact measurement: so let the data of administration be measured. Science is concerned only with facts: so let the 'facts' be sovereign" (1948, p. 21).

The specific meaning of bureaucratic expertise, however, elicits a general knowledge of administrative methods more than an extensive and specialized knowledge of issues or scientific disciplines. Professional civil servants must have a "functional balance" and "executive expertness" in all areas under the authority's jurisdiction (Wilson, 1941, p. 491). Competence is measured more in breadth than in depth, and functional knowledge of organizational procedures is most important. Furthermore, the posture of expertise is impersonal and apolitical, with an emphasis on "making the service unpartisan" (Wilson, 1941, p. 494). The superior knowledge of professionals justifies impersonal rule over the polity.

Task Specific Commission

An emerging form of land use control is the specialized commission having regulatory jurisdiction either over areawide land use, as in the case of the Hawaii Land Use Commission, or over unique natural resources, such as the California coastal commissions. Although relatively new to land use, the use of boards and commissions for administrative purposes stems primarily from the Progressive era. It has similar logic and purposes as the unitary bureaucracy (McCombs, 1924; Doyle, 1939; Trackett, 1937) and is usually associated with the center-periphery model of intergovernmental relations.

The central decision rule of maximizing welfare at large is similar to that of Progressive bureaucracy, but some recognition is evident in land use commissions of the need for "balancing" the interests of society. In concept, the commission sits as an impersonal board of objective observers following an irreducible set of first principles concerning societal betterment and equity. Motivated by practical reality and an assumption that society may not be as easily aggregated as Progressivism once set forth, the commission rule is to "intuitively" strike a balance among society's at-large needs. Although sometimes contrary to political realities, this is not supposed to involve a *de facto* compromise of private interests (Rawls, 1971, p. 36). Since society is still seen as a unit separate from individual preferences, demands of private interests are ignored unless they project a greater benefit for welfare at large. Hence, under intuitionist rules of general welfare, two premises exist: "first, they consist of a plurality of first principles which may conflict to give contrary directives in particular types of cases; and second, they include no explicit method, no priority rules, for weighting these principles against one another: we are simply to strike a balance by intuition . . ." (Rawls, 1971, p. 34).

The land use commission, therefore, is responsible for identifying and ascertaining the intensity of societal values as they relate to specific issues. Although this balancing procedure has no "factual" criteria for prioritizing values, certain common precepts associated with specific problems or issues are attributed to the task-specific commission. In reality, with the different power of affected interest groups, these precepts may correspond to individual political convictions and be less impartial than one would expect under a rule of institutional fairness. Indeed, most regulatory commissions exist in highly politicized atmospheres, and the intuitionist rule makes them vulnerable to "political necessity." In any case, the purpose of balancing is to spread the distribution of advantages more widely than would occur under the unitary at-large rule.

Under the commission system the separation of politics from administration is not nearly as distinguishable as in the case of bureaucracy. This is probably due more to the organizational structure of commissions than to a fundamental departure from Progressive logic. The task-specific commission consists of a number of members who sit as adjudicators over competing legitimate values. While the board may have a large staff to research issues and make recommendations, it is not attributed with comprehensive knowledge of all governmental activities like that of the unitary bureaucracy. The fact that the commission is task-specific limits its jurisdiction as well as its realm of knowledge and expertise. Consequently it relies heavily on interest groups and outside consultants to provide awareness of issues that may be either indigenous to the commission's area of competence or external to it but having overlapping areas of importance on specific problems. The problems are seldom the same when the authority is organized around issues rather than functional domains.

Although the commission pattern is more visible politically and depends on interest groups to pose needs for balancing and adjudication, it usually assumes exclusive or predominant authority over all issues within its scope. This unitary authority, while divided among board members, assumes a high degree of autonomy from the influence of private interests as well. The attempt is to remove politics from administrative decisions but, at the same time, recognize that political conflict is the basis for its public role. The result is a public hearing process where inputs from other agencies and the public may be used to identify contentious values, but where objective scrutiny of facts is reserved exclusively for the commission and staff. This poses a problem when the commission acts as a unitary authority outside the reach of any concurrent administrative arena. Required to act benevolently to protect several public interests, the commission form may reflect the stature of a philosopher-king. For example, in the case of nuclear energy, public interests include simultaneous needs for energy production, human safety, and protection of surrounding resources. Yet impartial judgment is expected to determine priorities and adjudicate values.

With the single authority for all issues in a specific task, the question of scale is often as evident in the commission pattern as in bureaucracy. Proposals for establishing or enlarging the scope and territory of commissions usually have been based on two considerations: (1) matching the commission's jurisdiction with the broadest boundary of the land use events being regulated, and (2) attempting to gain economies of scale. Some environmental groups, for example, have attempted to redefine the scope of public concern in terms of broad biological structures and processes (Ehrlich and Ehrlich, 1970). They become proponents of task-specific commissions because they "argue that only through regional authorities whose boundaries are based upon relevant bio-physical criteria can the complex and subtle ecological impacts be accounted for" (Warren and Weschler, 1972, p. 6). Consequently, more often than not, commissions acquire exclusive jurisdictions like bureaucracies on the basis of inclusive scale.

Concurrent Government

Probably the most complex pattern of land use control is a system of multiple, specialized jurisdictions which form coordinated networks of responsibility around publicly raised problems or controversies. Unlike Progressive bureaucracy and most task-specific commissions, this structure of administration attempts to maximize public access and promote public satisfaction by providing alternative authorities and forums of deliberation. As such, its focus is on fairness toward diverse interests and not a symbolic "public interest at large."

The intellectual heritage of this pattern is formed from a dual origin. The first is found in the concept of a "compound republic" formulated by the Founding Fathers, particularly Madison and Hamilton in the *Federalist* (Hamilton, Madison, and Jay, 1961; Ostrom, 1971; Madison, 1969; Padover, 1953). The second is found in the pluralist tradition starting with Tocqueville, who saw the multiplicity of overlapping associations as the distinguishing characteristic of the American political economy (Tocqueville, 1956). Following Tocqueville, the development of pluralist thought is found in the writings of such figures as Bentley (1908), Herring (1940), Truman (1951), and Latham (1952).

The nature of concurrent government in a plural society stems from a "pre-industrial" age where the habits of unitary control in government were not nearly so well developed. Indeed, political control was seen frequently through a distribution of power centers, associated as a whole only by ideological forces such as the unifying value of "manifest destiny" (Adams, 1961; Weinberg, 1935). In the practical lives of American citizens, diversity was extant and was so recognized by those who conceived the "compound republic." Madison said, for example, "As every State may be divided into different districts, and its citizens into different classes, which give birth to contending interests and local jealousies, so the different parts of the United States are distinguished from each other by a variety of circumstances which produce a like effect on a larger scale" (Hamilton, Madison, and Jay, 1961, p. 231). The vitality of this diversity was seldom seen in purely individual terms but instead was expressed through a multiplicity of private associations. "Feelings and opinions are recruited, the heart is enlarged, and the human mind is developed, only by the reciprocal influence of men upon each other . . . and this can only be accomplished by associations" (Tocqueville, 1956, p. 200).

Furthermore, the strength of such private associations in a "compound republic" was premised on their ability to form factions and act politically: ". . . political association singularly strengthens and improves associations for civil purposes" (Tocqueville, 1956, p. 205). The expression of diverse interests through political factions, however, posed serious problems of governance. "Complaints are everywhere heard . . . that our governments are too unstable, that the public good is disregarded in the conflicts of rival parties, and that measures are too often decided, not according to the rules of justice and the rights of the minor party, but by the superior force of an interested and overbearing majority" (Hamilton, Madison, and Jay, 1961, p. 77). How does a society deal with contending factions to maintain tranquillity? "There are two methods of curing the mischiefs of faction: the one, by removing its causes; the other, by controlling its effects" (Hamilton, Madison, and Jay, 1961, p. 78). The elimination of factional causes is the method of mass democracy made popular by the French Revolution. Madison raised this possibility by suggesting that "there are again two methods of removing the causes of faction: the one, by destroying the liberty which is essential to its existence; the other, by giving to every citizen the same opinions, the same passions, and the same interests" (Hamilton, Madison, and Jay, 1961, p. 78). The use of either of these methods would constitute subordination of diverse interests to a central authority (Hamilton, Madison, and Jay, 1961, p. 198). To the first, Madison concluded the remedy was worse than the disease; to the second, he recognized that the source of diversity recapitulates itself and does not melt in a pot.

In addition, governance based on a homogeneous majority created the risk of tyranny for minority factions. "When I see that the right and the means of absolute command are conferred on any power whatever . . . I say there is the germ of tyranny . . ." (Tocqueville, 1956, p. 115). This risk was especially salient to the Founding Fathers, most of whom were of the wealthy minority concerned about a hostile majority. "To secure the public good and private rights against the danger of such a faction, and at the same time to preserve the spirit and the form of popular government, is then the great object to which our inquiries are directed" (Hamilton, Madison, and Jay, 1961, p. 80). The architects felt the need for a strong union that protected minority rights, and they promoted the belief that "the liberty of association has become a necessary guaranty against the tyranny of the majority" (Tocqueville, 1956, p. 97). As such, concurrent government holds assumptions contrary to those of bureaucracy's symbolic at-large "public interest."

With no model governments that fostered both national strength and the protection of minority rights, the solution was necessarily a complicated one. "The inference to which we are brought is that the *causes* of faction cannot be removed and that relief is only to be sought in the means of controlling its effects" (Hamilton, Madison, and Jay, 1961, p.

80). That solution was referred to in the *Federalist* as a compound republic and was devised to be congruent with the multiple interests at all levels of society. It was "to sustain political solutions to problems concerning communities of interest flowing beyond the boundaries" of any particular geographical area (Ostrom, 1971, p. 114). With no single center of power, the compound republic was conceived as a system of limited and concurring regimes operating in coordination through a process of reciprocal checks and review. It is, therefore, based on the prevention of public monopolies and the provision of political competition through a multiplicity of authorities of different organizational scale commensurate with their individual tasks. As a noncentralized network, it is also at variance with the center-periphery model of Progressivism.

The logical advantage of such a governmental system is the securing of a fair representation of interests by providing the administrative means to search out alternatives acceptable to affected parties. In land use control, where external costs are problematic, a fair decision is one "that does not unduly favor or discriminate against any group as to the distribution of the costs involved" (Berry and Steiker, 1974, p. 415). With emphasis on innovation and under "the maxim, that everyone is the best and sole judge of his own private interest" (Tocqueville, 1956, p. 58), the fairness doctrine is equivalent to mutual improvement or positive sums.

Some would argue that decisions of mutual improvement constitute "watered down" compromises where progress on societal problems is sacrificed. Although the term "watered down" is misleading, its meaning is partly true. From the perspective of any single value or vested interest, a total set of desired preferences cannot be attained. The idea of mutual accords through concurrence implies that no single party can win all of its preferences from the public process. Instead, where conflicting interests are evident, each party represented in the process must prioritize preferences so that trade-offs can be made. The intent of fairness in the deliberation process is to allow advances through *innovation* but not through winner-take-all outcomes.

The Founding Fathers saw their proposal not as a perfect solution but as one that provided the closest fit to the plural needs of the nation as a whole. As such, they did not seek to maximize a single public interest or general welfare. A general or national public interest may or may not be involved in any given issue, but if it is, its claim stands among and not above a multiplicity of interests (i.e., specialized and general, local and national). Exceptions to this generalization are spelled out by the *Federalist* and tend to revolve around national security priorities and interstate commerce.

A "balancing" of such interests under the fairness rule is different from that usually associated with the commission form because the variety of specific partisan interests is not seen in a welfare-at-large context. Furthermore, under the premise that "a body of men are unfit to be both judges and parties at the same time" (Hamilton, Madison, and Jay, 1961, p. 79), the fairness rule does not rely on the benign omniscience of a *single* body of public officials. Without review of arbitrary discretion, public decision makers "have in too many instances abused the confidence they possessed; and assuming the pretext of some public motive, have not scrupled to sacrifice the [public] tranquility to personal advantage . . ." (Hamilton, Madison, and Jay, 1961, p. 54).

Unlike the two previous patterns of political economy, this expected arbitrariness is conditioned by a regulated system of interagency negotiation. Through a reciprocal review process among two or more separate agencies, value and factual questions are interrelated and deliberated simultaneously. Political issues are seen as indistinguishable from administrative issues. As a result, the measurement of each party's interests and strength of claims is not left to the judgment of a single body, but instead "the constant aim is to divide and arrange the several offices in such a manner that each may be a check on the other — that the private interest of every individual may be a sentinel over the public rights" (Hamilton, Madison, and Jay, 1961, p. 322).

The logic of concurrent government reflects a nonhierarchical structure that places power "not in a few, but a number of hands" (Hamilton, Madison, and Jay, 1961, p. 227). Contrary to the center-periphery model, "the administrative power in the United States presents nothing either centralized or hierarchical in its constitution" (Tocqueville, 1956, p. 63). Instead, the structure is more complex, consisting of at least three major characteristics.

First, the basic unit of authority is highly specialized, with its scale of jurisdiction limited by functional responsibility and the nature of the impact it oversees. Autonomy is not general but, rather, bounded by specific tasks (i.e., urban planning, wildlife management, marine preservation). "The local or municipal authorities form distinct and independent portions of the supremacy, no more subject, within their respective spheres, to the general authority than the general authority is subject to them, within its own sphere" (Hamilton, Madison, and Jay, 1961, p. 245). In addition to task specialization, these individual spheres are usually constituted for the protection of specific interests: ". . . an allocation of authority to an agency . . . will assign specific responsibility for the protection or pursuit of that value" (Lindblom, 1965, p. 230).

This denies the infinite-scales argument found in the unitary bureaucracy and implies that organizational size and jurisdiction are dependent upon the limited task. Moreover, it suggests that the structural arrangement of the federalist network will correspond to the different scales of problems associated with any complex public issue. In land use, where impacts may be felt on several ecological scales (i.e., air basins with boundaries different from watersheds, etc.) and where several regional or national interests are affected, agencies with different jurisdictional boundaries may be needed. Madison acknowledged the characteristic of multiple scales by noting that "the federal Constitution forms a happy combination in this respect; the great and aggregate interests being referred to the national, the local and particular to the State legislatures" (Hamilton, Madison, and Jay, 1961, p. 83). In short, the *Federalist* is arguing for a government that is extensive enough as a whole to include and rule all constituents but that is divided into a multiplicity of authorities and public forums to functionally represent segmented constituents.

Second, since multiple impacts are created by any specific issue and functional responsibilities cannot be isolated, an *overlap* of jurisdictions will occur for nearly every land use problem. The overlap, however, will vary from problem to problem and may involve different agency aggregations with spheres of authority covering both local, regional, and national *impacts* and such functional *issues* as energy resources, wildlife, urban services, and zoning. To account for phenomena inclusive of different aggregations of society, concurrent government may be both multitiered and multinucleated. Furthermore, while overhead costs of a single bureaucracy are incurred on a general allocation basis, costs for public agencies in a concurrent system may be allocated more specifically according to the issue or problem at hand.

Although the Progressive view interprets such overlap as creating unnecessary conflict and redundancy of task, others suggest that it more accurately implies "a concurrent structure with full redundancy of means and methods of operation but specialized as to function" (Ostrom, 1971, p. 21). The overlap of authority provides a more comprehensive decision process where a general question of public concern is regularly and systematically subdivided for in-depth evaluation. In contrast to the single bureaucracy or commission which views its expertise more as a "jack of all trades," concurrent government is an overlap of individual specialties. Such mastery of individual knowledge bases and values is necessary in land use where a variety of complex and interrelated impacts is endemic to a single problem.

Third, the coordination of individual specialties is accomplished by an integration process where "mutual adjustment" techniques including bargaining, negotiation, compensation, and mediation agencies may be used (Boschken, 1982; Lindblom, 1965). Unlike bureaucracy, where coordination occurs through central authority and standard procedures, nonhierarchical concurrent government accommodates a consortium of agencies with differing goals and interests through "reciprocal forbearances" (Hamilton, Madison, and Jay, 1961, p. 200). Conflict is a necessary part of coordination and promotes functional cooperation which leads to agreement among multiple agencies: "it is the relative lack of dominating power that turns participants in partisan mutual adjustment to seeking agreement on decisions or outcomes" (Lindblom, 1965, p. 209). Coordination occurs among concurrent regimes because individual agencies are forced to take each other into account in attempting to sustain agreeable and workable decisions for the government as a whole. They know that if they don't, the courts will act in their behalf by rendering winner-take-all decisions. "To the extent that they take each other into account in competitive relationships, . . . the various political jurisdictions . . . may function in a coherent manner with consistent and predictable patterns of interacting behavior . . . [and] may be said to function as a 'system' " (Ostrom, Tiebout, and Warren, 1961, p. 831).

The advantages of having such a concurrent system relate to representation and minimization of technical errors. First, because of the multiple arenas of deliberation, participation is encouraged for a broader number of affected interests. While the comparison of values for different people is made through negotiations among agencies, factional participation is essential for the broadest possible perception of interests by public officials. Noting the closer contact provided by concurrent government, Tocqueville argued that the "action of individuals, joined to that of the public authorities, frequently accomplishes what the most energetic centralized administration would be unable to do" (1956, p. 70). Individual groups in conjunction with specialized agency forums can better foresee and articulate interests than can the single omniscient observer holding comprehensive hearings.

Second, the system provides multiple arenas for confrontation among experts. Since facts are seldom clearcut or unbiased, "The oftener the measure is brought before examination, the greater the diversity . . . in those who are to examine it, the less must be the danger of those errors which flow from want of due deliberation . . . " (Hamilton, Madison, and Jay, 1961, p. 443). This interdependence among separate authorities is particularly important for land use control, since many public authorities including the unitary bureacracy do not have the resources to provide a staff of technical experts for every complex issue placed before them. Having multiple arenas of review with more contact with partisans, concurrent government tends to demystify the place of experts and open the process up to the questioning of fact. "The prospects for error-correcting strategies are enhanced when decision makers and interested parties have the opportunity to challenge prevailing assumptions, to propose alternative conceptions and sustain processes of reasoned deliberation" (Ostrom, 1971, p. 104).

Although concurrent government is not without societal cost, these two advantages generate a significantly different schedule of benefits from those provided by the unitary bureacracy or the task-specific commission. In what Follett (1924) called the achievement of "integration," the process of due deliberation and reciprocal review by concurrent government acts to account for external effects and minimize bias. Through a form of institutionalized competition, the structure provides internal checks and balances. "Where there is a consciousness of unjust or dishonorable purposes, [collusion] is always checked by distrust in proportion to the number whose concurrence is necessary" (Hamilton, Madison, and Jay, 1961, p. 83). Moreover, even though "there is no power on either side to annul the acts of the other [within their respective spheres] . . . [the] several constituent parts may, by their mutual relations, be the means of keeping each other in their proper places" (Hamilton, Madison, and Jay, 1961, pp. 206, 320).

Summary: Administrative Theory and the Patterns of Land Use Control

As paradigms of administration, the three patterns of land use control are not mutually exclusive interpretations of existing governmental institutions. Actual situations may adhere to variations and mixes of these patterns. It is not uncommon in land use, for example, to find a dominant, large bureaucracy assuming primary authority over an issue, but on occasion being forced to negotiate with more specialized agencies of lesser but overlapping authority. Nevertheless, in order to gain sufficient analytical perspective for the cases that follow, it is important to summarize and frame the essential characteristics of these patterns. Such a frame might look as shown in Table 1.

The nature of the problems in land use control is essentially one of administration in that they are related to decision-making processes and organization structure. Hence, even though the three patterns could be compared in many ways, Table 1 is laid out to show an affinity toward the modern schools of thought in administrative theory. Specifically, the bureacratic pattern (and to some extent, the commission pattern) may be associated with the formal theory of functional hierarchy, unity of command, and impersonal administrators described by Weber (Gerth and Mills, 1958), Gulick and Urwick (1937), and others. The Progressive logic emerged at about the time large-scale organizations in the private sector were demonstrating their ability to efficiently achieve

Table 1. Patterns of Land Use Control.

	Bureaucratic Pattern	Commission Pattern	Concurrent Pattern
Administrative Structure	Unitary hierarchy of authority	Commission/staff hierarchy of authority	Nonhierarchical interorganizational network; multiple public arenas
Intergovernmental Relations	Center-periphery structure	(see Note)	Noncentralized structure
Societal Assumptions	Homogeneous stable majority; static environmental factors	Stable aggregate groups; mixed factors	Plural overlapping associations in flux; complex environmental factors
Decision Rule	Welfare at-large	Balanced general welfare (intuitional)	Process-oriented fairness
Primary Performance Measure	Cost/unit efficiency	(see Note)	Effective delivery; minimal external effects
Expertise	Professional bureaucrat; general competencies	Technical staff; limited competencies	Specialized professionals; summation of competencies
Planning Function	Comprehensive/synoptic	(see Note)	Incremental

Note: Some characteristics like this one are not essential in distinguishing the commission from other patterns. Thus this characteristic may vary from case to case without confusing the structure, components, and behavior of task-specific commissions. Hence, for these characteristics, the commission sometimes may be submerged in the bureacratic context and in others as part of the concurrent pattern.

progress toward a unitary goal of material growth.[2] As Wilson said, government should be more "businesslike" in managing "the public interest" for a homogeneous majority. As a consequence, the organiza-

[2]A note of caution on the meaning of unitary goal is in order. In any specific context a unitary goal may be associated with development and materialistic values, but this is not always the case. Large-scale bureaucracies pursuing a single goal of environmental preservation also fit this pattern. Hence the essence of the meaning here does not revolve around development versus preservation but around a single value versus multiple values. At any point in time the welfare-at-large decision rule could favor either development or preservation, but the fairness rule is intended to accommodate multiple values through due process. Hence the problem of a unitary value approach has to do with its rigidifying effect on the organization and not with the substance of the value it advances.

tional style is essentially *closed* and the variety of forces outside the organizational boundary are usually ignored except as they may be used as support in achieving organizational goals.

On the other side, concurrent government more closely reflects the tenets of interorganizational network theory (Benson, 1975; Schmidt and Kochan, 1977) and the contingency model of administration (Thompson, 1967; Burns and Stalker, 1961). Concurrent government assumes diversity of interests and different scales of problems that are beyond the means and scope of unitary bureaucracy. As related to contingency theory, it advocates neither centralization nor decentralization but instead the arrangement of administrative units, big and small, to fit specific environmental and societal circumstances. Consequently, it reflects a more *open* structure of learning and adaptive systems.

Although the Founding Fathers saw themselves as designing a political solution around practical necessity, they may also have been unconsciously extrapolating the new pattern of political economy from an emerging but highly fragmented general theory of administration for the industrial age (Boschken, 1982). The noncentralized network of federalism fits the highly diverse and conflicting postcolonial society that was on the threshold of a complex transformation into the industrial age.

Relating these patterns to a well-established discipline of theory ties them to a wealth of more generally known concepts of administration. One can predict from this literature that universal solutions cannot be drawn. As the following cases will show, the usefulness of one pattern over another depends upon the specific land use circumstances. Unitary bureaucracy may work well under conditions of stability and minimal contention of interests, but it may be overwhelmed in complex and unstable settings. The same is true for commissions arranged around a center-periphery axis. Concurrent government, on the other hand, may be unnecessarily cumbersome under conditions of stability and homogeneity, but quite appropriate under conditions of uncertainty where complex decisions are needed.

The cases we will explore provide the means to examine these claims for land use control problems. Moreover, the analysis that follows them will show that the problems of administration (those of the individualistic public, human fallibility, diversity, and scale) are related to appropriate structure and organizational processes.

Part II | Three Cases in Land Use Control

CHAPTER 3

The Forest Service
at Mineral King

"The Greatest Good of the Greatest Number in the long run"
Gifford Pinchot

THE MINERAL KING case spans more than thirty years of deliberations. While it involved a variety of federal, state, and local agencies, the events were dominated by the U.S. Forest Service. Granted exclusive administrative authority over federal forestlands, the service acts essentially as a large unitary bureaucracy in a center-periphery pattern of intergovernmental relations. To this extent, the agency's structure and behavior closely reflect the methods and intent of Progressive values. Not only was it the first and most extensive experiment of the movement, but "the agency in fact stands as the prime administrative achievement of Progressivism . . ." (McConnell, 1966, p. 199).

The Forest Service became the first and enduring experiment by no accident. Gifford Pinchot, first chief of the Forest Service, was one of the leading Progressive philosophers during the movement. With his interest in resource management, he used forestry as a vehicle to implement his beliefs on administration and the role of government. A central theme in Pinchot's works, for example, is control over private forest enterprises by a public monopoly more responsive to the public interest (Pinchot, 1910).

Through the efforts of Pinchot and others, the concept of "conservation" was made a distinct element of Progressive values representing policy in the field of natural resources. In the first Forest Service directive, written by Pinchot over the Secretary of Agriculture's signature, the economic emphasis of conservation is defined as the "businesslike manner" through which natural resources may be efficiently used. "In the administration of the forest reserves . . . all land is to be devoted to its most productive use. . . . All the resources . . . are for use, and this must be brought about . . . under such restrictions only as will insure the permanence of these resources" (Wilson, 1905). Other values are relevant to the term only in the sense that regeneration periods afford an opportunity for natural resources to be utilized for "noneconomic" purposes.

A role for public forestry originally grew out of the federal government's land disposal policies and the "cut and run" philosophy of private lumbermen during the nineteenth century (Boschken, 1974, ch. IV). By the end of that century, dwindling forest resources created demands for public control of what remained. In 1891 President Harrison signed into law the forest reserve system, in 1897 agency jurisdictions were clarified by the Forest Service Act, and in 1905 the Forest Service gained its current status and authority under the Department of Agriculture. Its initial jurisdiction encompassed 60 million acres mostly in the western states.

The history of the Forest Service is full of color and ideology and is by no means short on conflict (Cameron, 1928; Ise, 1920; Smith, 1930; Pinchot, 1947). The sources of conflict came from its Progressive ties but usually have been seen as a struggle over forest uses. As a part of Progressivism, the conservation movement showed optimism and "abundant faith in technology as the key to human problems" (Hays, 1958, p. 41). Forests, therefore, only had value in a development sense. By contrast, the opposing idea of "preservation" holds to noneconomic values which would reserve the forests for more pastoral uses. Usually disposed toward minimizing the impact of man and technology on ecology, the naturalist promotes only limited forms of recreation. Although circumstances frequently unite these two orientations against wholesale resource extractions, the expansion of urban interests into the hinterland has tended to dichotomize these former alliances into warring camps.

The kinds of intense controversies that surround the agency today were not as evident in the early years. Instead of focusing on forest uses, conflicts tended to revolve around jurisdictions and interagency relations. Like Progressive efforts in general, the issues were over political territory (McConnell, 1959; Ise, 1920). For example, after six years of attempts to gain exclusive control for his agency over all forest-, range-, and parklands, Pinchot was fired by President Taft in 1911. This resolved an intense and bitter controversy with the Interior Department over whether federal land ought to be administered singularly by the Forest Service or divided among several agencies (Pinchot, 1947).

Today the federal forest reserves are administered by three agencies: the Park Service and Bureau of Land Management in the Interior Department and the Forest Service in the Agriculture Department. With jurisdiction over 187 million acres of these reserves, the Forest Service is by far the largest federal agency in land use management and controls the greatest variety of forestlands and their uses. With only vague directives from Congress, it handles its responsibility with a high degree of administrative autonomy and, except for economically oriented special-interest groups, minimal public involvement.[1]

The Mineral King controversy revolves around a question of whether to develop a fragile, almost forgotten valley into a center of skiing, resort activities, and valley conventions. Consequently it provides a useful setting to examine a unitary bureaucracy under complex and uncertain conditions. Although no single case is definitive, it does provide an effective way of dealing with the larger questions in depth. To this extent, Mineral King involved major policy decisions that required the active participation of foresters at all levels of the hierarchy including the chief and the Secretary of Agriculture. Further, with a Congressional directive to use the forests for multiple purposes, the case shows extensively the process of prioritizing values and devising methods for achieving welfare at large.

The Forest Service

The Forest Service is a welfare bureaucracy and has been among the most articulate in defining the welfare-at-large doctrine. In stressing "the permanent good of the whole people," the first Forest Service directive drafted by Pinchot states: "In the management of each reserve . . . the dominant industry will be considered first, but . . . where conflicting interests must be reconciled the question will always be decided from the standpoint of the greatest good of the greatest number in the long run" (Wilson, 1905). Although appearing as little more than a cliche, this high doctrine has served to form the terms of administration for the Forest Service. Even with its ambiguities, forest rangers point to it as their guiding criterion in making policy and operational decisions. Moreover, as seen in the Forest Service manual and other documents, the agency recognizes that its ultimate role is to define the public good by specific analysis and weighing all relevant factors. Since passage of

---

[1] A possible exception to this minimal public involvement was the RARE II process concerning designation and planning of wilderness areas. The Forest Service held numerous public hearings throughout the nation and claimed to have provided public access to all levels of the decision process. Nevertheless, as seen by several critiques of the RARE II process, Forest Service behavior toward public participation was not without controversy. For example, the California Resources Agency responded to the process by saying that it was "not based on adequate public involvement and basic needs beyond logging weren't given much consideration. . . . It's unfortunate that the latest Forest Service study continues past trends and practices" (1979). Forest Service use of the EIS under NEPA has drawn similar critiques.

NEPA in 1969, this has involved increasing reliance on computers and operations analysis (Walters, 1974), but not on public involvement.[2]

To operationalize welfare at large, the Forest Service has developed its directive through two specific concepts: "multiple use" and bureaucratic efficiency. "Multiple use" is a relatively new term but not a new concept for the Forest Service. The idea was first reflected in the Forest Reserve Act of 1897, and was codified as policy in the Forest Service manual redraft of 1921 (McConnell, 1959). In this early period conservation management involved primarily the uses of timber, forage, and water flow. The multiple-purpose nature of the agency expanded over time as urban influences generated new demands for natural resources, and in 1960 the concept and term were joined and enlarged by the Multiple Use/Sustained Yield Act. That act declared that ". . . the national forests are established and shall be administered for outdoor recreation, range, timber, watershed, and wildlife and fish purposes. . . . 'Multiple use' means: The management of all the various renewable surface resources of the national forests so that they are utilized in the combination that will best meet the needs of the American people . . . " (Multiple Use Act, 1960). Since passage of NEPA in 1969, the Forest Service has attempted to quantify "multiple use" through computerized planning and zoning techniques. This was seen as necessary "to coordinate uses and minimize conflicts between uses . . . to provide greater aggregate goods and services to greater numbers of people" (Walters, 1974, p. 5). Its use of computers and other operations planning techniques was especially evident in the RARE II process, completed in 1979.

An inherent problem of multiple use, however, lies in conflict among uses. While the concept reflects the accommodation of all uses not contrary to conservation, the reality of specific issues usually means a choice between contending uses. The need for establishing a hierarchy of uses for different situations, therefore, is an unstated part of managing multiple use. Nevertheless, Congress has given no specific criteria or limitations on prioritizing competing uses and, except for some new techniques used in RARE II, the Forest Service has not significantly updated its manual on the subject since 1911. In that year the manual

[2]In a workshop on organizational learning and change which this author did for the Forest Service in late 1979, the issue of computers versus public involvement was a recurring theme. Many recognized that use of operations research only represented a further isolation from forces external to the organization. In the words of one administrative officer, "Computers can solve technical problems, but cannot provide the means of setting goals and incorporating values." While many in the service know they have a problem of organizational rigidity, the bureaucratic structure limits the means of learning what to do. The service is clearly at a crossroads where the past provides few directions toward the future. Moving from the management of stability to the management of conflict has no obvious route.

stated that "National Forest land should not be devoted to an inferior use so as to preclude a higher use" (Forest Service, 1911, p. 11).

Furthermore, in prioritizing values for alternative mixes of use, no system exists for making explicit value and preference comparisons, and few measures, except cost/unit efficiency, are available for judging alternatives. Congress recognized this in 1960 and attempted to mitigate the limitless discretion in ordering that considerations be "given to the relative values of the various resources and not necessarily the combination of uses that will give the greatest dollar return or the greatest unit output" (Multiple Use Act, 1960). In reality, then, the ambiguity of multiple use, both in law and in Forest Service policy, obscures its application to specific instances and greatly limits outside scrutiny of decisions made in the name of either multiple use or general welfare.

Owing to its flexibility under multiple use as well as its long-established ties with business enterprise, Forest Service prioritizing of uses has tended to heavily favor economic values and interests (Nienaber, 1973; Kaufman, 1967; McConnell, 1959). Pinchot, for example, described the forest as a "factory of wood" and, in contrast to the Interior Department's preservationist tendencies, he believed in aggressive "tree farming" (Pinchot, 1947). Over the years this has come to be institutionalized through the Forest Service's posture in defining demands in terms of "industries" and market application.

Moreover, Forest Service reliance on private enterprise for help in bringing the resources to market (i.e., timber, ski resorts) has given agency personnel a sense of businesslike prowess and pride in economic cooperation with the private sector. This is reflected in the agency's consideration of costs in terms of revenue; it is one of the few economically self-sustaining federal bureaucracies. According to a Forest Service planner, it generates revenues equal to about 85 percent of its costs, mostly from timber and resort-type recreation (Walters, 1974, p. 3). This economic posture is further reinforced by local community support for revenue-generating projects. Under the Forest Reserve Fund Act of 1908, 25 percent of any national forest receipts are distributed to the specific local community affected, usually county government.

In addition to multiple use, the welfare doctrine is also adminstered through an emphasis on bureaucratic efficiency and autonomy. From its inception the Forest Service has considered efficiency as indistinguishable from the greatest good. Pinchot in his draft letter of 1905 emphasized this Progressive theme by saying that "continued prosperity . . . is directly dependent upon [the use of forest resources] under businesslike regulations, enforced with promptness, effectiveness, and common sense" (Wilson, 1905). The necessity of efficient methods simultaneously minimized the propriety of public involvement. Seeing public involvement as "a difficult thing for our agency to handle" (quoted in Nienaber, 1973, p. 175), the Forest Service has always advanced the need for "large powers and unhampered discretion" (Wilson, 1941).

Although the service maintains extensive public relations efforts, public hearings and public involvement are seldom required by policy. When they occur, they tend to be either "listening" sessions or instruments to promote the agency's decision. For example, although the agency says its RARE II process is its boldest attempt to provide public inputs, it has been criticized by many for not adequately using these inputs in allocating forestry uses. While not favoring public hearings and devices for broad participation, the agency has several public advisory committees. Members are primarily economic interests who articulate industry demands for forest resources (i.e., timber, grazeland, watershed, commercial recreation).

This degree of bureaucratic autonomy was assured early in Forest Service history. Most of Pinchot's struggles with Interior and his success in having the agency placed under Agriculture stemmed from his desire to attain greater independence. This sweeping discretion was legitimized by numerous congressional acts over the years that expanded the authority of the agency without hampering it with standards, limits, public scrutiny, or workable administrative checks. In achieving welfare for the greatest number, agency experts "know best" in questions of both policy formulation and decision making. Discussing Forest Service planning and policy techniques, one forester argued that the agency's success in developing and administering comprehensive plans was due largely to its bureaucratic discretion: ". . . as an agency with far greater control over plan implementation actions than most planning agencies . . . many of the classic arguments against comprehensive planning are less appropriate [for the Forest Service]" (Walters, 1974, p. 7).

In unison with the welfare-at-large rule, the internal structure of the organization is that of a large hierarchy with comprehensive authority. As shown in Figure 1, the organization tends to follow the traditional scalar principle, referred to by the Forest Service as "hierarchical specialization" (Kaufman, 1967, p. 209). Because the forests are its exclusive domain, centralized control over policy and operations is seldom subject to concurrence by other agencies. The organization chart reflects, therefore, the structure of primary authority as it is delegated down from the Washington, D.C., headquarters, through the regional offices, and to the individual national forest supervisors. This hierarchy of control is spread over five functional responsibilities:

1. The chief of the Forest Service reports directly to the Secretary of Agriculture and, in conjunction with his Washington, D.C., staff, forms the national leadership in forestry. His office is responsible for

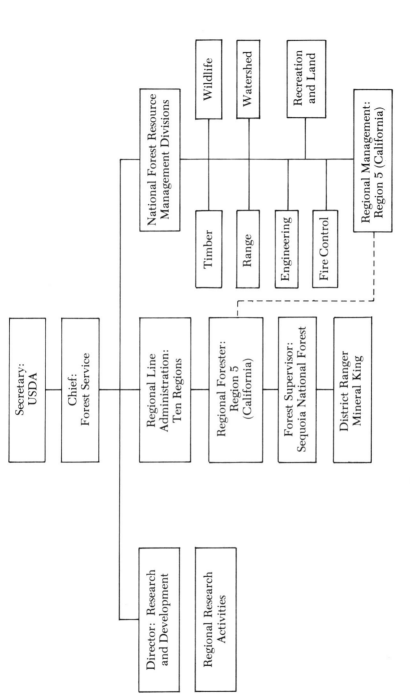

Figure 1. Partial Organization Chart of the Forest Service at Mineral King.

formulation of overall objectives and policy; direction for all programs, activities, and functions; preparation of major plans and agreements; program evaluation; and assistance to line units.

2. The staff units, consisting of research and development, forest management, and others, are separate from the line function of foresters. The largest staff group is forest resource management and is composed of individual advisory divisions (timber, watershed, recreation, and others). Their formal role is to fill a planning and advisory function, but practice in the past has varied from region to region. For example, during the Mineral King controversy the California regional head of recreation superseded his role by exercising great personal power over forest supervisors (line units). Recreation in the forests was a growing business, and budget allocations for this activity were controlled by the recreation division. Implementation of the Planning, Programming, Budgeting System (PPBS) minimized this to some extent.

3. The regional forester formulates objectives and policies and directs programs within his region. The Mineral King controversy occurred in the California region, known as Region 5, with headquarters in San Francisco.

4. The forest supervisor is responsible for short-range planning and execution of measures needed for protecting, developing, and utilizing the resources in the national forest. The Mineral King area is located in Sequoia National Forest, with headquarters in Porterville, Tulare County.

5. The district ranger is the lowest managerial unit in the organization. He helps formulate programs and carries out action related to his district.

In forming the linkages of command, the Secretary of Agriculture appoints the chief of the Forest Service. The position is somewhat competitive, since the position has classified status and appointments are reviewed by the Civil Service Commission. In practice, it is normally filled by promotion of one of the six assistant chiefs. Below the apex of this office, a formal unity of command is adhered to, with each level below responsible to the authority of that immediately above it. In the Mineral King controversy the essential decision to develop and promulgate subsequent plans was handled primarily at the regional office, with frequent correspondence with other levels.

With this type of "streamlined" decision structure, the Forest Service has always prided itself on the interchangeable character of its personnel. According to Kaufman, "The Service . . . shifts men to replace each other in what looks like a vast game of musical chairs, but for the serious purpose of giving them a wide range of experience in preparation for advancement to positions that require a broader understanding of national forest administration . . . " (1967, p. 176). Thus the agency follows its Progressive heritage in emphasizing the need for general bureaucratic expertise instead of scientific specialization.[3] Rotation generates uniformity of experience and organizational knowledge, which is further assured by hiring practices. About 75 percent of all professionals employed by the agency have general forester training rather than specialized degrees in life sciences or other technical fields. The vast number of positions, while having jurisdiction over specialized scientific matter, are filled by the generalist.

One might suspect that this orientation, which emphasizes knowledge or organizational norms and economic requirements, would produce less consciousness of environmental considerations — both socially and ecologically — than an organization of specialists. "The existence . . . of a single determinate individual formally empowered to issue decisions with respect to all functions . . . means that the competing claims of the several functional specialties will often be judged in terms of more general criteria of decision [i.e., bureacratic need]" (Kaufman, 1967, p. 210).

The national forest system is geographically dispersed throughout the United States, with heavy concentrations in the Rockies and Pacific Crest. The system is administered through nine regions (including Alaska) and about 150 national forests. Because of its geographical array and in spite of its hierarchy, the Forest Service has always referred to itself as a highly "decentralized" organization, with localized "on-the-ground" decision making (Wilson, 1905; Walters, 1974, p. 3; Kaufman, 1967; Forest Service, n.d., title 1000). According to one forester, ". . . the actual planning and supporting decisions are made on the basis of the judgment of local Forest Service officials most familiar with the situations involved" (Chief of Recreation Division, 1968).

Clearly the visible means for central coordination — proximity and reliance on ordinary daily contact — are somewhat absent, but the notion of decentralization is inaccurate. The Forest Service is certainly geographically decentralized, but the evidence does not support organizational decentralization. In order to see the difference, one must make a distinction between types of delegated authority. In order to create a hierarchy of decision, all organizations must delegate operating authority, but the term "decentralization" is reserved to the delegation of coordination responsibility and policy discretion. The Forest Service does not provide significant opportunity for either of these decentraliza-

---

[3] Owing to a change in civil service requirements, discretion to move personnel is no longer that of the organization. Individuals now have the formal right to apply for job openings and may not be forced to relocate. While pressures for reassignment remain great, some of the newer and younger generation of foresters and administrators have chosen to remain in a community indefinitely. This has not only thrown the bureaucratic logic of general knowledge into disarray but also represents a growing internal force for change away from hierarchical ways.

tion characteristics. Instead, agency procedures and rigid formal authority reveal a much greater desire for uniformity and conformity in all areas of decision making. Except for minor decisions or fire emergency, "virtually everything else is transmitted upward for approval and signature" (Kaufman, 1967, p. 103). In the case of orders handed down, "deviation is consciously discouraged, conformity deliberately encouraged" (Kaufman, 1967, p. 125).

Uniformity of decision and conformity to central command are assured through a number of techniques. Among the most important is the "preformed decision," which forms a decision hierarchy of predetermined rules, categories, and courses of action. For nearly every conceivable issue or topic, "events and conditions in the field are anticipated as fully as possible, and courses of action to be taken for designated categories . . . are described. The field officers then need determine only into what category a particular circumstance falls [and follow] the series of steps applicable to that category" (Kaufman, 1967, p. 91). The preformed decision is consequently used for both lower-level policy formation and operating circumstances. As a reflection of this downward communication of codified procedures, the Forest Service multivolume manual, known as the "bible," is among the largest and most detailed of any federal agency of comparable size.

A second technique to reinforce the central command includes a hierarchical chain of approvals and a system of auditing procedures. No decision of any unit takes effect without the necessary chain of approvals, and this serves as a means for higher-level officials to reshape or veto subordinate proposals. The auditing system, on the other hand, serves as what Pinchot called "the eyes and ears" of the chief. This is matched by regular inspections encompassing a broad range of items and is carried out by both the chief's office and the immediate level above the subject unit. Considering both the approval and audit requirements, the communications flowing to and from the districts, the forests, the regions, and Washington are voluminous and comprehensive. Although distrust is not the force behind the system, seeking approvals and furnishing facts through such a unitary hierarchy of command reveal how well individual officials conform to the standard procedures.

Making the formal authority techniques work, however, requires a favorable ideological disposition toward the agency's organizational needs. Although a number of outside forces create disintegrative tendencies, the Forest Service prides itself on a very high degree of solidarity, consistent behavior, and single-minded efficiency over the long run. To achieve this, a third technique is a well-organized socialization process which continues throughout a forester's career. The process involves recruiting compatible behavior types favorably disposed toward organizational demands; providing an elaborate "training" program (including orientation courses, refresher workshops, and intra-agency conferences); and making a conscious effort to socially inter-relate after hours. Over time, the forester comes to associate his identity and status with the agency and internalize its membership's perceptions, values, and bureaucratic methods. Although this may be changing somewhat, a sense among foresters is that the service provides a "one best way." If the forester is to succeed in this structure, therefore, he generally comes to recognize a dichotomy between "insiders" of the service and "outsiders." As a team participant, "only one thing gives any continuity, any structure to his otherwise fluid world: the Service" (Kaufman, 1967, p. 178).

Mineral King

The controversy over Mineral King swirled around a number of issues, most notably the demand for development versus the desire to shield a pristine ecological area from high-intensity recreation. The Mineral King area is located on the western side of the southern High Sierras, fifty-five miles east of Visalia and about equidistant from Los Angeles (228 miles) and San Francisco (271 miles).

Mineral King itself is a small subalpine valley surrounded by steep valley walls and high peaks. "Sidewalls of the valley generally have slopes averaging 50 percent, with the alluviated valley floor having slopes in the 2 to 10 percent range" (Forest Service, 1974, p. 35). Extending essentially in a northerly and thence westerly direction, the valley is about two and one-half miles long and one-quarter mile wide. The valley floor is about 300 acres in size, is traversed by the East Fork of the Kaweah River, and is the floodplain for numerous cascading tributaries in evidence along the valley sides. The entrance to Mineral King is at the northwest end where the Kaweah drains into a steep gorge extending twenty-five miles to Terminus Reservoir in San Joaquin Valley. Owing to severe avalanches, most of the valley is sparsely timbered except for aspens along the Kaweah and fir stands extending intermittently into the valley from the west side. Flora on the valley floor, however, provide a lush meadow groundcover consisting of ferns, wildflowers, grass, and high-altitude brush. Wildlife in the area is plentiful. Deer are among the most visible, especially during the seasons of fawning and summer grazing.

The terrain of the valley inclines gradually to the south where it terminates at Farewell Gap. Nearly twice as high as Yosemite, elevations start at 7,500 feet at Faculty Flat (entrance) and go up to 7,800 feet at Mineral King Village, 8,000 feet at Aspen Flat, and 10,588 feet at Farewell Gap. The surrounding valley rim provides a stunning backdrop of steep ridges and peaks which maintain permanent glacial formations. The east wall of Mineral King is the Great Western Divide and includes the noted Sawtooth Peak and Florence Peak, the highest point in the area at 12,405 feet (5,000 feet above the valley floor). The west side, known as Miner's Ridge, is less spectacular but has considerably more forestation and lush undergrowth.

Mineral King Valley is the focal point of a much larger area encompassing 15,630 acres of surrounding ridges, peaks, mountain basins, and twenty-one lakes (see Figure 2). Known officially as the Sequoia National Game Refuge, most of this terrain lies along and west of Miner's Ridge (west side). Within the confines are several large bowls including Farewell, White Chief, Eagle, Mosquito, and Mineral. All except Farewell have pristine lakes fed by glaciers, but Mosquito to the west is the largest with a chain of five lakes terracing down toward the north and paralleling Miner's Ridge and Mineral King Valley. Beyond this designated area lies wilderness. To the east of Mineral King is the Kern drainage with numerous lakes, meadows, and treeless ridges. To the south is the Kern Plateau and the Little Kern River. In the west and north is more wilderness with several stands of the giant sequoia redwood.

Jurisdiction over the area appears as a geographical anomaly. Ecologically, Mineral King has a greater affinity toward parkland than it does to the lower-altitude, lumber-oriented forestland. As shown in Figure 2, however, the area was administered until 1978 by the Forest Service as a game refuge connected to Sequoia National Forest by a narrow "corridor." Protruding into the southern portion of Sequoia National Park, Mineral King was surrounded on three sides by parkland. Consideration for park inclusion was made in 1926, when Congress incorporated adjacent lands as additions to the park, but Mineral King was excluded because of the visible remnants of marginal lumbering and mining activities (Kirby, 1973). In lieu of park inclusion, it was granted refuge status in recognition of its parklike characteristics. Administration was left to the Forest Service with the understanding that it would be governed by park values and policy (U.S. Department of Justice, 1971, p. 52).

Although having a rich history reminiscent of the Old West (Kirby, 1973; Gudde, 1969), the valley since 1890 has been an almost forgotten place. It is presently used as a small summer home settlement and a staging ground for back-country outings. Facilities include two campgrounds at the entrance (thirty-three campsites total), a cluster of sixty-six cabins, pack-horse stables, a ranger station, and a public telephone. A small store and post office are located at nearby Silver City. Entrance to the valley is free and parking is provided for about 100 cars. According to the Forest Service, the valley sees about 6,000 visitors

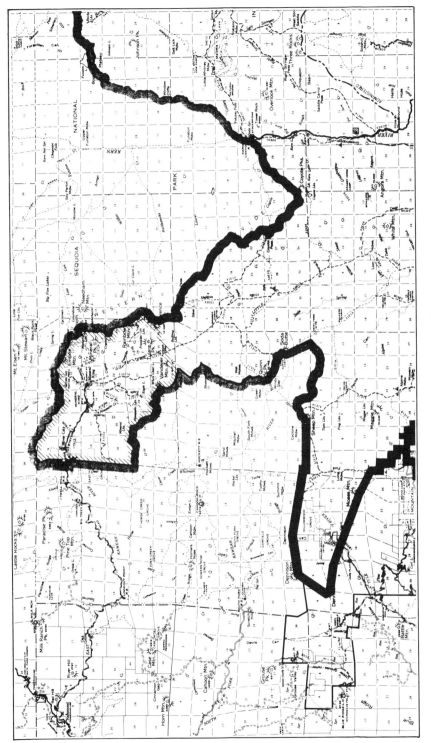

Figure 2. Map of the Mineral King Area

a year, and with trails leading in virtually every direction, most either pack into park wilderness to the north and east, pass through Farewell Gap to the south, or frequent the Mosquito Lakes chain to the west.

The narrow, winding road into Mineral King extends twenty-five miles from the main highway at Hammond, and takes from sixty to ninety minutes to drive. Modified only slightly since it was first constructed in the 1870s, the road has a low standard blacktop surface but is not suitable for winter snow travel. Consequently it is closed from about mid-November to April, leaving Mineral King inaccessible except to those with over-the-snow devices. This access route, first constructed by Chinese labor to support the short-lived mining boom, is maintained by Tulare County, an empoverished area which derives little economic gain from existing Mineral King uses and activities.

The Decision to Develop

Mineral King, like many hinterland areas, became ripe for development primarily as a result of the post–World War II era of spreading affluence which included more leisure time and better transportation. The Forest Service felt these new demands in the form of a "recreation boom." Skiing was one of the activities that gained high visibility. Although never enjoyed by a large portion of society, it nevertheless became a source of avant garde identity for those feeling the security of increasing leisure time, expanding middle-class incomes, and family-oriented pursuits. The push for more outdoor recreation facilities became a mandate of the "greatest good" for the Forest Service, and after 1945 mass recreation facilities in national forests grew to become the second largest activity, behind timber management. Ski resorts and other concessionaire-type recreation have been particularly appealing to the Forest Service because of the large revenues they generate. By contrast, campgrounds and trail maintenance are provided at a net cost by the agency. Further, large commercial recreation sites promised a new clientele and meant expanded budgets, activities, and public support. Thus socioeconomic factors dovetailed with agency policy.

Early postwar consensus demanded that ski resorts be of high quality and coincide with other recreational forms to make year-round use practical (Brower and Felter, 1948). In California a number of potential sites were identified, but those viewed with greatest interest tended to be near the Southern California market. The most immediate interest was centered on the north slope of the 11,500-foot Mt. San Gorgonio, located in a primitive area of San Bernardino National Forest. Situated just east of the Los Angeles basin, the area was first proposed for winter sports development in 1947. A fierce fight ensued, and the Forest Service decided that "the area has higher public value as a wilderness and watershed than as a downhill skiing area" (Forest Service, 1974, p. 20).

The issue was raised again in 1963 and rejected, but in 1964 and 1965 bills were introduced in Congress to allow development (*Rutgers Law Review*, 1970, p. 120; Forest Service, 1974, p. 20). In order to effect a "balance" between competing demands, the bills would have permitted 3,500 acres of the 33,398-acre San Gorgonio Wilderness Area to be set aside for winter sports. Because of strong opposition, the idea was again defeated. Intermittently during this twenty-year period, Mineral King was raised as a possible alternative to San Gorgonio. The Sierra Club, for example, originally accepted Mineral King development to save San Gorgonio. It maintained that the ". . . ideal defense would be to point out where else they could ski better and on finer ski terrain . . ." (Brower and Felter, 1948, p. 97). Anticipating a small project, the club left the Mineral King option open until 1965.

Mineral King was a suitable winter sports site for a number of reasons. First, although it was a five and one-half hour drive from Los Angeles, it was still the closest point except for the less reliable San Bernardino Mountains. The next closest locations are at least another hour farther. As such, it was seen as having the most promising regional affinity to Southern California (Elsner, 1972).

Second, the size and character of the terrain would provide exceptional skiing opportunities. The ridges and peaks surrounding the valley contain at least eight Olympic-size bowls, all of which have a northern exposure for consistently good snow conditions. The area is so vast that it would "provide ski terrain equivalent to six Squaw Valleys" (Walt Disney Productions, 1969, p. 13) and thus solve Southern California's ski problems all at once. Stressing quality, the Forest Service contended that the Alps were the "only known counterpart" (Hasher and Gibson, 1948, p. 5) and suggested that "the challenging slopes . . . and the relatively high elevation . . . combine in such a way that together they offer the potential of being one of the finest winter sports areas in the country — if not the world" (Forest Service, Feb., 1969, p. 3).

Third, in contrast to most winter sports areas, Mineral King would be suitable for year-round use because of its spectacular scenery and ecological variety. For both the Forest Service and local people of Tulare County, this "playland" potential meant satisfaction for large numbers and big revenue inflows. As early as 1947, estimates of 15,000 people and 2,000 cars per day were cited (*Visalia Times-Delta*, Jan. 11, 1947; *Fresno Bee*, July 30, 1953). Although spoken of in noble or honorific terms by the Forest Service and others (Fox, 1952; Miller and Frank, 1952, pp. 2-3), the local people were explicit. "We can put ourselves on the map with a resort that is unequalled in this world. . . .

It can ring the cash register for every man, woman and child in Tulare County" (Walters, 1947).

With such extensive possibilities, publicity and public pressure to develop Mineral King were intense during the active consideration periods of 1945-53 and 1960-69. As early as 1947, Mineral King was being viewed in the local press and by national ski magazines as "a treasure of White Gold" (*Visalia Times-Delta*, Jan. 11, 1947). The image held and was reinforced by the enthusiasm of numerous professional skiers. In 1949 the Forest Service contributed to the euphoria by writing letters to ski magazines, encouraging them to give editorial visibility to the Mineral King area (Gibson, 1949; Barnum, 1949). This precipitated organized efforts by ski associations and a huge letter-writing campaign. By 1953 the euphoria was so high that it led one forester to say, "We are somewhat concerned that enthusiasm for development may have clouded the major issues requiring careful study of all public benefits" (Wetzel, 1953). After subsiding in late 1953, the publicity and pressure resurfaced in 1960 with the prospect of new developer interests.

The first interest in Mineral King as a ski resort area apparently dates back to the late 1930s, but the first recorded correspondence was from a Major Wade, who in 1945 wrote: "I understand that the [Forest Service] plans to open certain areas for the development of winter sports, after the war. . . . I believe [Mineral King] to be the best ski terrain in the western [Sierras]" (Wade, 1945). Forest Service interest at this time was directed elsewhere; citing Mineral King's poor access and hazardous avalanches, the agency responded, ". . . we have given very little consideration to the Mineral King area . . ." (Norris, 1945).

In the succeeding months after this correspondence, the Forest Service was subject to so much discussion of the area's potential that it sent James Gibson, a respected agency ski expert, into the area to "obtain some first hand knowledge of that country" (Barnum, 1945). Gibson returned, concluding that "it might be deemed desirable to develop Mineral King primarily as a winter sports center, regardless of the summer values which might be injured or destroyed. On the other hand, this area represents one of the few remaining spots of its kind in California. Furthermore, ski developments for large masses of people can perhaps be directed to other, more readily accessible areas" (Gibson, 1945). On this basis, the agency decided ". . . that for the present at least we will not consider Mineral King as a winter sports area" (Elliott, 1945).

Developer interest remained high, however, and in June, 1946, the Forest Service received communications from what would become its first solid development opportunity — the Lawrence Company of Los Angeles. The firm represented the Mineral King Committee, a consortium of businessmen including Fay Lawrence, Cortlandt Hill, and Alexander Cushing, a New Yorker who "cashed several hundred thousand dollars worth of securities in order to have available cash to invest . . ." (Lewis, 1947). In the ensuing months this group carried on numerous discussions with the Forest Service and generated much publicity in Tulare County in an attempt to convert the agency's non-committal posture into one of advocacy. A year later, in August, 1947, that position was forthcoming and represented a commitment which would last three decades. Writing to Lawrence, the San Francisco regional office said, ". . . all Forest officers who are engaged in winter sports development in California, as well as the top skiers, are agreed that the area justifies development. The next question is 'How'?" (Barnum, 1947). Lawrence's response emphasized, ". . . the first job was to collect the present irrefutable evidence that Mineral King is potentially the greatest ski area in, . . . quite possibly, the world. The evidence is here" (Lawrence, 1947). In making the decision, the record shows that the Forest Service received no major opposition and, without active search or solicitation, presumed that none existed contrary to development.

During this period the Lawrence group also carried on a lobbying campaign in Sacramento to get better road access (Sieker, Oct. 3, 1947), and in Tulare County to organize a comprehensive snow survey. Although road funding failed to materialize because of the state's overcommitment to highway construction, success did come for the survey when the county board of supervisors committed $5,000 for a team to spend the winter of 1947-48 collecting data in Mineral King (Hasher and Gibson, 1948, p. 1). The Forest Service promised that if this cursory survey "supported the contention that the area is well suited to winter sports development, the Forest Service would be willing to make public its intention to permit the development, by private capital, of the winter sports facilities and accommodations necessary and desirable for maximum public use of the area" (Sieker, 1948). Led by Gibson, the service's ski expert, and Hasher, a noted professional skier, the party wintered at the Mineral King ranger station collecting ski condition data, monitoring avalanche activity, and making publicity films (Hasher and Gibson, 1948; Hill, 1947). Although the winter was abnormally mild, the conclusion was that adequate snow was available especially at higher levels and that avalanche was a surmountable problem.

With this, the Forest Service first speculated about granting the private consortium a use permit without competitive bidding (Barnum, 1948), then halted in favor of a prospectus for bidding. At first the agency tied development to road access, saying, "If and when a satisfactory all-weather road is assured we will publish a prospectus stating the public needs in Mineral King and setting forth the minimum develop-

ment needed" (Watts, Mar. 26, 1948). Then, concerned about im-
mediacy, the service abandoned the condition and in September, 1949,
published a prospectus which envisioned a year-round "interim" project
to be completed prior to a new access and requiring "over the snow"
transportation (Barnum, 1949). Suggesting a "total cost probably exceeding $300,000," the prospectus announcement said, ". . . the
development plan includes a resort hotel accommodating 150 persons, a
chair lift one mile long, a 'T-bar' lift 2100 feet long, and other facilities. . . . All construction must be completed within two years"
(Forest Service, 1949). For a number of reasons the Lawrence group's
proposal (Hill, 1947) never materialized into a bid. The lack of road access made the "interim" project a speculative rich man's retreat,
violating Forest Service objectives for mass recreation (Sieker, Oct. 3,
1947a; McArdle, 1953); statistics indicated little real demand at
Mineral King (Hasher and Gibson, 1948, p. 1); and the consortium
believed the agency use fees were "unreasonable" (Fox, 1952).

By this time (1951), however, the Forest Service was no longer simply
responding to developer influence. Internalizing the need to develop,
the agency commenced an active search, contending that since "neither
Mr. Hill nor any of his associates were sufficiently interested to secure a
permit and we had no other applications, we are free to negotiate for a permit . . ." (Barnum, 1951). A year later this effort generated a new inquiry by two wealthy Los Angeles real estate and oil men by the names
of Frank and Miller. Reflecting great enthusiasm, one forester said in an
office memo, "They possess a remarkable knowledge of what is involved. . . . Their approach is much more practical than that proposed by the Hill Corporation . . ." (McNutt, 1952).

After a cursory evaluation of the area the two men determined that adequate road access was a necessity for financial success. Stipulating this
as a prior condition, they submitted a proposal in October, 1952, which
dispensed with the "interim stage" and revised upward the resort scale
and ski-lift capacity. With an initial investment of $725,000, the new
plan called for lodge (100 guests), inn (250 guests), and dormitory (400
guests) accommodations for 750; an unspecified ski-lift system for 600
persons per hour, and additional T-bar and rope tows; and several
stores and eating facilities including one on the ridge adjacent to the lift
terminus (Miller and Frank, 1952). With no completion date specified,
but with an investment "considerably more than $1,000,000" (Forest
Service, 1952), final phase capacity was estimated to accommodate "at
least 2000 persons," offer ski-lift capacity for 1,800 persons per hour,
and provide nonskiing activities such as a "cinema," churches, gas stations, and ice rink (Miller and Frank, 1952).

Although a new draft was circulated within the agency, the assistant
chief decided that "it will not be necessary to issue a new prospectus for

general public notice since only the Mineral King Corporation evidenced any interest in the last prospectus" (Cliff, 1952). During this entire period of evaluation and search, the Forest Service had considered the question of development as entirely an internal matter: "we are not at liberty to make . . . information . . . available to the public" (Barnum, Jan. 8, 1953). No hearings occurred and only formal announcements were made. This and widespread animosity toward both the Lawrence group and Frank and Miller spawned resentment in Tulare County.

The local groups were concerned that the Forest Service was making tacit arrangements with the developers that might ultimately close out the Tulare people from any economic benefits (McArdle, 1953; Wetzel, 1953). The Lawrence group, for example, was quoted as saying that they were not "interested in the general public but in the skiers that would come and stay two weeks or longer" (Wetzel, 1953). The Frank and Miller group alienated the local community when they referred to local opposition as selfish political interests. According to the Forest Service, "these people are mostly prominent local leaders and strongly resent the selfish insinuation" (Wetzel, 1953).

This public skepticism and alienation, especially from local business associations, resulted in strong demands for access and a Forest Service public hearing (Rosenberg, 1953; Radoumis, 1953). A Forest Service office memo reflected concern, saying, "The Mineral King development is receiving considerable local attention. Mixed sentiments prevails [*sic*]." But wanting to avoid an undesirable precedent and fearful of invoking public scrutiny at such a fragile point, the memo concluded, "We do not believe the subject of Mineral King development has reached the stage of public hearing" (Wetzel, 1953). Instead, the agency encouraged informal discussion groups among those favoring development. Responding to this, the Tulare County Chamber of Commerce organized a "semi-public hearing" (Rainwater, 1953) that all agreed would serve to promote development and entertain sentiment concerning the project scale. The "hearing" was held in March, 1953, and, although conducted by Congressman Harlen Hagen of Visalia, was not subject to public notice. Instead, eighty-two invitations were sent out, primarily to business organizations and ski clubs. Only three went to conservation groups.

The central theme revolved around road access and the choice between two alternative development plans: one for light development (Lawrence group plan and first prospectus) and the more extensive Frank and Miller proposal. The Forest Service opinion was that justification could only be made for a project on at least the scale of that proposed by Frank and Miller (McArdle, 1953). The question of whether the project should be located at Mineral King was not on the agenda, and the Forest Service would later argue when the question was raised that the "hearing" disclosed "no opposition" (Connaughton, 1965). Two weeks after the "hearing" Frank and Miller attempted to accommodate local sentiment by offering to combine forces with Ray Buckman, a local resident and owner of the Mineral King stables. The Forest Service, seeing a possible breakthrough in the stalemate, showed approval: "We believe tieing of local people to a development has certain immeasurable value. . . . By Mr. Buckman becoming an active proponent in the development of the Mineral King area it is possible to carry out our basic concepts for the development" (Barnum, Mar. 24, 1953).

The project, however, never materialized from all these maneuvers. From the start, the need for an all-weather access route was an overriding barrier. In 1947 new road construction costs were estimated at $3 million, a figure ten times the proposed resort investment of the Lawrence group. In 1953 the figure was raised to $5 million (Wetzel, 1953), which was more than five times that of the Frank and Miller plan. The high cost was compounded by the need for concurrent review by and negotiation with the state highway department (which had jurisdiction over funding and construction) and the Park Service (which maintained jurisdiction over the parkland right-of-way). Recognizing these requirements as early as 1945 (Gibson, 1945), and deciding in 1948 that it was unable to fund the road itself (Watts, Mar. 26, 1948), the Forest Service was unsuccessful in 1953 in placing the new road in Governor Knight's ten-year highway program (Wetzel, 1953). With the developers unwilling or unable to commit the funds, the Forest Service suspended active consideration, leaving development plans dormant for seven years (Sieker, 1959).

For many reasons the Mineral King project was always somewhat tenuous. With all the economic, political, and ecological side effects it would create, the Forest Service had need of a "first class" developer, one who had a good business reputation and a popular image. The two developers of the early 1950s had questionable credentials and a money-hungry tinge. Regarding the Frank and Miller group, one forester cautioned, "Our concern would be to assure ourselves that no stock selling promotion scheme is involved. . . . I am always skeptical about possible promotion schemes organized on the strength of a Forest Service permit. However, one of these days someone is going to promote an outstanding ski development in California . . ." (McNutt, 1952). That "someone" finally came in the form of Walt Disney in the spring of 1960. Knowing that no one carried a more invincible image than Disney, the Forest Service was euphoric. Greatly "impressed with Mr. Disney's sincerity and realistic approach," the regional head of Forest Service recreation said, "He has succeeded in almost everything he has ever undertaken, and has surrounded himself with the most qualified men available for all his enterprises. Since we have had an overdose of experience with permittees who operate on a shoestring, I hope it will be possible to further stimulate his interest in the Mineral King area" (Davis, July 8, 1960).

The Disney Proposal

Disney's initial interest stemmed both from his desire to extend activities into the resort/recreation business and from his contact with a number of professional skiers during the 1960 Winter Olympics. After a cursory review of possibilities Disney decided to pursue "a first-class winter recreation area, without overnight accommodations. . . . The area should preferably be less than three hours drive from the users, and have dependable snow for at least three months each year" (Davis, July 8, 1960). Having specific knowledge of the Los Angeles area, he chose San Gorgonio as his first target. In a June, 1960, meeting with the Forest Service he pressed his need for this area, suggesting that some compromise with wilderness interests would be possible. The Forest Service discouraged this approach and offered Mineral King as an alternative. Uninterested in the area because of distance and poor access, Disney ended the discussion by saying, "Well, let's forget it" (Davis, July 8, 1960).

Not wanting the opportunity to slip by, the Forest Service wrote letters to Disney and his ski associates. Suggesting that Mineral King development was an inevitability, the regional chief of recreation wrote, "I regret that our meeting with Walt Disney did not turn out more favorably but plan to do as much as I can to further stimulate his interest in the Mineral King project" (Davis, July 11, 1960). Nevertheless, another four years elapsed before Mineral King received renewed interest. Disney remained intent on San Gorgonio and pursued the 1963 hearings and 1964 congressional interest in reclassifying the area. Exhausting these possibilities, he turned his interest to Mineral King along with several others in 1964. By December the Forest Service was aware that "it may be necessary to prepare some form of prospectus to test the extent of the interest and provide background data for negotiations" (Davis, 1964). Disney's interest, however, was already confirmed by his $5 million purchase of substantially all the valley's private holdings (28.5 acres) during 1964. The firm would later contend in its official bid that the acquisition placed it in the most favorable position as the likely developer, since such exclusive control assured "orderly development of Mineral King" (Walt Disney Productions, 1965).

The prospectus was issued in February, 1965, and represented the third time in twenty years the Forest Service would commit itself to providing "an area and facilities to accommodate many visitors in pursuit of scenic, high elevation, summer and winter outdoor recreational experience" (Forest Service, 1974). The agency claimed that "Mineral King is the only remaining area where high quality, large scale winter sports opportunities can be provided . . . to Southern California. At the same time it can help meet needs for . . . a compact area of high visual quality" (Forest Service, 1974). It further pointed to the state's rapid growth, increasing leisure orientation, and overcrowded ski areas: "The public needs the development, almost desperately" (Forest Service, Feb., 1969). Reinforcing this was an agency prediction of large economic inflows to Tulare County and the state, culminating with a fifteen-year "total [private] expenditure . . . of ONE BILLION DOLLARS" (Forest Service, Feb., 1969).

The prospectus conditioned its calls for bids, however, by requiring access improvement as an essential first step: "the successful applicant will find sufficient incentive, without obligation on the part of the Forest Service, to solve the winter access problem . . . " (Forest Service, 1965). Establishing an initial investment "conservatively estimated at three million dollars," the Forest Service envisioned facilities that would include lifts or tramways with a 2,000-person-per-hour capacity, parking for 1,200 automobiles, resort with overnight accommodations for at least 100 individuals, and support facilities. In soliciting bids, the agency announced four criteria for selection:

1. The suitability of the proposed development in terms of meeting the public need (pursuit of the greatest good).

2. The bid fee based upon percentage of receipts with no consideration of bids less than 2 percent (revenue/public enterprise criterion).

3. Sufficiency of developer's financial resources (organizational size and financial connections).

4. Proof of experience, character, and ability (good public image).

Six bids were received that met or exceeded Forest Service considerations but, concerned about "shoestring operators," the regional office eliminated four immediately. The two remaining were those of Walt Disney and Robert Brandt, a financial expert, film producer, and husband of actress Janet Leigh. Disney, a Republican, and Brandt, a Democrat, both had strong national political connections in addition to good reputations. Although inclined toward Disney because of his public image, the service had no easy way of eliminating Brandt. Fearing a controversy, the agency submitted its evaluation and recommendations to Secretary of Agriculture Orville Freeman to assure itself broad support (Cliff, Oct. 7, 1965). Recognizing the importance of the issue, Freeman called the two bidders to Washington and assumed responsibility for the decision. Although questions exist as to Disney's influence and the propriety and fairness of the selection process (Brandt, Dec. 30, 1965; Forest Service, 1965, p. 4; Nienaber, 1973, pp. 73–77), the choice of Disney was made in December, 1965, without controversy. Seeing the culmination of a twenty-year search for a progressive corporation, the Forest Service stated, "For the first time, we have a developer planning everything from scratch, and planning it far better than any ski development has been planned before. We're happier with Disney than a frog in a mud puddle" (Hano, 1969, p. 56).

Disney was issued a three-year planning permit and in January, 1969, submitted a master plan "essentially the same" as the firm's 1965 proposal (Walt Disney Productions, 1969). In the interim, the Forest Service and Disney had carried out a comprehensive planning program that cost Disney more than $500,000 (Forest Service, Feb., 1969). In announcing approval, the Forest Service said that Disney had "combined innovations in outdoor recreational facilities, with the best features of existing complexes now found in the United States, Europe and South America" (Forest Service, Jan. 27, 1969).

An ambitious project in its own right, it was also being planned simultaneously with the firm's new Disney World in Florida. The plan envisioned a development of vast size and scope, costing an estimated $35.3 million (nearly twelve times the investment suggested in the Forest Service prospectus) and generating an initial revenue of $23 million annually. Handling two projects of such magnitude was no problem for Disney during this period. As shown in Table 2, the corporation was growing rapidly between 1965 (the year Disney made its proposal) and 1969 (the year the Forest Service accepted the bid). By nearly tripling its asset base, Disney was on the threshold of becoming one of the few hundred largest U.S. industrial corporations with broad financial capacity. While Mineral King would have represented 40 percent of company assets and 21 percent of sales in 1965, other ventures like Disney World would have diluted each of these figures to about 15 percent in 1969.

Describing the development as the biggest and best in the world, Disney said that the "facilities in Mineral King equal or surpass any Alpine recreation area in terms of master planning, visitor accommodations, activities for all ages, operations and conservation techniques" (Walt

Table 2. Size Indicators: Disney Corporation.

	1965	1969
Assets (in millions)	$ 88.2	$238.2
Net Sales	109.9	148.4
Net Income	11.4	15.8
Mineral King:		
Revenues as a Percent of Total Sales	20.9%	15.5%
Investment as a Percent of Total Assets	40.0%	14.8%

Source: Disney Corporation, *Annual Report* (1973).

Disney Productions, 1969, p. 7). The initial phase was to be spread over a five-year period starting with the scheduled opening date in the winter of 1973. Long-range plans for expansion beyond the initial $35 million were also developed, but no specific dates were ever given.

The plan called for a year-round recreation area to accommodate, at full operation in the initial phase, an annual visitation rate first estimated in 1965 at 1.7 million. This was revised down to 986,000 when inexpensive summer accommodations and most camping sites were eliminated from the 1969 final submission (Walt Disney Productions, 1969). Of the total visitation, 35 percent were expected to come from out of state; in terms of seasons, 66 percent were to be during the summer period (240 days) and 33 percent during winter (120 days). Disney and the Forest Service further projected that average daily visitation would be 5,000 people (8,500 in the final phase) in the winter and 14,000 in the summer, 74 percent of which would not stay overnight (Walt Disney Productions, 1965).[4] Concerning market segment, the plan quite literally included every desirable middle-class image: "families," "single persons," and "college students." The Mineral King lodging mix, however, was to be developed primarily for "organized groups" and conventions (Walt Disney Productions, 1969, pp. 20, 41).

Access for such large numbers was to be over a new, twenty-mile, two-lane highway with occasional passing lanes, built to accommodate speeds up to fifty miles per hour and capable of handling 1,200 cars per hour in each direction (U.S. Department of Justice, 1971, p. 6). The 1969 estimated cost ranged from $23 to $30 million and was to be financed primarily with state funds (Walt Disney Productions, 1969). Disney also envisioned some supplemental group transportation and registered the names "Mineral King Airways" and "Mineral King Stagecoach Lines" with the state of California (Nienaber, 1972).

The master plan called for four groupings of facilities and activities. The first of these was the "auto reception center," to be located at the valley entrance known as Faculty Flat. Situated on thirty-five acres, the center was to include an eight-to-ten story parking structure located "in a deep, natural depression," capable of handling 3,600 vehicles. It also was to contain a railroad station with a train maintenance shop, general store and post office, secondary lodging for up to 2,700 guests, two restaurants with 300-seat capacity, service station, employee housing, hospital and fire station, warehouse, 60,000-square-foot central commissary and food preparation center, gondola lift station, ski shop, and administrative offices (Walt Disney Productions, 1969).

[4]These average daily figures are inconsistent with Disney's total visitation of either 1.7 million or 986,000. Using a weighted average for the 5,000 winter and 14,000 summer figures, the figures are consistent with a total visitation of 3.9 million annual visitors.

The importance of the reception center was based on Disney's banning of automobiles from the valley itself. Although the firm contended this was "to avoid distraction from [Mineral King's] beauty," the actual motivation for exclusion arose out of the European experience of auto congestion and pedestrian hazards around resort facilities (*Rutgers Law Review*, 1970, p. 111). In lieu of autos, guests were to transfer at the reception center to "colorful excursion trains" with a peak hourly capacity of 3,000 persons (4,000 in the long range). These trains were "planned to use an electrically-powered cog rail system to carry Mineral King guests from the sub-level auto reception center to the main village a mile and a quarter further up the valley" (Walt Disney Productions, 1969, pp. 44, 49).

The "village" composed the second grouping of facilities and, designed with an "American-Alpine" style, was to be arranged to create "an illusion of smallness" (see Figures 3 and 4). As the project's focal point of attractions, the village was to "recreate the charm, character and environment" of European resorts, and provide "inter-related, conveniently located accommodations, shops and recreation facilities" (Walt Disney Productions, 1969). Covering between twenty-five and fifty acres and located at the confluence of Monarch Creek with Kaweah River (known as Harry's Bend), this area was to contain hotels varying in height up to five stories and providing 2,400 beds in 1,030 rooms for up to 3,310 persons; a variety of restaurants and snack bars with a seating capacity of 1,700; a variety of shops; open and enclosed ice rinks, swimming pools, gondola lift center, chapel, theater, convention center, "teen center," and adjacent equestrian facilities.

Ski facilities represented the third grouping and were to be spread over a total of 13,000 acres and extend four miles out into the surrounding wilderness, primarily to the west (see Figure 5). Planning to satisfy over 80 percent of all 1985 unmet ski demand in Southern California, these facilities were to include twenty-two lifts and gondolas (twenty-seven in the final phase) with a total lift capacity of 22,000 skiers per hour; a 350-seat "buffeteria" at the Midway Gondola Terminal atop Miner's Ridge; and a 150-seat coffee shop at the lift terminal atop Eagle's Crest (Walt Disney Productions, 1969). At full operation in the initial phase, five bowls were to be developed (eleven in the final phase) including Farewell, Eagle, White Chief, Mineral, and Mosquito. Mosquito, the largest and most central, was to provide a run of over four miles with a vertical drop of 3,700 feet. Snow play areas were also to be provided for tobogganing, sled rides, and "specially designed" snow amusement equipment.

With Disney and the Forest Service expecting the largest crowds during the summer, the fourth grouping of activities was to be "an extensive

Figure 3. Mineral King Village: Rendering 1.

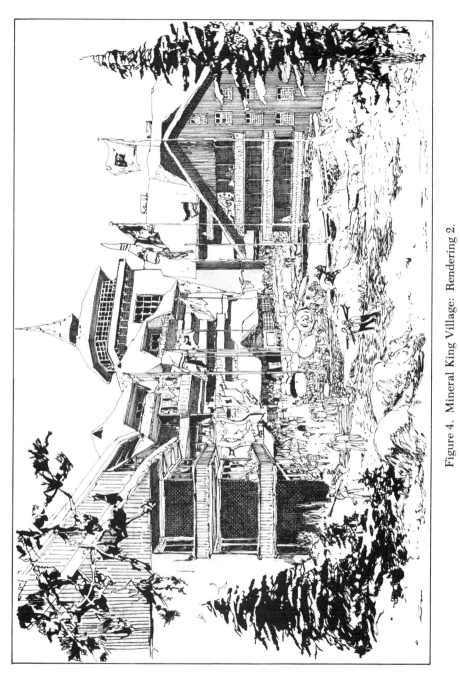

Figure 4. Mineral King Village: Rendering 2.

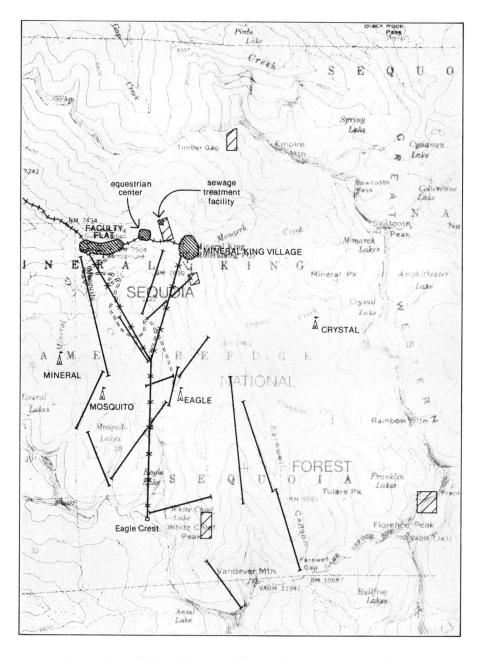

Figure 5. Land Use: Village and Ski Lift Facilities at Mineral King.

summer recreational program which will be based upon five major activities: fishing, an equestrian center, picnicking, hiking and camping" (Walt Disney Productions, 1969, p. 15). Access to mountain activities would be provided by fifteen miles of new hiking trails and use of lifts and gondolas. Close-in programs would feature "western-style" entertainment including hay rides and chuck wagon dining, square dancing, folk concerts, and "unique" facilities such as "a hay barn representing a new concept in playground operations" and a swimming pool built to look and feel like Huck Finn's "old swimming hole." Disney also raised the possibility of including a three-par golf course and tennis courts (Walt Disney Productions, 1969).

To support the vast crowds and extensive development features, the plan called for a complete water system capable of generating one million gallons per day in the initial phase from the Kaweah River; electrical power supplied by a 66,000-volt overhead power line from Three Rivers; a central tertiary treatment sewer system; garbage collection for eleven tons per day; medical facilities; and a video monitoring system for "crowd control," telecasting special events, and announcing "the arrival of Very Important Persons at Mineral King" (Walt Disney Productions, 1969). Ecological safeguards included flood and debris control by rechanneling the Kaweah and tributaries, and altering valley walls and ski slopes by blasting and earth moving to minimize avalanche hazard.

When the above proposal was made public, many viewed it as a "rural Disneyland." It was a compelling image, since many saw Disney's genius as his ability to create spectacular artificiality in films and in his adaptation of the amusement park to a grand scale. Using computer modeling and planning techniques adapted from Disneyland and Disney World, numerous features clearly mirrored the Disney style. Although the proposal suggested that Mineral King would benefit from the transfer of "knowledge and ability gained" at Disneyland (Walt Disney Productions, 1969, p. 64), the firm and the Forest Service adamantly denied the image, maintaining that "Disneyland is *entertainment;* Mineral King will be *outdoor recreation*" (Forest Service, Feb., 1969, p. 7).

Hence, from the modest requirements of the 1949 prospectus for a $300,000 resort and the 1965 prospectus for a $3 million project, the Forest Service accepted Disney's $35 million proposal two weeks after its 1969 submission date. With this quantum jump in size, the Forest Service anticipated $600,000 annually in agency receipts at full operation in the initial phase (Forest Service, Feb., 1969). Consuming over 500 acres for permanent structures and altering or affecting 13,000 additional acres, the Forest Service summarized the impact by saying, ". . . the project represents an essentially permanent land use that commits Mineral King to relatively high intensity recreation use" (Forest Service, 1974, p. 213).

Multiple-Agency Involvement

In the years prior to 1965, evidence shows little involvement of public agencies in the Mineral King planning and decision process other than the Forest Service. Environmental quality agencies had not yet been enabled, and multiple-agency activity was muted by the exclusive jurisdiction granted the service over the site area under the 1926 Game Refuge Act. Consequently, the only opportunity that arose for concurrent review was linked to road improvement to the area, and that did not occur until Disney's solid commitment in 1965. Even though these review capabilities were not introduced until late in the decision process, the Forest Service had been apprehensive over this sharing of powers, saying as early as 1945 that "some difficulty might be encountered in gaining all of the necessary approvals" (Gibson, 1945). Nevertheless, in 1965, with development close at hand, the trade-offs fell in favor of the new road and the necessity for concurrent review.

Agencies with jurisdiction over some aspect of the project were few in number but included all levels of government shown in Table 3. The first level of multiple-agency involvement included activities by Tulare County and the state of California. These activities were mostly favorable to the development and were sustained by lobbying efforts on the part of Disney, Brandt, and the Tulare County Chamber of Commerce. Lobbying had been important to Mineral King development from the beginning (Sieker, Oct. 3, 1947; Cliff, 1952), but the effort was intensified by Brandt's influence with Governor Brown and the Democrats, and Disney's with Reagan and State Senator Burns (then chairman of the Public Works Committee and president pro tem). Although Disney claimed, "We don't do any lobbying" (Hicks, Apr. 26, 1969), evidence indicates that the firm was very influential, especially after the 1966 Republican triumph in California.

Consequently, with bipartisan support, the road ceased to be a problem in July, 1965, with a legislative commitment to construct a new access (Forest Service, Feb., 1969). This was accomplished by means of a last-minute rider on another bill, and provided for the road to be included in the state highway system. Pursuant to this, the State Highway Commission adopted a $22 million plan for financing the route and instructed the highway department (Caltrans) to complete route studies (California Division of Highways, 1967). At the August, 1967, department hearings on the route, the agency described its new two-lane highway, designating it Highway 276.

Table 3. Public Decision Authorities: Mineral King.

Project Impact	Public Agency	Certification Authority
Economic	U.S. Forest Service	Forest resource planning; multiple-use policy making; letting of concessionaire contracts
	California legislature	Highway appropriations bill for project access
	State Division of Highways (Caltrans)	Highway planning, construction, and maintenance
	Tulare County	Employment development; property assessment and planning on nonfederal lands
Public Services	U.S. Forest Service	Avalanche and fire control; resources management
	State Division of Highways (Caltrans)	Highway construction and maintenance
	Tulare County	Provision of unemployment services; fire and police in adjacent areas
Land and Water Environments*	U.S. Forest Service	Resource management and environmental control of forestland
	National Park Service	Protection of park values and resources; maintenance of facilities; determination of right-of-way on parkland
Air Environment*	U.S. Forest Service	Air basin quality over forestland

*The State Air Quality Control Board and Regional Water Quality Board were being empowered at the end of the controversy, but took no active roles. Today they would exercise some concurrent authority over pollution impacts outside forestland boundaries.

The second area of review authority lay at the federal level with the Park Service and its parent agency, the Department of Interior. The Park Service was drawn in as a review agency because the new road was to cross about eleven miles of parkland and was to substantially affect the park ecology, especially around significant stands of giant sequoia. Unlike the state, however, the federal agencies were not as favorably disposed toward the development proposal.

Being a smaller agency in a smaller federal department than the Forest Service, the Park Service has a much more specific administrative charge. In preserving park values, its task is esthetically oriented: "The Service . . . purpose is to conserve the scenery and the natural and historic objects and the wildlife . . . by such means as will leave them unimpaired for the enjoyment of future generations" (Park Service, 1971, p. 17). This objective is reinforced by Congress's charge to Interior to ". . . provide for the preservation from injury of all timber, mineral deposits, natural curiosities or wonders within said park, and their retention in their natural condition . . . [and] shall provide against capture and destruction, for the purpose of merchandise or profit" *(Rutgers Law Review,* 1970, p. 106). Hence, with both a philosophical and a legal affinity toward an environmentalist position, the Park Service provided an avenue for review based on values different from those held by developers and the Forest Service.

The first appearance of concern for the Park Service occurred at its 1966 wilderness hearings for Sequoia and Kings Canyon national parks (Park Service, 1966). Although the hearing ostensibly was to deal with wilderness proposals, it was turned into an open hearing on Mineral King by the project proponents and opponents. The issue turned primarily around whether the Park Service should leave a wide corridor or a narrow one in anticipating the development's access and expansion needs. Disney and ski associations, supporting the greater flexibility of the wide corridor, substantiated the need for the project. As designated representatives, two Disney officials also read statements of support from U.S. Senator Murphy, Governor Reagan, and Mayor Yorty of Los Angeles. The opposition, consisting of several national affiliations, supported wilderness boundaries at the existing right-of-way without a fringe. They argued that, without narrow limits, the Forest Service and developers would "chip away" at the "wilderness threshold" and create an access corridor inconsistent with wilderness and park values.

Although the Park Service ultimately provided for a wide corridor, both it and the Interior Department became actively concerned about the road and overall project impact on parklands. Withholding final approval of the new right-of-way, in January, 1967, the Park Service requested detailed evaluative studies on ecological impact and studies of alternative means of access across its jurisdiction, including tramways, cog-assist railways, and monorails (Park Service, 1967). Through Disney, the Forest Service responded with a cost comparison of these alternatives, claiming that only the road was feasible (Tatum, 1967). Unconvinced by Disney's assertions, the Park Service said, ". . . our outlook remains unchanged concerning the need to consider alternative means of access . . ." (Montgomery, 1967).

Equally important to the Park Service was the project's overall impact, which would affect not only the access corridor but parklands surrounding Mineral King Valley. Although agreeing "that suitable recreational development of Mineral King is appropriate," the Park Service in a position paper maintained its desire "to make sure that those measures necessary to develop the area . . . are planned and carried out in such a way that they will not adversely affect important nearby National Park values" (Park Service, 1967). Fearing criticism from environmental groups, the Park Service urged the Forest Service to consider ways of minimizing adverse project impacts, especially regarding siltation and waste pollution in the Kaweah and the impact of crowd overflow into adjacent park areas (Udall, 1967).

As 1967 progressed, review and interagency negotiations greatly intensified. The Park Service, using its authority over new access as leverage, sought to gain guarantees and project alterations necessary to internalize potential adverse impacts on the park. The Forest Service, on the other hand, sought to maintain its unilateral control over development plans, and was reinforced by Disney pressures to sustain the agreed upon project size and intensity. Disney, fearing a reduction in scale, stressed to the Forest Service that if project investment was cut back toward the prospectus figure of $3 million, "the State would not consider the building of a road costing over $20 million" (Hicks, 1967).

In August, the proceedings drew in the concerns of the two department secretaries. Udall of Interior in a letter to Freeman of Agriculture asserted, "We are troubled by the side effects of the Disney plan as well as by the plan for a new highway into this beautiful but fragile valley . . . and I am honestly worried by the thought that we will not be honored 25 years from now if we make a decision to violate this valley . . ." (Udall, 1967). Freeman responded, "I am very disappointed by your letter. . . . The conspicuous failure of our two great Departments to reach agreement on as simple a matter as improving a few miles of existing road must be a growing source of embarrassment to the Federal Government" (Freeman, 1967). Although under great pressure by development interests and state political figures, Udall and the Park Service did not relent in their efforts to maintain review authority.

Concurrent with this review process, the Johnson administration, represented by the Bureau of the Budget, had been attempting to work out a settlement with the state of California for a new Redwoods National Park along the north coast. Governor Reagan's position on the proposal had been negative and was captured in his comment, "If you've seen one redwood, you've seen them all." Given Reagan's reluctance, the BOB saw a strategic opportunity for compromise by yielding to the governor's desire for Mineral King in trade for the new park. Offering this trade-off, the BOB wrote, "It is in the interest of the Administration and the State that the Mineral King area . . . be . . . developed . . ." (Hughes, 1967).

Consequently, in the fall as the two department secretaries became more embroiled in the controversy, the BOB intervened. Contending no urgent or compelling reason existed for delay, the budget agency over-ruled the Park Service's right to review and decided the Forest Service should pursue its plans without further restraint. Even though the BOB stipulated that its decision was based on public benefit and government revenue flow, Udall refused to issue an endorsing statement (Nienaber, 1973, pp. 100-101, 119). Hence, concurrent review at the federal ad-ministrative level ended here with the issuing of a BOB public statement that all parties had reached agreement. A year later, although finding design standards for the road unacceptable, the Park Service approved the new route (Hummel, 1968).

In addition to those formally endowed with jurisdictional authority, the Forest Service solicited the interest of several other agencies, primarily to fund joint research and gain support for the project. Although "given an opportunity to contribute" (Forest Service, 1974, p. 233), most responded without concern, since they had no independent authority to participate. The State Department of Fish and Game was one exception, responding that "in an extensive development such as the Disney proposal, considerable wildlife habitat would be lost . . ." (quoted in McCloskey and Hill, 1971, p. 4). The Forest Service countered with an offer of joint research. An exception of positive response was Tulare County. Thirsting for the potential economic im-pact, it cooperated in a number of ways under the premise that the pro-ject "will be good for California, the entire western part of the United States and the world" (Hillman, 1968).

Besides administrative inputs and authority, the influence of political figures was also conspicuous. Almost from the beginning, this had been an important source of promotion and instrumental support. Con-gressman Hagen of Visalia, for example, was responsible along with the Tulare County Chamber of Commerce for organizing the 1953 "public hearing" which publicized Mineral King's development poten-tial. With the growing possibility of development during the early 1960s, this political activity increased. The fact that funding for road access passed the legislature as a rider and without a hearing was due to the influence of Fresno's Hugh Burns, then president pro tem of the state Senate.

Probably the staunchest advocate, however, was Governor Pat Brown, who gave the project substantial visibility. In April, 1966, he submitted a proposal for supplemental funding of the road to the Federal Economic Development Administration, and in December received a $3 million grant (California Division of Highways, 1967). Accepting the grant, Brown referred to the project as "a creative work-ing partnership" (Walt Disney Productions, 1969, p. 5). In September, 1966, he accompanied Disney and a news crew to Mineral King. Flying in by helicopter, he captured the moment by saying, "I hope that ten years from today I can stand with Walt Disney again and look around at the wonderland that will have been created" (quoted in Hope, 1968, p. 75). When Reagan took office in 1967, he carried Brown's plans forward.

Other public advocates included California's two U.S. senators, George Murphy and Thomas Kuchel. Kuchel, who was chairman of the Senate Committee on Interior and Insular Affairs, promoted a trade-off between Mineral King and his proposed Redwoods National Park by writing an article in *Western Ski Time* magazine. Opposed to the development were a number of state and federal elected representatives. Among the most vocal figures in the legislature was Assemblyman Alan Sieroty (Los Angeles), who assailed the new road as a misallocation of state funds. At the federal level opposition grew to the point where eighteen California congressmen and twenty-three from other states sponsored a variety of bills to transfer authority for Mineral King to the Park Service (*Sierra Club Bulletin*, 1974).

The freeway proposal, which provided the opportunity for intergovernmental review and public access on Mineral King, was ultimately altered. Owing to Park Service concern, the high road cost compared to project investment, and state financing problems, the upper two-thirds of the new route (including that portion traversing the park) were deleted by the California legislature in August, 1972 (California Division of Highways, 1969; Forest Service, 1974).

Public Opposition

Political partisans were readily visible throughout the thirty-year decision process of Mineral King and were exemplary of the postwar enlarged regional influences. Most of these influences came from Los Angeles, and had affected not only Sierra ski resorts but also a number of other projects such as Oroville Dam and the California Water Project.

The source of concern came from questions of "public interest." The nature of the project posed a number of implications locally, regionally, and nationally, and thus stirred interests on a broad front. Protesting against the potential adverse effects, the opposition questioned the appropriateness of Forest Service methods in defining and achieving the greatest good. "Federal officials, assuming they know what is in the public interest and that they can handle all problems, have barged ahead without answers to any basic ecological questions" (McCloskey and Hill, 1971, p. 1).

Reluctance to intervene and competing environmental controversies combined to minimize action on Mineral King until the magnitude of the 1965 Disney and Forest Service plans became known. The most energetic of the opposition interests was the 78,000-member Sierra Club, founded by John Muir in 1892. When the idea of a Mineral King ski resort was first conceived in the late 1940s, the club saw the area as a reasonable alternative to San Gorgonio "because it foresaw a modest development which would not do violence to the landscape and the nearby wilderness . . ." (McCloskey, 1967).

By 1965, however, the growing scarcity of wilderness and the quantum jump in the project's proposed size combined to cause the club to reverse its position. The first major concern of the club was expressed by the Kern-Kaweah chapter in January, 1965, when it announced the completion of a comprehensive study on Mineral King (Harper, 1965). In May the club's national board of directors resolved that "the Sierra Club opposes any recreational development in the Mineral King area . . . [and] requests that no action be taken on any bid . . . until after public hearings" (Siri, 1965). From that point on, Mineral King grew to become the club's major issue, surpassing opposition to the SST, cutting the redwoods, polluting the Everglades, and damming the Grand Canyon (*Sierra Club Bulletin*, 1974).

Joining with the Sierra Club were a number of other groups both large and small. The most prominent included the 34,000-member National Parks Association, the 35,000-member Wilderness Society, the National Audubon Society, and the Federation of Western Outdoor Clubs. All reflected naturalist values and advocated the "need for a spacious and beautiful environment" to replenish and foster "growth of the human spirit" (Park Service, 1966, p. 29). Like that of the Sierra Club, their purpose in protesting the Mineral King project was to sustain "a balanced conservation program essential to the survival of our culture" (Wilderness Society, 1966, p. 1). In conjunction with the Sierra Club as opposition leader, the coordination of groups engaged in a variety of activities including (1) participation in the Sequoia National Park wilderness hearings and the California Highway Department hearings on the new freeway access: (2) development of ecological studies, films, and position papers on Mineral King; (3) a letter exchange with the Forest Service to promote public hearings; (4) written critiques of the project's environmental impact statement; and (5) picketing the Disney Studios in Burbank.

The specific concerns of the opposition were many and were compounded by the project's ambiguous plans and lack of limits on scope. Referring to the 1974 environmental impact statement, the Sierra Club contended, "Where the plan exists only as a concept, the detailed analysis of environmental impact . . . cannot be performed" (McCloskey, 1975). Nevertheless, the problem areas fell into three categories. First, considerable concern developed over the need for a large ski resort in a near-pristine mountain area. Although the Forest

Service saw the project as primarily fulfilling excess ski demand, the industry and Disney were talking in terms of a highly competitive and seasonal market where many large and small ski resorts were consistently near financial failure. Moreover, Disney, with its national media connections, envisioned large expenditures on promotion of the resort similar to that done in advertising Disneyland and Disney films. As a consequence, the opposition feared that Mineral King would be transformed by a project that could successfully sustain itself only by "creating a demand." Holding the position that the resort was not economically justifiable, the Sierra Club maintained that "if Mineral King is developed as proposed it may be a commercial success, but at the expense of other ski resorts . . ." (McCloskey, 1975).

A second concern was over the impact of project size and the detrimental effects of unrestrained technology: ". . . historically the Service has assumed that the bigger the project is, the better" (McCloskey and Hill, 1971, p. 8). The adverse possibilities were viewed in both extensive and intensive dimensions. From an extensive standpoint, the opposition expressed fears that the project would create pressures for satellite or concentric growth and degrade the surrounding wilderness with urban-oriented activities and conveniences. Believing that satellite development is "one of the most adverse impacts of a major ski area development," the Sierra Club argued that the problem was inevitable at Mineral King (McCloskey, 1975, p. 6). To illustrate, the club pointed to the fact that following announcement of the Disney plans, another private party in Silver City (the small community two miles down the road from Mineral King) requested a county zoning variance to accommodate its 160-acre planned unit development, which was to contain high-density lodges, condominiums, and a village shopping center. With regard to degrading the adjoining wilderness, the club asserted that because of large numbers of people and the comfortable access provided by summer use of ski lifts, "it is obvious that the effect on the backcountry will be very significant" (McCloskey, 1975, p. 4). To the opposition, the project was "one cancerous growth of commercial devastation" (Harper, 1965).

From an intensive standpoint, the opposition was concerned about the premise that "you can vastly increase visitation and still maintain a reasonably natural condition by skillful design and cosmetics." The club countered by saying, "The project has grown to such a size that all other values are in danger of being overwhelmed" (McCloskey and Hill, 1971, pp. 1, 3). This threat of a "crushing impact" stemmed from the concentration of individuals on the confined valley floor and the dispersing pressures along trails and the surrounding landscape.

A number of comparisons were made. The valley floor population density was related to that of New York City and to overcrowded

Yosemite, where valley floor density was half of what Mineral King's would be (McCloskey, 1967; Mineral King Task Force, 1974). In addition, the 1,700-room lodging facilities were compared with the 1,500-room Biltmore (the largest in Los Angeles at the time) and the 608-room Disneyland Hotel (Rettenmayer, 1969). According to the Sierra Club (and later confirmed by the Forest Service), the effect on vegetation, lakes and streams, and wildlife would have been substantial. "The Mineral King basin is simply too restricted in its physical and environmental dimensions not to suffer irreparably from the envisioned [project]" (Harper, 1965).

The third concern of the opposition was over the multiple impact of the new freeway. The most important impact, and the one which gained the greatest public attention, was environmental. Construction of the new route would require removal of eight million cubic yards of soil and would necessitate locating the roadway alongside two unique giant sequoia groves. Unsure of the consequences, the highway department and the Park Service each commissioned independent studies. Both reports emphasized major reservations over environmental safeguards and the threat to as much as 45 percent of the redwoods (Hartesveldt, 1966, p. 41; Clarkson Engineering Co., 1967). Feeding on this, the Sierra Club said, "Removing *any* giant sequoias or encroaching on their potential habitat is always lamentable, but destroying them for non-park purposes is inconsistent with the park established for their preservation . . ." (McCloskey, 1975, p. 11).

This position was further compounded by the belief that the new road was being promoted for use as a catalyst for private development and "that the current design is merely a foot in the door . . ." (McCloskey and Hill, 1971, p. 6). Pressures will generate "quickly for expanding the improved two-lane 28 foot roadway into a divided highway, with two 40 foot roadways" (McCloskey, 1967). Combined with alleged faulty inducement of growth, the opposition also argued that the road costs could not be justified in the public interest because funds would be reallocated away from more urgent needs in Tulare County and Southern California. "Why should the taxpayers undertake to subsidize a deadend road designed to service a monopoly concessionaire?" (McCloskey, 1967).

In total, the concerns amounted to the possibility that the Forest Service was sponsoring "a gaudy mountain carnival" (Park Service, 1966, p. 219) and that "making wilderness accessible to millions [was] a little like carving up Michangelo's statue of 'David' so that each of us might own one small chip of marble" (Burton, 1969). Consequently, "When weighed against our long-standing principles . . . there could be little doubt that we had to oppose major commercialization and development of Mineral King" (Siri, 1965). As an alternative, the opposition argued that "Congress has made it clear that it wants this land treated more as a park than as regular national forest" (McCloskey, 1965), and thus proposed that the area be granted "National Park status as the best long-range solution . . ." (Sierra Club, 1969).

Since the Forest Service decision process on Mineral King had reached the advanced stage of commitments prior to significant public knowledge of the details and implications, the organized opposition's initial efforts from 1965 to 1969 represented a rear action strategy to stall for evaluation time and public awareness. Having failed at this attempt, the environmentalists found themselves in 1969 with much public support but also with the Forest Service's immediate intention to sign the final thirty-year contract with Disney. Left with no other avenues, the Sierra Club filed suit in federal district court against the Secretary of Agriculture, the Forest Service, and the Secretary of Interior in June, 1969, asserting that "the secret and closed nature of the whole process left the critics with no recourse but the courts" (McCloskey and Hill, 1971, p. 9).

Relying on the right to request a judicial review, the club asked for a declaratory judgment on the legality of the administrative decision and requested injunctions to stop further progress (*Sierra Club v. Morton*, 1972). Directed primarily at the Forest Service, the suit alleged four categories of violations including arbitrary and capricious action concerning the new freeway and development of the valley and surrounding slopes (*Sierra Club v. Morton*, 1972; *Rutgers Law Review*, 1970; Ferguson and Bryson, 1972). Among the allegations, the issue of greatest concern was that the Forest Service had exceeded its statutory limits in issuing permits to Disney. Under a 1956 statute the service was allowed to grant thirty-year permits covering a maximum of eighty acres (prior to 1956, the maximum was five acres). At its inception the eighty-acre limit was seen by the Forest Service as providing "for such public and semipublic uses as landing fields, resorts . . . and ski lifts . . ." (Morse, 1955). Nevertheless, when ski resort developers requested larger parcels, the service routinely granted them by combining the long-term permit with a three-year revocable permit.

According to the agency, "These two permits can be considered as one permit for most practical purposes . . ." (Forest Service, 1952). Such action was taken to accommodate large-scale development, but the Sierra Club saw the procedure as a "clear and patent effort to circumvent" the law (McCloskey and Hill, 1971, p. 10). It further represented a persistent trend in Forest Service thinking, which in 1948 saw that issuing a revocable permit for a large investment "might embarrass us if cancellation became necessary in a year or two" (Watts, July 8, 1948). Consequently the Sierra Club argued that the land covered under the three-year revocable permit was an integral part of the entire project and was not really subject to revocation. In Disney's case revocation would have required removal of all ski lifts covering access to 13,000 acres and would have severely impaired the $35 million investment.

The district court granted a preliminary injunction on August 4, 1969, and rejected the government's challenge that the Sierra Club did not have "standing" (i.e., legal right) to sue in the name of the public interest. Specifically speaking to the dual permit system, the court said the eighty-acre limit was intended to contain all structures including ski lifts, and that "to hold otherwise would be to assume that the Congress . . . contemplated that it could be circumvented, even nullified, by the device . . ." (quoted in Ferguson and Bryson, 1972, p. 527). The court further ascertained that the Forest Service had not prepared an environmental impact statement. The government appealed and the Ninth Circuit Court of Appeals reversed on September 16, 1970, ruling that the Sierra Club did not have proper standing because it was not directly affected by the administrative decisions. Regarding the dual permits, the court noted that at least eighty-four recreational developments were in existence under such a combination and therefore were "convincing proof of their legality" (quoted in U.S. Department of Justice, 1971, p. 8).

The case was again appealed by the Sierra Club to the U.S. Supreme Court. This time the Court addressed itself only to the question of standing and on April 19, 1972, determined in a four-three decision that the club did not show that it had been sufficiently affected to bring suit. However, the Court noted that "our decision does not, of course, bar the Sierra Club from seeking in the District Court to amend its complaint" to avoid the problem of standing (*Sierra Club v. Morton*, 1972, p. 8). The club did amend but then failed to proceed, favoring instead a campaign in Congress to remove Mineral King from Forest Service jurisdiction. From the suit's beginning, mixed feelings were evident on the part of those being sued. The Park Service, for example, said, "Should the courts ultimately determine our proposals to be unlawful, we shall cheerfully adapt ourselves to any such determination" (Bowen, 1969). The Forest Service, on the other hand, was not so accommodating.

During the entire period of public opposition to Mineral King, the Forest Service in conjunction with Disney reacted strongly against requests for public hearings, environmentalist concerns, and general anti-development activities and opinions. Stating that "the Sierra Club stands alone in opposing Mineral King," the San Francisco regional forester lamented, "I have asked the Sierra Club for constructive advice and to work with us. . . . They have chosen, instead, to bring this suit" (Deinema, Oct., 1969). To counter the growing opposition, the Forest Service also produced a number of "position" papers, promotional pieces, and "news releases." Disney, on the other hand, assumed an apolitical posture at first, saying that it was "simply the agency by which the public land is developed for public use" (Park Service, 1966, p. 103). But when it was clear that the firm's reputation was at stake, the Disney project manager organized an active campaign, claiming that "it is unfair to think that Disney did a good job at Disneyland, but will do a bad job elsewhere" (Hicks, 1969).

Sparked by the rhetoric of the contesting parties, public opinion and the press assumed an active but mixed posture toward the controversy, and grew from a pre-1965 local level to attain a national scope. Referring to "private greed, bureaucratic empire building, and official ir-responsibility," the *New York Times* asked, "Have the Forest Service bureaucrats no sense of shame about taking a wonderful portion of the nation's rapidly dwindling natural heritage entrusted to their care and surrendering it to the exploiters?" (Feb. 2, 1969).

Finally, after seven years of protest and lawsuits, the Forest Service made some modifications to the project that it formerly had said were not feasible for cost and convenience reasons. Most important among them was the substitution of a cog-assist electric railroad in May, 1972, to replace that portion of the new freeway crossing parkland (about 13.3 miles). Financing was to be by revenue bonds issued by Tulare County. In addition, incremental reductions in the project's original capacity and investment were made, but no limits were placed on future expansion. Objections to the project remained unchanged; as the Sierra Club commented, the ". . . project is still huge, and we have seen no guarantee that it won't grow even larger" (Sierra Club, May 3, 1972).

With no apparent end in sight to the litigation proceedings and with a tarnished image, Disney announced in July, 1975, that it had placed its plans for Mineral King "in dead water," and moved its attention to a 10,000-acre site on private land near Independence Lake, northwest of Lake Tahoe. Although not flatly abandoning Mineral King, a firm spokesman said "it will have to wait until the Independence Lake resort is finished" (*Los Angeles Times*, July 22, 1975). Concurrently, the Forest Service announced in August, 1975, that all development in the valley had been abandoned and that a scaled-down version of the facilities would be constructed two miles down the road at Silver City. Access to the ski slopes would be by six to nine ski lifts originating at the new village (Forest Service, 1975). No public hearings were planned (Wychoff, 1975), but circumstances made it apparent that what had seemed so promising for over thirty years was close to abandonment.

In 1978 Congress passed an omnibus parks bill which provided for the transfer of Mineral King to Park Service jurisdiction. In the end the Department of Agriculture supported the transfer, saying that the valley's ecological state, surrounding park wilderness, and visitor access were all "logical arguments for addition to the Park" (Cutler, 1978).

CHAPTER 4

The California Coastal
Commissions at San Onofre

"Controversy and criticism are not signs of failure: they are
signs of public involvement in a democratic process."

M. B. Lane, Chairman
California Coastal Zone
Conservation Commission

THE COASTAL ZONE is an important example of
land use control in the United States. In 1972 Congress passed the
Coastal Zone Management Act, which established among other things a
federal grants program for states to establish agencies to govern the
coast. Because of this support and the influence of environmentalists,
most coastal states developed varying degrees of activity. The most
prominent among them has been the California Coastal Zone Conservation Commissions. Originally fashioned as a temporary control and
planning authority, the set of commissions came into existence in
January, 1973, after success of a voters' initiative known as Proposition
20. They were mandated as an experiment in land use planning and
control over California's 1,100-mile coastline. With a primary objective
of making a coastal plan, the commissions were given a limited existence of four years.

The coastal zone embodies major land use concerns because of its
relative scarcity and the variety of competing demands for its diverse
resources. Confined as a narrow strip, the coastline is unlike other land
which can be expanded in a two-dimensional plane by the square of the
distance from its urban core. Coastal resources are limited to linear expansion. Yet in California, where 84 percent of the state's twenty
million population live within thirty miles of the coast, multiple uses are
intense and frequently conflicting. Competing demands include
residential, recreational, industrial, and commercial activities; waste
disposal; energy generation; food production (aqua and agri); natural
preserves; and limited-access governmental uses such as military bases.
Resource scarcity is compounded by public access problems. Of the

1,100-mile coastline, 61 percent is privately owned and 10 percent is government owned but closed to the public (California Coastal Zone Conservation Commissions, 1973; hereafter cited as Coastal Commissions). The 29 percent residual (about 300 miles) has forced noncoastal residents into high concentration areas.

What all this has meant is a deteriorating natural resource base and stress on the coast's ecological carrying capacity. Congress found in the 1972 coastal act that "increasing and competing demands . . . have resulted in the loss of living marine resources, wildlife, nutrient-rich areas, permanent and adverse changes to ecological systems, decreasing open space for public use, and shoreline erosion" (Coastal Zone Management Act, 1972). In California this condition grew in part out of local government's inability to handle powerful development forces moving into its jurisdictions. From this awareness came the initiative establishing the commissions.

The new statewide agency did not involve a dissolution of local authority but, instead, added state discretion concerning adverse impacts on regional and statewide interests. Further, the new authority was not vested with a synoptic planning format but was provided with a more complicated incremental process of policy deliberation, regulation, and planning. As a result, the commissions proved to be one of the most advanced state-level attempts to deal with land use and scarce resource allocation. In the process they also became among the most controversial.

Minimizing impacts and improving the quality of development have been the central thrusts of coastal management. These tasks have addressed two levels of problems that placed the commissions in different authority positions. The first has to do with regulating incremental additions to coastal housing stock prior to adoption of the coastal plan. In the absence of other state reviews, this activity placed the commissions in a dominant position over local government. Much of the criticism about the agency's "dictatorial" behavior stemmed from this set of relationships.

The second level of problems concerned large-scale development including huge planned unit developments like the Sea Ranch case, harbor development, and manufacturing. Within this category, however, probably the most important and complex problem revolves around electric power plant siting, construction, and operation. This becomes even more critical when dealing with nuclear energy. The particular case under study deals with the planning and approval process of a nuclear power station at San Onofre, located along an isolated stretch of San Diego coastline. It involves a land use conflict between energy needs and nuclear reactors on the one hand, and concern for nuclear safety and natural resource preservation on the other. It also represents a microcosm of the commissions' decision processes for control of large-scale development.

The controversy occurred during the "energy crisis" of 1973–74 and thus involved the additional conflict suggested by the *Federalist* between short-run public emotionalism and the need for administrative due process. Feeling these pressures, the state commission staff director said the energy "shortage may have more impact on coastal-zone planning than any other single factor" (Bodovitz, Nov. 17, 1973). The case was the largest to come before the commissions during their initial four-year existence. The state commission staff summarized the case as involving "a more complex array of issues than any matter yet before the Commission; on many . . . questions there is disagreement among experts" (Coastal Commission, Oct. 15, 1973). Similarly, the environmentalists argued that "it is the most significant environmental case now pending in Southern California" (Coastal Commission, Oct. 18, 1973, p. 63).

The California Coastal Commissions

Control over coastal resources in California has been frustrated by uncoordinated public jurisdictions. Until Proposition 20, the coast was separately managed by fifteen counties, forty-five cities, forty-two state agencies, and seventy federal agencies (Douglas, 1973). No grouping of these agencies had developed any significant reciprocal arrangements for dealing with adverse environmental impacts or accounting for multiple interests.

Concern in California for coastal resource management dates back to two legislative reports in 1929 and 1931, but widespread awareness was not apparent until the rise of environmentalism during the 1960s. Late in that decade several gubernatorial and legislative marine advisory commissions were established. Through legislative action over a five-year period, the state established the Bay Conservation and Development Commission (BCDC) to control land fill and development along San Francisco Bay (Scott, 1975).

Broader legislation, however, was not forthcoming. In 1970, 1971, and 1972 bills were introduced to establish some form of administrative structure for the entire coastline, with state, regional, and local agencies sharing some measure of the responsibility. Owing to strong lobbying efforts by the League of California Cities, developers, large corporations, and labor unions, they were all defeated. From this failure in coastal legislation emerged a force of disgruntled environmentalists called the California Coastal Alliance. Composed of thirty-four groups including the Sierra Club and the Planning and Conservation League, this organization formed a campaign in 1971 known as "Save our

Coast." When the legislature found itself in mid-1972 unable to act on proposals, the alliance moved the campaign to a voters' initiative. In less than two months 418,000 valid signatures were collected to qualify the initiative, and in November, 1972, Proposition 20 became law with 55.1 percent of the vote.

Opposition to the initiative came predominantly from development interests and was organized through the various real estate, manufacturing, and building trade associations. Campaign funds came from a dozen large corporations. Of the six top contributors, three were nuclear power plant companies: Bechtel Corporation, General Electric, and Southern California Edison (Scott, 1975, p. 357). Had the environmentalist movement not been near its apogee, Proposition 20 might easily have succumbed to the opposition.

Known as the California Coastal Zone Conservation Act of 1972, the new law was essentially constructed from the bills that failed in the legislature (Douglas, 1973). As an innovation in land use control, it encompassed two critical assumptions. First, it recognized the need for multiple-interest representation in the allocation of coastal resources. Second, it assumed that coastal resource demand was the result of an interdependence with activities outside the zone. The act therefore declared, ". . . in order to promote the public safety, health, and welfare, and to protect public and private property, wildlife, marine fisheries, and other ocean resources, and the natural environment, it is necessary to preserve the ecological balance of the coastal zone and prevent its further deterioration and destruction . . . " (California Coastal Zone Conservation Act, 1972; hereafter cited as Coastal Act). As an enabling law, the act included a policy mandate and specification of administrative structure and process.

The policy stance stipulated that the state had an obligation "to preserve, protect, and where possible, to restore the resources of the coastal zone for the enjoyment of the current and succeeding generations . . ." (Coastal Act, 1972). In so doing, it set forth a central role for planning, a role which recognized that coastal resources were not subject to standardized treatment or a single public interest mandate. Said the state commission's director, "A coastal zone plan . . . must deal both with the coastal zone as a whole, and with the region-by-region variations . . . " (Bodovitz, Mar. 29, 1973). What makes this case even more interesting, however, is the fact that planning was viewed as an incremental policy process. Synoptic planning was seen as inappropriate because it presented "a single package" that usually escaped the interactive advantage of partisan mutual adjustment: ". . . coastal zone planning, to be successful, must educate as many people as possible as to the issues and controversies affecting the coastal zone and must win approval for the solutions proposed so as to result in a final plan having statewide public support" (Bodovitz, Mar. 29, 1973).

To achieve this logic, the coastal act granted a dual function to the commissions of regulation and planning. These were viewed not as separate activities involving a division of labor but as a single reinforcing process where interim development during the four-year planning period was not to be detached from or inconsistent with the ultimate plan:

> As the planning proceeds, decisions on permit applications can help carry out the plan. And, of equal importance, decisions on plan recommendations grow out of the permit experience. . . . This insures that the plan is not prepared in ivory tower isolation but instead is prepared on the solid foundation that comes from understanding the very real conflicts over conservation and development in the coastal zone. [Coastal Commissions, 1973, p. 9]

Planning for the coast, then, meant that policy guidelines would emerge from the regulatory process. Although this may seem chaotic to the synoptic planner, the desire was to create "a living policy plan, not a document like a city or regional plan . . . " (Bodovitz, June 14, 1973, p. 10).

The policy of incremental planning was also meant to extend to public access and deliberation. The act required plan preparation "in full consultation with all affected governmental agencies, private interests, and the general public . . . " (Coastal Act, 1972). Intergovernmental and public participation was advocated to generate a broader knowledge base on complex issues and create the widespread public support essential to assure perpetuation by the 1976 legislature.

The authority vested in the commission structure by Proposition 20 reflected the reality of existing multiple jurisdictions and thus was limited to a specialized function. This meant that multiple interests were to be handled by several agencies having overlapping authority rather than a single agency exercising discretion over uses as at Mineral King. Where land use was subject to intense noncompatible uses and where the upper bounds of ecosystem carrying capacity were being reached, the coastal commissions' role was to minimize adverse impacts. From this perspective, the act defined "the following objectives:

> (a) The maintenance, restoration, and enhancement of the overall quality of the coastal zone environment. . . .
> (b) The continued existence of optimum populations of all species of living organisms.
> (c) The orderly, balanced utilization and preservation . . . of all living and nonliving coastal zone resources.

(d) Avoidance of irreversible and irretrievable commitments of coastal zone resources.
[Coastal Act, 1972]

Likewise, criteria for interim permit regulation stipulated that "development will not have any substantial adverse environmental or ecological effect" and will be consistent with the act's planning objectives (Coastal Act, 1972).

The act further established two methods to deal with adverse effects. The first had to do with voting requirements, which stipulated that "no permit shall be issued without the affirmative vote of a majority of the total authorized membership" of the commission (not just those present), or a vote of two-thirds where a direct impact such as dredging, reduction of public access, or irreversible harm to other economic interests was likely to occur (Coastal Act, 1972). The second method was related to the findings of the commission and required that the permit applicant (i.e., developer) "has the burden of proof on all issues" (Coastal Act, 1972). Like affirmative voting, forcing development interests to prove conformance to the act gives the question of adverse effects greater visibility and thus encourages a more balanced weighing among competing values.

In addition to the policy stance, the act created an administrative structure and process that reflected a blend between the need for political legitimacy and the demand for specialized expertise. This consisted of a bi-level commission system that provided overlapping jurisdictional boundaries to account for both regional and statewide interests and for interregional influences and spillover effects (i.e., the construction of a coastal nuclear power facility in one region that was necessitated by energy demand from other regions). This bi-level structure included six regional commissions, of which San Diego County is one, and a statewide commission headquartered in San Francisco. The accepted logic for having regional commissions was that a single agency would be too remote. "The Regional Commissions are better able than the State Commission to achieve extensive involvement of large numbers . . . because they are more directly accessible to the people, and because coastal problems and solutions are most easily comprehended as they affect one's own region of the State" (Bodovitz, June 14, 1973). Likewise, the purpose of a state commission was to provide "a forum for statewide policy" and to assure implementation of state interests (Scott, 1975, p. 39).

With regard to the permit review process, the bi-level commissions operated with identical sets of decision discretion and policy guidelines but were linked to each other on an appeal basis. The regional commissions were the points of original jurisdiction and they maintained responsibility for both regional and statewide considerations. If any party to the process was dissatisfied with the regional outcome, appeal was open to the state commission, which "may affirm, reverse, or modify the decision of the regional commission" (Coastal Act, 1972). In some regions, especially San Diego and Los Angeles, the state commission had to adopt a watchdog approach over regional commissions because of serious nonconformity with the act. A similar relationship was also adopted for coastal plan preparation, but the act reserved exclusive authority over plan development for the state commission. "The State Commission is responsible for preparation and adoption of the final plan, and the Regional Commissions are responsible for making their recommendations . . . before final actions are taken" (Bodovitz, Mar. 29, 1973, p. 2). In this unique incremental process, then, the regional commissions carried the essential responsibility for assuring that interim coastal development would be compatible with the ultimate plan.

The bi-level commissions consisted of eighty-four voting members, of whom twelve were state commissioners. Half of the state commissioners acted as representatives from the six regions, and the other half were selected as "general public" representatives. In the San Diego region the commission consisted of twelve members, four selected by the county, one by the city of San Diego, one by the regional Council of Governments (COG), and six as representatives of the "general public." All "general public" members in the system were selected equally by the governor, the Senate Rules Committee, and the Speaker of the Assembly. All commissioners were part-time and served without pay except for $50 per diem.

The mix of appointments was seen as providing broad representation and fostering multiregional communications. Further, to promote an environmental advocacy role, all "general public" members were to be selected based on evidence that they were "exceptionally well qualified to analyze and interpret environmental trends and information, to appraise resource uses in light of the policies set forth in the [Act], to be responsive to the scientific, social, aesthetic, recreational, and cultural needs of the State" (Coastal Act, 1972). Despite the appearance of environmental advocacy in the act, perspectives varied widely across the commissions. While the state commission was generally influenced by environmentalists, the regional commissions ranged from strong environmental advocacy in the North Central Region (San Francisco) to strong developer bias in the San Diego Region.

The differences, of course, reflected regional socioeconomic and political infrastructure manifested in commission makeup. At the time of the San Onofre controversy the San Diego Regional Commission consisted of five members who openly opposed Proposition 20, one who headed a real estate firm exclusively in the coastal zone, one who headed the local carpenters' union, and another who was an executive for Gulf General Atomic (maker of nuclear reactors). None would disqualify themselves for the San Onofre vote. Although the commission's staff represented a general pro–Proposition 20 stance, only three of the twelve commissioners were considered favorable to the act. The regional representative to the state commission and central figure on the regional commission was Jeffrey Frautschy of Scripps Institute of Oceanography. Although not the regional commission's chairman, most members looked to him for advice and leadership. As a declared advocate of nuclear power (Frautschy, 1975), Frautschy played a dual role as both commissioner and expert witness during the regional deliberations on San Onofre (San Diego Coast Regional Commission, Aug. 10, 1973). Summarizing the regional commission's record going into the San Onofre case, a pro–Proposition 20 commissioner said, "I think we have given developers the green light, and our only hope is that the State Coastal Zone Conservation Commission can put on the brakes" (Keen, 1973).

The environmental posture of the state commission was widely recognized given that eleven of the twelve commissioners had voted for Proposition 20. Equally evident was the prestigious and professional backgrounds that several brought with them. Perhaps the best known was the commission's chairman, Melvin Lane, publisher of *Sunset* magazine and a director of the Bay Area Council (a prominent organization of corporate executives). Although an environmental supporter, he was also a rigid parliamentarian. He once said, "As chairman, I think in terms of procedures and commission's time and our ultimate acceptance in Sacramento" (Lane, May 15, 1974). This pragmatic emphasis was applauded by most, but it frustrated many environmentalists whom he frequently closed off. For example, at the San Onofre hearings Lane interrupted the environmentalists' chief counsel, ruling him out of order. The counsel responded, "Mr. Lane, I've appeared before you four times. On each of those occasions, you have interrupted me" (Coastal Commission, Feb. 20, 1974, p. 22).

Other notable members included Mrs. Ellen Stern Harris, a Los Angeles journalist and staunch preservationist; Richard Wilson, former head of the Planning and Conservation League; Fred Farr, a former state senator who chaired the powerful Natural Resources Committee; Ira Laufer, a Ventura radio station owner; and San Francisco Supervisor Robert Mendelsohn, who would become the key arbitrator in the San Onofre case. Mendelsohn along with Lane brought prior shoreline experience to the commission, both having been members of BCDC, the San Francisco Bay agency from which Proposition 20 had been fashioned. Frautschy, the San Diego regional representative, was viewed as one of the more development-oriented members and at the San Onofre hearings became the utilities' nuclear advocate (Coastal Commission, Dec. 5, 1973, p. 85). Reinforcing the commissioner's environmental predilection was a highly competent staff of specialized experts led by Joseph Bodovitz, former director of BCDC.

The permit review and planning process involved scrutinizing much scientific information and dealing with complex ecological and social issues. However, in comparison to Forest Service autonomy over a broad geographical area, the coastal commissions had a more limited and specialized scope. The coastal act specified two geographical zones of discretion, a planning zone and a "permit zone." The larger planning zone (defined as the "coastal zone") was viewed as that area necessary to be inclusive of the natural ecological system of the coast. The act defined its boundaries as extending seaward to the state's three-mile jurisdictional limit and landward to the crest of the first coastal mountain range or a maximum of five miles inland, whichever was closer. The incremental planning process was to culminate in December, 1975, with "a comprehensive, coordinated, enforceable plan" to be submitted to the legislature for adoption and implementation (Coastal Act, 1972). The second and smaller "permit zone" was authorized to provide interim land use control in the immediate coastline area. It extended out to the three-mile limit but was limited to 1,000 yards landward from the mean high tide line.

During the life of the commission system, anyone who wanted to develop within this permit area was required to obtain coastal approval, subject to certification that the project would not likely thwart the mandate and intentions of the eventual coastal plan. The regional permit process involved a sequence of (1) regional staff review of a detailed application, (2) an open public hearing, and (3) a vote by the commission membership. If a case was appealed, it would follow a similar course at the state level. In processing permits, the commissions tried to divide the task into a fact-finding role for commission staffs and a political role of value judgment for the commissioners. As evidenced at San Onofre, the quality of review and depth of analysis by the staffs offered a major point of contrast between the two commission levels. Although sacrificing long hours without overtime compensation, the regional staff in San Diego usually relied on data and conclusions of the permit applicants or other approving public agencies. The state staff, on the other hand, was more scrutinizing in the pursuit of data, in the reconciliation of information anomalies, and in its preparation of comprehensive assessments and recommendations. When issues were unique, outside specialists were used to complement areas in which the staff felt inadequate. Noting the rigorous contribution of the state staff, chairman Lane said, "I know of few governmental agencies where so much work is done for the taxpayer's dollar" (Coastal Commissions, 1974, p. 2).

Another difference between the regional and state staffs was dominance. The relationship varied from region to region: the San Diego staff often had a difficult time emphasizing environmental requirements, and staff recommendations were frequently ignored by the pro-developer voting majority. By contrast, the state staff exercised much dominance over commission proceedings and greatly influenced voting patterns. This was evident enough to lead a pro-developer commission member to say, "We have a good staff, but it . . . is giving the Commission direction. . . . The tail seems to be wagging the dog" (Osenbaugh, 1976). Hence, while the separation of political and administrative roles was intended by the act, the dominant elements on the different commissions exercised a mixture of both. Speaking on state staff dominance, Bodovitz said, "We recognize that by having these great powers we have to use them wisely. I think we will be judged on the stewardship of that power . . ." (Bodovitz, Aug. 13, 1973).

A highlight of the commission process was public access. The purpose of the commission system has been to promote visibility of public policy making, but Proposition 20 introduced an unprecedented openness to California land use planning by requiring widely publicized public hearings on all project applications and providing on-going public forums for plan preparation. Chairman Lane argued that no "statewide planning program ever conducted in California has made such a strong effort to secure full and open public participation" (Coastal Commissions, 1974, p. 2). The open hearings and planning-draft reviews enabled all interested parties to present their concerns, preferences, and recommendations, and to criticize the thinking and objectives of their opponents. This was reinforced by the staffs' generally open deliberation and solicitation of partisan inputs, especially at the state level.

A final point deals with the coastal commissions' role as an "added layer" in an intergovernmental system. The commissions were created in the midst of a number of other existing state and local agencies that had some degree of authority over aspects of coastal resources (Gamman, Towers, and Sorensen, 1975; Scott, 1975, pp. 209–17, 254–56). The need for another agency specializing in coastal land use came from the belief that the existing system had not improved use patterns as they related to environmental quality. Although anti–Proposition 20 forces argued that "it's just an unnecessary level of government . . . " (Kronberger, 1974), the commissions provided a functional role because "most state agencies have their own bias and their own clienteles" different from those of the coastal commissions (Crandall, 1975). At times, however, the new authority did not appear as a coordinated part of the larger intergovernmental system. The inconsistency was due in part to a "last-in-line" policy adopted by the coastal agency. "A permit application may not be filed with the Regional Commission until . . . [all

other state and local agencies] have granted . . . approval in concept . . . " (Coastal Commission, Oct., 1973). This established a sequential approach for the commissions which isolated them from intergovernmental reciprocal reviews. As they gained experience with the
other authorities, conformity to the policy was relaxed, allowing for
better integration into interagency deliberations.

San Onofre and Nuclear Energy

In addition to environmental quality, the San Onofre case was also
part of the national controversy over generation of electricity by nuclear
power. Growth in construction of nuclear power plants was occurring
at an exponential rate by 1973 to match the utilities' projected electrical
demand. With this, uncertainties over nuclear safety and proper siting
grew as well. Although not accepted until Three Mile Island six years
later, proliferation of nuclear reactors increased the probability for a
nuclear disaster. Concern over San Onofre impacts was further enlarged by the Atomic Energy Commission's use of political power and
lack of sufficient emphasis on nuclear safety.

San Onofre was at the forefront of the larger controversy for two
reasons. First, the generating station's first reactor, which started
operation in 1967, was embroiled in both state and national adjudica-
tions over its emergency backup systems for nuclear disaster prevention.
At the state level a group called the People's Lobby was fighting in the
courts and at the state Public Utilities Commission to have Unit One
shut down until nuclear safety assurance could be made (*The People's
Lobby v. SCE and SDG&E*, 1973). At the national level the Ralph
Nader organization was attempting in federal courts to have nearly all
commercial nuclear reactors including San Onofre shut down for
similar reasons (SDG&E, 1973, p. 18). The second reason for San
Onofre's visibility had to do with project size. With the proposed addi-

Table 4. Size Indicators: SCE and SDG&E (1973 Data).

	SCE	SDG&E*
Assets (in millions)	$3,889.7	$758.0
Gross Revenues (in millions)	1,079.3	227.8
Net Income (in millions)	147.7	27.7
Electric Generating Capacity (in Mw)	12.3	2.3
Service Area Population (in millions)	7.5	1.6

*About 75 percent of the assets, revenues, and income figures are from electric generation.

Sources: Southern California Edison, "Prospectus" (Oct. 30, 1974); San Diego Gas and
Electric, "Prospectus" (Nov. 19, 1974).

Table 5. Percentage of Electricity Generated by Energy Source at SCE and SDG&E (1973 Data).

	SCE	SDG&E
Oil	45%	54%
Natural Gas	21	29
Coal	15	—
Hydroelectric	9	—
Nuclear	3	5
Purchased Electricity	7	12
	100%	100%

Sources: Southern California Edison, "Prospectus" (Oct. 30, 1974); San Diego Gas and Electric, "Prospectus" (Nov. 19, 1974).

tion of Units Two and Three, the facility would become the largest commercial nuclear complex in the world. This was made even more significant by the fact that the proposed addition was the first nuclear request to come before the coastal commissions.

The San Onofre nuclear station was jointly developed by San Diego Gas and Electric (SDG&E) and Southern California Edison (SCE), with the latter having responsibility for operating the facility. Since the two utilities were among the first to use nuclear power, both had made long-term commitments to its future development. However, with regard to coastal zone preservation, they took opposing positions. SCE, the bigger of the two, was the sixth largest contributor to the anti–Proposition 20 campaign and propagandized against the initiative with supplements to its regular customer billings. SDG&E, on the other hand, was the only utility in the state that remained neutral on the initiative. The company's president recalled, "I didn't win any popularity contest among my colleagues . . . but it seemed to me that the concept behind Proposition 20 . . . was a necessary thing" (Zitlau, 1974, p. 99).

Both utilities, as shown in Table 4, were large corporations and maintained regulated monopolies over nine million people in Southern California during the 1973 San Onofre deliberations.

The co-owners in 1973 had joint assets of $4.7 billion, revenues of $1.2 billion, and net income of $175.4 million. The joint service areas covered more than 55,000 square miles spread over twelve counties from Mono in the north to San Diego in the south (the city of Los Angeles was excluded since it operates a public utility).

As shown in Table 5, electricity in 1973 was generated from a variety of energy sources, but the largest contributor was oil. No solar or geothermal alternatives were employed at that time. Although nuclear fuel represented only a marginal contribution, the commitment to nuclear reactors as the major source of future energy was reflected in the companies' considerable depth of knowledge in nuclear technology, especially SCE.

The need for additional nuclear generating capacity was initially expressed in terms of trendline projections for population growth in Southern California and the nation. Although the emotionalism of the energy "crisis" accentuated immediate need, the projected demand relevant to the proposed addition was for 1980 and beyond. Implying that the future would be essentially like the past, the utilities set projections on the fact that the United States accounted for about one-third of world energy consumption and that the rate of increase was among the highest in modern nations. Between 1950 and 1970, U.S. population grew at about 1.5 percent annually, while energy demand grew by 3.6 percent annually and electricity as a subcategory grew by 7.0 percent annually (AEC, Nov., 1973a). This meant that in the postwar era electrical demand doubled about every twelve years. In Southern California it doubled every eight years. In order to keep up with this demand, SCE and SDG&E had to build as much new capacity in eight years as they had in all their previous history.

Demand in Southern California has been due principally to two factors: population growth and increasing affluence. The utilities argued that even though immigration and births in California dropped off significantly by the early 1970s, the most important consideration was improving the standard of living. SCE president Horton maintained that "an improved quality of life for all depends upon a growing electric energy supply" (SCE, 1972, p. 3). One SDG&E senior vice-president argued further that his company felt an "obligation and responsibility" to those "working hard to elevate themselves to a higher standard of living" (San Diego Coast Regional Commission, Aug. 10, 1973, p. 10).

Compounding this growth was the utilities' belief that electrical demand was essentially inelastic and that people were basically unable to adjust their needs under resource scarcity. Citing a Stanford Research Institute report, an SCE vice-president said, "Elasticity . . . was extremely small . . . [and] the effect of price on demand . . . was negligible (San Diego Coast Regional Commission, Aug. 10, 1973, p. 168). This argument, as well as the overall logic for demand, fits a pattern of belief made popular during the San Onofre controversy. The belief was that world population was far outstripping the ability of technology and resource availability to provide for a healthy world order (Meadows *et al.*, 1972). Recalling the images of famine, pestilence, and war, the "limits to growth" scenario implied that existing democratic allocation systems would have to be suspended in favor of a more centralized order committed to technological advancement and population control.

The argument was compelling to large corporations, especially utilities, because it was modeled by computers and MIT quantitative techniques. Furthermore, since large corporations were the crucibles of technology, it also seemed to promise a greater societal role for corporate management. SCE frequently alluded to this role at public information meetings, and the utilities industry in general argued that "our country's ability to do the work that needs to be done will depend on an adequate supply of electricity. There's no time to waste" (Power Companies, 1973).

With such urgency in mind, nuclear power offered three advantages. First, nuclear fuel was said to be more plentiful and cheaper. SCE estimated an annual fuel cost savings from the nuclear addition of $250 million. Second, with the "crisis" of petroleum scarcity, nuclear fuel would conserve remaining oil supplies for more dependent uses such as automobile travel and petrochemicals. The annual savings of oil from San Onofre was equivalent to running "the entire state for 20 days" (*San Diego Union*, Dec. 5, 1973). Third, the utilities believed that "nuclear power is the cleanest, safest, most reliable source of energy presently available to serve you and the needs of the environment" (SCE, 1972, p. 10). If San Onofre was blocked, "utilities would be forced to rely upon overworked fossil fuel plants . . . thereby adding to air quality problems" (SCE, Feb., 1972, p. 21). According to SCE, using oil-burning facilities instead of San Onofre would increase air emissions in Los Angeles by 83.4 percent and in San Diego by 53.2 percent (Fogarty, 1974).

The utilities further argued that curtailment of the San Onofre additions would ultimately bring havoc to the social order. "Some environmentalists and other single-purpose groups have succeeded in blocking construction of much needed new facilities. But . . . we need more electricity on the order of several magnitudes just for environmental clean-up" (SCE, 1973, p. 5). The threat of blackouts was also of concern, with SCE contending that without new facilities, "power shortages in certain areas or an embargo on some new hookups" was possible (SCE, Feb., 1972, p. 5.). In the larger scope, deferment of nuclear development was even dangerous to national security (Ward, 1974).

In addition to future need, SCE and SDG&E developed much of their logic around cost factors. Nuclear reactors require several times the capital investment of a conventional fossil fuel plant, but 1973 operating and fuel costs were considerably less than in oil-fired plants when operating continuously at designed capacity. Consequently the utilities argued that a fundamental need for San Onofre was to replace existing fossil fuel plants with nuclear power for "base load" generation. They were viewed as the future "wheelhorses of any generating system," reserving fossil fuel plants as "peak load" units only (AEC, Mar., 1973, p. 12-1).

The two utilities shared the San Onofre facility, with SCE getting 80 percent of the electricity and SCG&E receiving the remainder. All investment and costs were shared on a similar basis. The location of San Onofre was conveniently near the border of the two service areas approximately sixty-two miles south of downtown Los Angeles and fifty-one miles north of San Diego. The site, which also contained the existing Unit One, was eighty-four acres in size and was situated on the northwest end of the eighteen-mile shoreline of Camp Pendleton Marine Base. The utilities were granted an easement from Congress in 1963 that lasts until May 12, 2023. As shown in Figure 6, primary considerations for location on the base shoreline included minimizing "sociological and aesthetic impacts" and providing "adequate cooling water in an otherwise arid service area" (AEC, Mar., 1973, p. 1-3).

Although the nuclear station was along an isolated beach, a variety of land uses existed within a five-mile radius. Just landward from the nuclear station was the San Diego Freeway (Interstate 5) and mainline railroad tracks. The 196-square-mile Marine base (95 percent unimproved) was used for military maneuvers and wildlife preservation. To the northeast, about 1,200 acres of truck crops were under cultivation, and some beef cattle and sheep grazed on the Marine base. The seacoast north and south of the site is an extensive natural undeveloped area "considered to be a unique and scarce recreational resource" (AEC, Mar., 1973, p. 2-11). Under a fifty-year lease to the State Parks and Recreation Department, the coastline includes precipitous eroding bluffs and a coarse-sand beach about eighty feet wide. The continental shelf in this area is about five miles wide and generally shallow, offering excellent surfing conditions and water temperatures ranging from 50° F to 73° F. Average daily attendance at the state beach in 1973 was about 4,000 persons.

The nearest population centers included San Clemente (population 17,063) four miles north and Oceanside (39,100) seventeen miles south. President Nixon's Western White House was located about three miles northwest of the site. The greatest local public concern about and subsequent opposition to the nuclear additions came from San Clemente, a community of wealthy upper middle-class professionals and retirees.

The completion date for the two new nuclear units was set for around 1980, with construction costs estimated at $1.3 billion. Supply of nuclear fuel, which cost about one-fifth of most fossil fuels in 1973, was contracted for through 2008. In comparison to San Onofre Unit One, which had an electrical generating capacity of 430 megawatts, the two new units were to have a capacity of 1,140 megawatts each. The increase in each utility system's projected 1982 capacity from the two

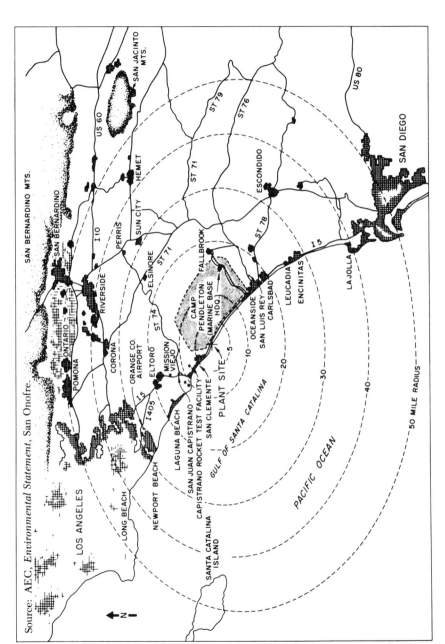

Source: AEC, *Environmental Statement*, San Onofre.

Figure 6. Site Location: San Onofre Nuclear Station.

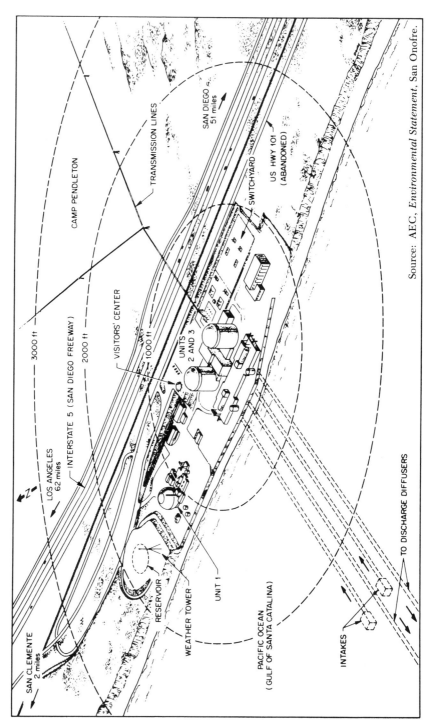

Figure 7. San Onofre Nuclear Station Proposed Additions: Units Two and Three.

Source: AEC, *Environmental Statement, San Onofre.*

units amounted to 8.1 percent for SCE and 9.6 percent for SDG&E.
With all three units operating, the nuclear generating station could supply power for a city of two million people. As shown in Figure 7, Units
Two and Three were designed to be an integrated power plant and consequently were to share a variety of ancillary facilities spread over 80
percent of the eighty-four-acre site. The units were to be located about
200 feet from the beach at an excavated elevation of thirty feet. Major
structures were to include two circular prestressed concrete containment buildings for the reactors, an auxiliary building, fuel-handling
buildings, safety injection system buildings, and turbine buildings.

The construction phase was scheduled to take six years. The nuclear
reactor and steam supply units were designed and fabricated by Com-
bustion Engineering, and the turbine generators and secondary components were supplied by General Electric Company of England. Chief
engineer and general contractor was the Bechtel Corporation, a large
international construction firm. During construction about 1,000 yards
of the state beach were to be closed to the public, and excavation at the
site was to remove about 2.7 million cubic yards of existing land forms.
Part of the earth was to be deposited in the ocean to replenish beach
sand, while the rest was to be placed across the San Diego Freeway to
conceal the site's construction supply yard from view.

The nuclear reactor process involves the "fission" of uranium atoms,
which generates heat. The type of reactor used for Units Two and Three
is called a "pressurized water reactor" (PWR), and was recognized as
the least efficient, most dangerous, but most operational form used in
the United States for high power output ratings. Europeans, by contrast, use a smaller but safer and more efficient system known as the
"high temperature gas-cooled reactor" (HTGR). As shown in Figure 8,
the pressurized water reactor confines water under pressure to prevent
it from boiling as it is heated by fission.

The heated and pressurized water is pumped out of the reactor and
into a steam generator where it heats water contained in a separate
system. From there the pressurized water is pumped back into the reactor for recycling. The water in the steam generator, after turning to
steam, rushes past the blades of a turbine electric generator. After passing through the turbine, the steam is channeled into a condenser and
returns as water to the steam generator for recycling. The steam condenser and heat dissipation systems were to operate by drawing
seawater from the Pacific Ocean. Operating on a once-through basis,
the seawater cooling system was designed to draw 830,000 gallons per
minute for each unit through two eighteen-foot-diameter underwater
conduits extending 3,400 feet out in the ocean. After passing through
the condenser, the heat-exchanged water would return to the ocean.
The entire generating process was to be monitored and controlled by a

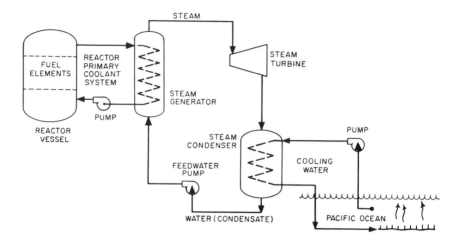

Figure 8.   San Onofre Nuclear Generating System: Pressurized Water Reactor.
Source: AEC, *Environmental Statement*, San Onofre.

computerized operations center and, because of advanced technology, the entire nuclear station was planned to use only 130 personnel (AEC, Mar., 1973).

Since excessive nuclear radiation poses a significant health hazard, a number of precautionary measures have been adopted for nuclear power stations. Under normal operation, radiation exposure from electric generation adds little to that from natural sources. The real concern, however, is with accidents. The reactor fission process is controlled by movement of reactor vessel rods which intervene in the atomic chain reaction. Although the fission process can be shut down immediately by total insertion of these control rods, residual heat generated by the nuclear "decay" process remains, necessitating continuous water cooling. Although San Onofre was designed against earthquake, sabotage, or accident, if an uncontrolled rupture occurred in the reactor vessel cooling pipes, the radioactive fuel core would overheat and melt. In the worst case, called the "China Syndrome," the core would melt through the reactor vessel and through the containment floor into the earth, spewing radioactive gases. This is what nearly happened in the Three Mile Island accident, but radioactive gases were spewed into the atmosphere even though a total meltdown did not occur.

To maximize safety, a number of redundant features have been designed to control this potential "loss-of-coolant accident," and prevent meltdown gases escaping to the atmosphere. The most important safety feature, however, is the "emergency core cooling system" (ECCS). In the event of such an accident the ECCS is designed to inject cold water into the reactor vessel at a rate in excess of the amount being lost by the pipeline rupture. Units Two and Three at San Onofre were to have separate ECCS units that were capable of operating over a range and combination of break sizes (AEC, 1972).

In addtion to system accidents, radiation hazard is also contingent upon the disposal of nuclear wastes; hence the utilities have developed procedures and mechanisms to avert excess exposure from this source as well. In magnitude, the type of accidents that could occur from either coolant pipe ruptures or nuclear wastes range from minor to catastrophic, but the utilities believed the potential for severe accidents at San Onofre was negligible. SDG&E said that, "viewed with some background of knowledge, radiation loses the ominous connotation given it by alarmists" (SDG&E, n.d.).

In addition to minimizing land use implications for radiation hazard, the utilities also contended that Units Two and Three were located and designed to be environmentally and economically sound in the long run. To substantiate the environmental claims, the companies emphasized the most visible impacts. Besides the fact that nuclear plants produce no visible pollution, the companies also said they can be made "esthetically pleasing" by minimizing "visual clutter" and making structures "complimentary [sic] to the sea coast environment" (Coastal Commission, Oct. 18, 1973, pp. 17–21). The intention to excavate 0.7 mile of erosion-sculptured bluffs, however, was not generally associated as an offsetting visual loss to the architectual accounterments.

The most extensive and complex environmentally related feature of the nuclear facility was the plant cooling systems, which, as shown in Figure 9, included seawater intake and discharge conduits extending over a mile out into the ocean. The PWR nuclear plants convert only about one-third of the fuel energy to electrical usage as compared to about 40 and 50 percent for the HTGR and conventional fossil fuel plants respectively. This inefficiency combined with plant size creates greater heat dissipation requirements and necessitates using a larger volume of water heated to a higher temperature (in this case, 830,000 gallons per minute per unit at a temperature 20°F above the ocean).

With this large volume of heated seawater, two major marine ecology problems existed: entrainment of fish and plankton (larval-stage, near-shore micro-organism) and thermal pollution. With regard to mortality caused by entrainment heat and turbulence, no device was planned to save plankton, but the utilities proposed to reduce the fish kill by installing a "velocity cap" on intake ports and special "screenwells" which catch and return fish to the ocean. The velocity cap prevents vertical flow intake which fish cannot adequately detect and, according to the

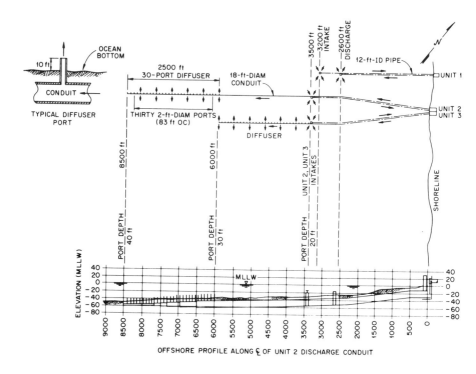

Figure 9. Undersea Cooling Conduits and Diffusers for San Onofre Units Two and Three.   Source: AEC, *Environmental Statement*, San Onofre.

utilities, might reduce entrainment by 60 to 80 percent. With regard to minimizing thermal pollution, the two units were to be equipped with a staggered multiport diffuser system. Costing an extra $26 million, the system was to consist of thirty two-foot-diameter dischargers spread over a 2,500-foot length of undersea conduit for each unit, and was designed to achieve maximum dilution resulting in lower ocean temperature increases than single-point dischargers. Consequently the utilities saw no appreciable marine ecology changes occurring.

The last major impact discussed by the utilities was economic. Although comparable to fossil fuel facilities, short-run benefits included about $300 million in construction wages, while long-term benefits included about $2 million annually for operating salaries and $18 million annually in local taxes. A secondary and less assessable economic impact was growth inducement in the larger service area. However, because of the energy crisis, this new source of demand was not emphasized by utility spokesmen.

San Onofre Opposition

In contrast to the utilities and their proponents, a number of interest groups opposed further San Onofre expansion in the belief that while additional electrical capacity might be worthwhile, the advantages of nuclear power along this part of the coast were offset by serious social and environmental externalities. Different opposition groups tended to be more visible at different stages of the multi-agency process, but those especially active during the coastal commission deliberations included Groups United Against Radiation Dangers (GUARD), Environmental Coalition of Orange County, Friends of the Earth, Scenic Shoreline Preservation Conference, and the Sierra Club.

GUARD and Scenic Shoreline provided the central energies, while the Sierra Club, divided by internal disagreement over the issue, adopted a "neutral" position. A few of the club's leaders testified in "a questioning posture," but not until January, 1974 (after coastal commission deliberations), did it officially oppose "new nuclear reactors utilizing the fission process" (Sierra Club, Jan., 1974). Besides the active groups, opposition appearances at the state commission hearings were also made by several California marine research scientists, and a member of the Union of Concerned Scientists, an MIT group of atomic physicists. To organize the opposition's thrust, the groups hired the Center for Law in the Public Interest, a Los Angeles law firm specializing in land use cases.

The priority of concerns over San Onofre expansion included nuclear safety, the environmental impact on land and coastal waters, and the control exercised by the two corporate utilities over electrical demand for San Onofre. All had important implications for land use, but safety seemed to dominate the discussion. Radiation, especially the gamma rays produced by reactors, was of concern because of the far-reaching hazards for humans. Radioactive materials are dangerous in minute concentrations, but are especially pervasive because they reach humans through a multitude of ecological pathways. Specific concern over safety arose with respect to both atmospheric releases from reactor meltdown and aquatic releases from disposal of nuclear wastes.

Concern over reactor safety can be traced back at least to 1965, and its salience was brought to the forefront partly by Edward Teller, father of atomic energy. Giving a hint of the uncertainties present, he remarked that "nuclear reactors . . . are clean as long as they function as planned, but if they malfunction . . . they can release enough fission products to kill a tremendous number of people" (Teller, 1967). Safety during such a malfunction is greatly dependent on reliability of the emergency core cooling system. Supported by partial evidence, the San Onofre opposition believed that temperature increases from a coolant rupture would occur with such great intensity that any amount of emergency coolant would simply be evaporated and expelled from the overheated core. To compound the problem, any measure of control also depended on whether the emergency coolant reached the core within the maximum sixty-second limit after primary coolant loss.

The problematic nature of ECCS reliability stemmed from several sources, but nuclear opponents at San Onofre frequently referred to AEC-sponsored tests done in Idaho in 1970. In a nine-inch model of the reactor core with an electrical heating element instead of nuclear fuel, the ECCS failed six out of six times. Although an AEC internal memorandum concluded that "no assurance is yet available that the emergency systems will provide enough water and in a timely way to prevent a meltdown accident," the AEC publicly argued that "no direct extrapolation of the results from this test to a reactor" can be made (Coastal Commission, Oct. 18, 1973, pp. 101, 125).

While San Onofre proponents were optimistic about the system's integrity and argued that no atmospheric escape would occur even in the event of meltdown, the opposition raised enough questions to make any conclusions tenuous. A cartoon appearing in the *Los Angeles Times* during the San Onofre controversy depicted the severity of the issue and expressed the mood of many Southern Californians. Showing a nuclear power plant in the background and a public address system in the foreground, the caption read, "In case of emergency repeat after me: Our Father . . . " (*Los Angeles Times*, Mar. 13, 1974).

The nuclear waste problem was a secondary issue for San Onofre, but plant expansion was seen as contributing to its severity. Nuclear wastes, which include spent fuel and exposed materials, are a critical problem to land use because they take thousands of years to decay and necessitate some form of long-term secure storage or deep underground disposal (AEC, Nov. 1973b). Since wastes accumulate at the rate of about one and one-half tons per 1,000 megawatts of power, several opponents of San Onofre wondered how safe storage and transfer by the utilities would be when reported cases like the Hanford, Washington, seepage problem continued unresolved.

SDG&E President Zitlau maintained that "man will discover how to use all of it beneficially just as we recycle . . . other products" (Zitlau, 1974, p. 59). Unconvinced, an opposition scientist testified that the "wastes represent a legacy to hundreds and thousands of generations who will achieve no benefit from whatever power was generated . . . " (Coastal Commission, Oct. 18, 1973, pp. 104–5).

What the opposition feared was a Faustian bargain: with nuclear technology, society could gain some added conveniences but in exchange would get a much increased potential for catastrophe. For both safety issues, the stakes in the bargain went up as new reactors were

built. Although SDG&E's Zitlau claimed, "It's a shame that these un-
warranted fears are slowing down our progress into the nuclear age"
(Zitlau, 1974, p. 57), an opposition scientist disagreed. "The experience
to date has been so minuscule that it's hardly sufficient to support . . .
the safety assurances for . . . the hundreds and ultimately a thousand
[reactors] that are expected by the end of the century" (Coastal Commission, Oct. 18, 1973, p. 103).

The second important issue raised by the opposition was environmental, including the coolant system's impact on marine ecology and
destruction of the 0.7 mile of bluffs and beach. The less efficient PWR
nuclear plants discharge about 40 percent more heat than comparable
size fossil fuel plants and require a vast amount of coolant water. At San
Onofre the combined discharge volume for Units Two and Three was to
be 1.66 million gallons of seawater per minute and would displace
ocean water equivalent to one square mile fourteen feet deep every day
(Coastal Commission, Dec., 1973, p. 7). From this, two marine impacts
were seen by environmentalists. The first was the effect of heat on kelp,
which is a commercially harvestable crop and habitat for other marine
organisms. Known to diminish at water temperatures above 70°F, the
outer extremities of the San Onofre kelp beds were located only 700 feet
from the nearest discharge diffuser. During warmer months, when ambient ocean temperatures approach 70°F, the added 20°F from coolant
discharge could badly damage or kill the beds.

The thermal plume effect was also known to create a secondary problem by drawing organisms toward the coolant system vicinity (Jensen,
1970), thus accentuating the second marine impact caused by entrainment. To most environmentalists, the entrainment of fish and plankton
was the more serious of the two impacts because of its complex and unknown effect on ecological balance. Although marine scientists did not
know whether organisms were as good dead as alive in the overall near-
shore ecology, the San Onofre opposition argued that 142,000 pounds of
fish per year and ten times that weight in plankton would be killed by
the "heat shock," pressure, and turbulence of entrainment.

Of even greater significance was the possibility that the coolant
system would act as a river, transporting plankton out and away from
their near-shore "nursery" environment. From the operating experience
of Unit One, which had its intake port 600 feet farther offshore than its
single-point discharger, the utilities found a near-shore enrichment of
plankton life believed to be due to induced transport through the coolant system. As shown in Figure 9, the much larger Units Two and Three
were to have just the opposite scheme with discharge diffusers extending
over one and one-half miles offshore. Arguing that the system "will suck
in waters from both sides along the shore and transport these waters in a
huge river going out to sea," an opposition marine biologist offered the

possibility that this might eliminate the reproductive capacity of near-shore areas and create a localized "marine desert" (Coastal Commission, Oct. 18, 1973, pp. 75–76). Most of the answers to this and other marine ecology questions were unknown, but most authorities including the AEC agreed that the utilities' study on marine impact was unsatisfactory.

The second environmental concern was over excavation plans for the bluffs and beach. Although not visible from the nearby freeway, the site's bluffs and intricate canyons were in many ways unique. The erosion-caused canyons formed a "complex labyrinth of spectacular proportions and beauty, consisting of deep, narrow, twisting canyons, pinnacles, and natural bridges" (Coastal Commission, Dec., 1973, p. 6). While this esthetic resource was not the only one of its kind along the coast, the opposition believed the strange sculpturing and chocolate marbling effects made it incomparable to others. Despite the utilities' contention that the formations were recently caused by freeway runoff, the environmentalists insisted that the nuclear expansion would meet the purpose of Proposition 20 only if Units Two and Three were moved back from the bluffs and across the freeway (Sierra Club, 1974).

The final opposition concern was with corporate power. Until the late 1960s utilities enjoyed a nearly autonomous position in society from their status as legal monopolies. As a result, they were not generally accustomed to dealing with partisan interests on an equal basis. Consequently, to offset an autonomy eroded by environmental and antinuclear activists, the utilities formed two nationwide political consortiums known as the American Nuclear Society and Reddy Kilowatt, Inc. Through these associations the utilities distributed a variety of pamphlets, lent support to utilities under siege, and trained utility executives on how to confront the opposition and "defuse the emotional aspects" of nuclear energy (*Wall Street Journal*, Apr. 4, 1974).

SCE and SDG&E were both active participants in these public relations efforts, but in addition they were also known by the opposition for their attempts to overshadow public deliberations. A variety of examples pertaining to San Onofre were raised, but four were particularly salient. First, during the state coastal commission hearings San Onofre Unit One had a major breakdown in its turbine generator that activated the ECCS. Although not needed on this occasion for emergency cooling, the system failed to operate properly. Contrary to utility agreements and legal requirements, SCE in conjunction with the AEC did not report the incident to the general public. The coastal commission was not informed of it until the opposition accidentally discovered mention of it in the Federal Register (a reporting system for government notices). Second, during the 1973 People's Lobby effort to close down Unit One, SCE attempted to prevent opposition arguments from being legally heard before the state PUC by disrupting the proceedings (*People's Lobby v. SCE and SDG&E*, 1973). The exasperated PUC examiner continuously overruled SCE legal manipulations during the four-hour session. Third, SCE carried on an active campaign of what the opposition described as "blackmail" and deception. For example, during both the energy "crisis" and coastal commission deliberations, both utilities were advertising nationally to urge new companies and people to locate in Southern California (*Forbes*, Sept. 15, 1973). Yet they argued before the state coastal commission that "failure to receive approval for San Onofre Units Two and Three would . . . [add] greatly to the likelihood of service interruptions to our customers" (Coastal Commission, Oct. 18, 1973, p. 55). Fourth, in an apparent effort to thwart a state Water Resources Control Board timetable to reduce thermal pollution, SCE failed to do required studies and submit work plans to confirm compliance (Coastal Commission, Feb. 20, 1974, pp. 19, 29).

Beyond these examples, considerable evidence showed a general disinclination, especially by SCE, to respond adequately to significant public issues at San Onofre and elsewhere (AEC, Oct. 15, 1973). Regarding information requests from the utilities, a GUARD member commented that the companies went "around the barn and ignored them . . . or gave such obviously misleading answers that you just don't accept them" (San Diego Coast Regional Commission, Aug. 10, 1973, p. 127). Instead of recognizing opponents' legitimacy, the utilities were seen as using their organizational influence to confront "uncommitted" public agencies with "intimidation" and deception. The Sierra Club stressed that "if Edison is successful in forcing the commission to bend the law, other developers will be equally successful in the future" (Sierra Club, 1974).

San Onofre opponents were also skeptical of the utilities' arguments for inelastic electrical demand and the emphasis placed on nuclear economics. The question of demand was raised in two lights. The first was timing. Initially, at least, much of the utilities' justification for nuclear expansion revolved around the urgency of the 1973 energy "crisis." A Sierra Club member said that "even if Units Two and Three are constructed and completed on time, they will not contribute to the solution of either the present or near-term needs for electrical energy . . ." (Coastal Commission, Dec. 5, 1973, pp. 42–43). With a start-up date of 1980, the applicable supply and demand circumstances seemed some distance off.

The second aspect concerned the ability of society in the long run to adjust to changing resource availability. The utilities had based much of their reasoning for nuclear demand on the *Limits to Growth* scenario, but as critics pointed out, the model was badly flawed and incomplete (*London Times Literary Supplement*, 1973; Day and Koenig, 1975). In particular, the Meadows team, consisting of scientists and engineers, overlooked human capability to adapt to change. This caused a "failure to incorporate negative feedback loops representing such crucial factors as the way the economic system responds to changes in relative prices, and the way that the goals and the attitudes of people, and the policies of governments, change over time in response to the circumstances and problems that confront them" (*London Times Literary Supplement,* 1973). Ignoring the flaw, the utilities adopted future projections based on a market incapable of adjusting to prices and a society unable to reduce or change its consumption patterns.

Pointing to the utilities' limited view of the future, the opposition called for examination of alternative futures. A Sierra Club member queried, "The testimony given so far indicates that the alternative is either we have these nuclear plants right now or we burn more fuel oil . . . [but] is that really the alternative? . . . Could we not get by with what we have already?" (San Diego Coast Regional Commission, Aug. 10, 1973, p. 88). Citing studies by the Rand Corporation and others which showed substantially different projections from those of the utilities, the individual argued that adaptive behavior left open the possibility of adopting energy conservation measures. At the coastal commission deliberations one SCE vice-president finally acknowledged that although "our position is still the same as far as San Onofre is concerned," his company was about to reduce future projections of need from its reported 6.2 percent compounded annual growth rate to 4.5 percent (Coastal Commission, Dec. 5, 1973, pp. 66–67). One month after the utilities secured coastal commission approval, SCE announced major nonnuclear expansion cutbacks (*Los Angeles Times,* Mar. 14, 1974).

Placed in a land use context, the opposition had suspected that the utilities were shifting to an all-nuclear system to eliminate the air pollution factor and thereby reduce public concern over the impact of their growth-inducement policies. With this foresight, another Sierra Club member urged the regional coastal commission to impose "very strict conditions upon this power plant to ensure that it will only be operated at a level that is consistent with the actual demand and not at a level which is merely being used [as] a growth-inducing [mechanism]" (San Diego Coast Regional Commission, Aug. 10, 1973, p. 98).

The other impact from overshadowing corporate power revolved around the operating economics of nuclear reactors. The image promoted by utilities during the preliminary years of nuclear power was one of great hope for unbounded electrical supply. Inwardly, the utilities also recognized the central role this would bestow and the enormous influence that would come to them as the captains of nuclear technology. The promise was enlarged by what appeared to be operating cost

advantages over fossil fuel plants. Original assumptions were that nuclear plants would operate at 80 percent of capacity as compared to 75
percent for fossil fuel plants, and that uranium fuel would cost about $8
per pound, a fraction of the cost for oil.

The actual operating experience, however, not only failed to verify
the assumptions but also revealed a number of hidden costs. With
regard to operating efficiency, reactors were never able to achieve the
80 percent factor. Although the figures ran somewhat higher for San
Onofre Unit One, the average capacity factors for all nuclear plants ran
at about 50 percent (Comey, 1974). Moreover, nuclear plants were
designed to last thirty years or more, but evidence for all plants showed
that after a three- or four-year break-in period, the plants reached a
submaximum peak and then dropped off rapidly because of aging problems (Comey, 1974). The implication drawn by the opposition was that
this placed extraordinary financial penalties on nuclear users and might
eventually lead to corporate bail-outs by government.

With regard to the cost of fuel, the price of uranium started
skyrocketing in the early 1970s because of nuclear plant build-up and
diminishing fuel supplies. Although SCE and SDG&E claimed to hold
supply contracts for uranium through 2008, scarcity had quadrupled
the $8 price by 1975, and forced domestic enrichment plants to break
contracts. Measuring ore reserves against planned nuclear expansion,
the U.S. Energy Research and Development Administration (ERDA)
estimated that by 2000, uranium demand would be twice what could be
supplied domestically (*Wall Street Journal*, June 7, 1976).

In addition, the opposition pointed to other hidden social costs, including the expense of storing radioactive wastes indefinitely, the lack
of appropriate insurance for people in the event of a nuclear accident,
the unamortized cost resulting from plants lasting less than their designed lives, and the resource cost of using energy faster than necessary.
The nuclear shutdown suit by Nader, for example, argued that in 1972
it took nearly as much energy to make uranium usable (6,100 mw) as
was produced by nuclear plants (6,873 mw), thus leaving only a tiny
residual for end use (von Haden, 1973).

SDG&E recognized the implications of the explicit and hidden costs,
saying that "the central issue [is] allowing the price of energy to reflect
its real economic and social costs. . . . All of these are rising, and consequently, the price of energy *must* rise as well" (SDG&E, 1972, p. 8).
Nevertheless, when questioned by one state coastal commissioner, the
utilities gave no definitive response as to their certainty of nuclear cost
advantages or to what societal implications might result from unexpected cost increases (Coastal Commission, Feb. 20, 1974, pp. 35-39).
By early 1975, however, the cost difficulties had become so apparent to
other utilities that two-thirds of those reactors that had been scheduled

for construction were either delayed or cancelled (*Wall Street Journal*, Feb. 3, 1975).

The contrasting perspectives of the utilities and their opponents reflected the substantial issues and insufficient knowledge with which the public deliberation process would have to deal. On the one hand, the utilities were proposing the largest nuclear complex in the world for the needs of a heavily urbanized region. On the other hand, the opposition concluded, "We are not suggesting that no more power plants be built and we are not advocating a policy of no growth. We are simply saying that the Coastal Zone Conservation Act does not permit the construction of this nuclear power plant at this time at this site" (Coastal Commission, Oct. 18, 1973, p. 112).

Public Deliberation Process

At San Onofre a score of overlapping state and federal authorities had concurrent jurisdiction over plant expansion. As shown in Table 6, the public deliberation process occurred between June, 1970, and July, 1974. Although some agencies exercised authority over more than one project phase or impact, the process did not reflect much interagency coordination. Moreover, coastal commission deliberation came at the end of the process after other agency decisions were made.

Most of those state agencies involved were known to favor the needs of development over environmental considerations. Excluding the coastal commissions, the most active were the Public Utilities Commission, the San Diego Regional Water Quality Control Board (SDRWQCB), and the California Water Resources Control Board (CWRCB). The PUC, which issues "certificates of convenience and necessity" to utilities after determining cost and adequacy of service and public need, held hearings in San Clemente beginning in October, 1970. The certificate was issued without restriction in March, 1971. Like the coastal commissions, water resource management is governed in California by a bi-level regional/state structure. The San Diego regional board, which acts as the regulating authority, held hearings on San Onofre and deliberated over a range of issues including sand disposal in the ocean and thermal effects from the plant cooling systems. Following public hearings, a permit was issued for sand disposal in September, 1970. Additional hearings were held for water discharge and a separate permit was issued in July, 1972, subject to the results of a continuous monitoring program to detect long-term discharge effects on marine ecology. The CWRCB, which certifies compliance to its water quality control plan and standards, issued a certificate in October, 1970. However, following a request by the utilities for a thermal discharge exemption to exclude excess heat created during system clean-

Table 6. Public Decision Authorities: San Onofre.

Project Impact	Public Agency	Certification Authority	Application File Date	Agency Final Decision
Economic	Atomic Energy Commission	Need for additional electrical capacity; financial and engineering qualifications of utilities	6/1/70	Construction permit issued 10/18/73
	California Public Utilities Commission	Need for additional electrical capacity	7/16/70	Certificate granted 3/9/71
	California Coastal Commissions	Need for additional electrical capacity	7/3/73	Overall permit issued 2/20/74
Radiation Hazard	Atomic Energy Commission	Reactor safety; nuclear waste disposal; radiation monitoring	6/1/70	Construction permit issued 10/18/73
	California Public Health Department	Radiation monitoring	9/21/70	Monitoring program approved 9/28/70
Land Environment	Atomic Energy Commission	Construction laydown area; public safety exclusion area	6/1/70	Construction permit issued 10/18/73
	U.S. Marine Corps	Transmission line easement	6/18/70	Issued 8/7/70
		Soil disposal	9/15/70	Granted 9/15/70
		U.S. Highway 101 right-of-way	10/15/70	Access and relocation granted 1/26/71
	California Highway Department	U.S. Highway 101 right-of-way	10/15/70	Access and relocation granted 1/26/71
	California Parks and Recreation Department	Construction laydown area; access road	4/18/72	Approved 6/15/71
	California Coastal Commissions	Conservation of bluffs, canyons, and beach without substantial adverse effect	7/3/73	Overall permit issued 2/20/74

Table 6. Public Decision Authorities: San Onofre. *(continued)*

Project Impact	Public Agency	Certification Authority	Application File Date	Agency Final Decision
Marine Environment	Atomic Energy Commission	Thermal discharge; entrainment; water flow; cooling system construction	6/1/70	Construction permit issued 10/18/73
	California Lands Commission	Sand Disposal	7/8/70	Granted 3/4/71
		Offshore conduit easement and construction	4/6/72	Granted 12/1/72
	Army Corps of Engineers	Sand Disposal	9/2/70	Approved 1/28/71
		Construction of conduit and discharge in navigable waters	2/24/72	Granted 7/31/74
	San Diego Regional Water Quality Control Board	Sand disposal	7/10/70	Granted 9/21/70
		Industrial waste discharge	2/14/72	Granted 7/31/72
	California Water Resources Control Board	Compliances with water quality standards	2/14/72	Certification issued 10/7/70; revised for thermal exemption 2/15/73
	California Coastal Commissions	Conservation of coastal waters without substantial adverse effect from thermal chemical discharge and entrainment	7/3/73	Overall permit issued 2/20/74

ing operations, the state board held new hearings and allowed the exemption in a revised certification dated February, 1973. In addition to their individual authorities, all state agencies were supposed to comply with the newly passed California Environmental Quality Act of 1972 (CEQA).

At the federal level the Marine Corps, Corps of Engineers, and Coast Guard were marginally involved, but the central agency in deliberations was the Atomic Energy Commission. The agency was originated by the Atomic Energy Act of 1946 in response to demands to redirect atomic war technology toward peaceful uses. To this end, the act directed the AEC "to make the maximum contribution to the general welfare . . . [and] increase the standard of living" (Office of the Federal Register, 1969, p. 399). To do this, the agency was given independent status and was governed by a five-member board appointed by the president. Below it stood a large-scale unitary bureaucracy composed of two arms directed by a general manager who served as the chief executive officer of the agency. The dominant arm included research, development, manufacturing, and promotional functions. The subservient arm provided all regulatory functions for commercial development. As a result of this arrangement, the AEC ruled as both advocate and judge in the field of nuclear energy, and the subordinate position of regulation provided a clear advantage for development interests.

Although not designed to be a land use agency, the AEC dominated San Onofre proceedings. Its involvement, however, came at a time when it was under intense public scrutiny for widespread mismanagement. With its dual role under a single hierarchy, the agency frequently had a conflict of interest between promotion and regulation. By the time of San Onofre, pro-development administrators had established a pattern of concealing or minimizing the severity of issues (especially safety) that posed threats to continued development. Known by opponents as the "Good News Agency," the AEC suppressed information by blocking opposition hearing testimony, "laundering" reports on nuclear health and safety, threatening concerned agency employees who wanted to testify on safety hazards, lying to the public, and hiding information under the guise of "national security" (Metzger, 1972; Coastal Commission, Oct. 18, 1973, pp. 91-110).

Besides the suppression issue, the agency also resisted inclusion of environmental considerations. Until the 1971 federal court decision on Calvert Cliffs, the AEC refused to conform to NEPA requirements in completing environmental impact statements (Bieber, 1973). In assessing AEC behavior toward NEPA, the federal court remarked that the agency "made a mockery of the Act" (quoted in Dolgin and Guilbert, 1974, p. 245). For nuclear plants sited along the coast, the agency also circumvented the federal Coastal Zone Management Act, which required that all federal agencies "cooperate and participate with state and local governments and regional agencies" in preserving coastal resources (Coastal Zone Management Act, 1972, Sec. 303).

In 1975 the agency was reorganized by breaking the two arms into separate authorities. Regulatory responsibilities became the sole function of the Nuclear Regulatory Commission, but as seen in the Three Mile Island accident, many of the pro-development values and procedural patterns survived the reorganization.

At San Onofre the AEC maintained discretion over three areas including economic need, environmental impact, and nuclear safety. For safety, the agency held exclusive jurisdiction over a variety of issues associated with ECCS, fuel transportation and storage, earthquake proofing, plant protective systems, and emergency planning. AEC deliberation occurred between June, 1970, and October, 1973, and included three public hearings in San Diego and Sam Clemente. Although the AEC usually determined unilaterally what issues would be heard, it yielded in this case to significant opposition pressure by accepting nine issues as "contested" (AEC, Oct. 15, 1973). Through the AEC regulatory staff's impact statement, the agency nevertheless refuted all issues in favor of the utilities (AEC, Oct. 20, 1972; Mar., 1973). Acting on this, the AEC licensing board affirmed the staff conclusions (AEC, Oct. 15, 1973) and issued a construction permit on October 18, 1973. An appeal for reconsideration was denied by the AEC appeals board.

When the coastal commissions entered the deliberations, they transformed what appeared to be a pro-development process into an open and controversial review. Although the regional commission generally accepted the proposal as routine, the state commission saw the decision as coterminous with developing its coastal plan. Consequently it expended considerable time on public hearings and in establishing a working dialogue with other agencies. Subject to much pressure by the utilities, which claimed delay costs would run $5 million a month, the coastal commission took an additional eight months to complete its reviews. This additional review was diminished, however, by the AEC's exclusive jurisdiction over nuclear safety. In spite of Proposition 20's mandate "to promote the public safety, health, and welfare" (Coastal Act, 1972), the coastal commissions were prevented by a prior federal court decision from considering the effect of nuclear safety on coastal land use patterns.

Application to the San Diego Coast Regional Commission was made on July 3, 1973, and the decision was rendered on September 7, 1973, a month earlier than required. A public hearing was held on August 10, 1973, but most of the process lacked rigorous review. As one observer put it, the proposal "kind of floated through" (Stark, 1974). Prior to the public hearing, staff activity involved preparing a project summary and handing out copies of the AEC environmental statement to commissioners. Believing that the AEC report and the public hearing would provide "adequate information on which to base a permit decision"

(Crandall, 1973), the staff limited post-hearing activity to preparation of a four-page recommendation and package of comments offered by the utilities in response to hearing testimony.

To avoid a controversy over its pro-development bias, the commission agreed "to *not* limit testimony. . . . This will prevent accusations being made that we have ignored some portions of the . . . California Coastal Zone Conservation Act" (Crandall, 1973). Open rebuttal or cross-examination, however, was not permitted. The all-day hearing commenced with an hour-long presentation by the utilities covering electrical need, the "oil crisis" imperative, technical aspects of the proposal, and construction phase activities. This was followed by a question and answer period between commissioners and utility representatives. Commissioner Frautschy then provided his expertise on the advantages of nuclear power and gave a discourse on why coastal siting was mandatory over inland siting.

The remaining half of the hearing was consumed by state agency representatives from Air Resources, Water Quality, Fish and Game, Parks and Recreation, and finally by a dozen opposition groups. Among the participating agencies, only Parks and Recreation voiced major concern over the project. In what would become the major restriction imposed by the regional commission on its approval, the parks representative requested that the coastal agency "grant conditions which will assure that the construction and operation of the utilities there will not in any way inhibit the planning, development, operation, or enjoyment of San Onofre Bluffs State Beach . . ." (San Diego Coast Regional Commission, Aug. 10, 1973, p. 78). Unlike the utilities, the opposition was unable to adequately organize and moderate its sequence of testimony. They argued that sufficient information on most issues was not available and that no commission decision should be made until the utilities could satisfy the coastal act's burden-of-proof requirement.

The regional commission voted on September 7 to approve the project, by a margin of nine to one (two members were absent). Although the opposition stressed that other agency approvals "shouldn't be a reason why a permit should be given here" (San Diego Coast Regional Commission, Aug. 10, 1973, p. 116), the commission felt that "much expertise" had gone into prior approvals and the coastal agency had no "real need to try to add anything . . ." (Keen, 1974). The sole dissenting commissioner argued that "we should postpone the matter . . . until we can understand what the problems are" (*San Diego Union*, Sept. 8, 1973), but he also recognized that "there wasn't much real interest on the part of our commission [to do so]" (Keen, 1974). The commission placed four conditions on its approval, all of which were either covered by other agency jurisdictions or had no legal effect. The fourth condition, for example, stipulated that the utilities had to pay a use tax on the facilities "if such fee or tax is determined appropriate by the California State Legislature, Congress of the United States, or other agency authorized by law to impose such a fee or tax" (San Diego Coast Regional Commission, Sept. 4, 1973).

Unsatisfied with the regional decision, a group of opponents, including GUARD, Environmental Coalition of Orange County, Friends of the Earth, and Scenic Shoreline Preservation Conference, appealed the case to the state commission. As provided by the coastal act, an appeal could not be heard unless the case posed a "substantial issue" for statewide interests or adversely affected the coastal planning effort. The opposition claimed that the project endangered public health and safety and would create a degrading and irreversible impact on coastal resources (Coastal Commission, Oct. 15, 1973). The state commission deliberated over the appeal for five months and did not reach a final conclusion until after an array of events including a public hearing, much staff research activity, an original decision to deny construction, and reconsideration of that denial under pro-utility pressures.

The appeal hearing was held in San Diego on October 18, 1973, and included half a day of testimony. It opened much as had the regional hearings, with a formal presentation by utility executives and engineers. Similar issues were covered, but the utilities concentrated on areas (such as ECCS, bluffs excavation plans, and the "marine desert") made vulnerable by opponents at the regional hearing. The utilities further argued that since other agencies had made thorough reviews, the coastal commission need not delay approval. A departure from the earlier hearing was the opposition testimony. In order to match the orderly progression of utility testifiers, the environmentalists hired Fredric Sutherland, an environmental attorney with the Center for Law in the Public Interest. At the hearing he acted as opposition moderator, integrating a half-dozen scientists and laymen into an organized presentation. A surprise witness for the opposition was Dr. Henry Kendall, a nationally known nuclear physicist and member of the MIT-based Union of Concerned Scientists. As one of the central figures who exposed AEC mismanagement, he provided an expertise at least comparable to that of the utilities on the implications of nuclear power.

Owing to the complexity of issues and the interest in resolving a variety of questions, the commission staff gained an extension on the sixty-day appeal period limit from the reluctant utilities, thus postponing the original decision until December 5, 1973 (Bodovitz, Oct. 24, 1973). During this extended period the staff carried out an open search for information in hopes of resolving the critical issues. Requests were made of other agencies for interpretations of information and positions on individual problems. Communications were also established with partisan interests, including Gulf General Atomic concerning different types of reactors, and Scripps marine scientists concerning cooling system impact. During this staff review the cover-up of Unit One's breakdown also came to light. The accident, which occurred on October 21, was not discovered by the public until late November and prompted speculation that SCE and the AEC were trying to conceal the occurrence until after the coastal commission decision (*Los Angeles Times*, Nov. 22, 1973). In an editorial the *Los Angeles Times* said, "The most disturbing thing about the accident . . . is that a deliberate effort seems to have been made . . . to keep news of the problem and the closure from the public" (Nov. 26, 1973).

A week prior to the commission vote on December 5 the staff released its recommendation to deny approval of the project. Concerned with the conflicting and inadequate information and suspicious of utility behavior, the staff detailed its findings on a variety of unresolved issues. One concern, for example, was over the value of the bluffs and canyon area. The utilities had argued that the canyons were dangerous and should be destroyed. In response the staff said, "Such a position is similar to asserting that the Grand Canyon should be filled because someone could fall into it" (Coastal Commission, Dec., 1973). Viewing the bluffs as a unique coastal resource, the staff further concluded that "our society is not yet so poor that we must chop down our cathedrals for firewood" (Coastal Commission, Dec., 1973). Without considering the question of nuclear safety, the staff supported its recommendation, contending that the coastal act planning "goal should be both enough energy *and* a healthy environment. By this standard . . . the project in its present form does *not* qualify for a permit . . . " (Coastal Commission, Dec., 1973). Although the utilities responded that "we are greatly disappointed [and] greatly concerned that the staff has taken this position" (*San Diego Union*, Dec. 3, 1973), the staff recommendation offered a number of areas for compromise. To reduce the project's external impacts, these compromises included placing the reactors across the freeway, using an HTGR nuclear generator with lower cooling requirements than the PWR generator, and using a cooling discharge system that would not require near-shore water.

During its regular December 5 meeting at Newport Beach the commission allowed a four-hour open discussion on the staff recommendation prior to voting. Staff director Bodovitz started the session with a review of the recommendation, stressing that staff concerns could be greatly mitigated if the utilities adopted the recommendation's proposed alternatives: "We're suggesting that with amendment and with changes, this could be converted into an acceptable proposal, but in its present form . . . it is not" (Coastal Commission, Dec. 5, 1973, p. 20). Displaying impatience, utility executives followed with a lengthy contention that the recommendation was unprofessional, full of improper value judgments, and lacked knowledge of the issues. For the first time SCE's top executives were present, and the senior vice-president addressed the commission on why the staff compromises were not feasible and in any event would only create unnecessary delay. He said,

> To be quite direct, [we] do not have any potential [alternative] sites . . . on which these proposed San Onofre units could be developed with less than a four- to six-year delay. . . .
>
> The installation of HTGR's at this existing San Onofre site would involve delays of not less than four years. . . .
>
> . . . there is absolutely no substantial credible evidence that a deep water intake would represent a meaningful environmental improvement. [Coastal Commission, Dec. 5, 1973, pp. 25–26]

From the utilities' arguments the discussion moved to Sutherland, the environmentalists' spokesman, who argued that SCE was attempting to obscure the issues by introducing new information at the meeting that could not be evaluated by the staff prior to the commission vote. He further stressed that so much uncertainty existed in the proposal that the coastal act precluded approval.

A number of the commissioners voiced concern over the project's ambiguous impact and spent considerable time in exchanges with SCE executives. Finally, after failing to reach agreement on what conditions would be appropriate under the act, the commission voted against approval. Although project proponents argued that a majority of the commission voted for approval (six of eleven present), it failed to get a majority of the total membership and, more important, failed to get the necessary two-thirds vote (eight of the twelve members) required by the act in situations of "irreversible impacts."

The consortium of environmentalists seemed to have won the day, but the utilities and their supporters brought immediate pressure for reversal of the vote. The utilities filed suit in San Diego, claiming among other things that the commission had illegally considered nuclear safety. In the political arena they exerted influence through public sympathizers. For example, a pro-development member of the San Diego Coast Regional Commission said that "to disregard the critical need for additional electrical energy because of an insignificant effect on . . . [the] bluffs . . . is a ridiculous tradeoff [made by] a very small minority of appointed officials from out of our area . . . " (*San Diego Evening Tribune*, Dec. 7, 1973). The *San Diego Union* complained that "the commission was vetoed by its own staff which does not answer to either the voters or the Legislature" (Feb. 20, 1974). The lieutenant governor called the vote "a tragic and irresponsible decision. It could well result in blackouts . . . " (*San Diego Union*, Dec. 6, 1973). Key legislators further let it be known that if the decision wasn't reversed, the commission would have a tough time staying in existence.

As a result of the utilities' success in politicizing the decision, commission members came to express regret at the outcome. Commissioner Mendelsohn argued that "what we really said December 5 was not that we didn't want it, but that we wanted to minimize the environmental damage . . . (*San Diego Union*, Jan. 23, 1974). Commissioner Lane expressed hope that "we can find a combination of things that will make it possible to satisfy the [utilities] and the staff" (*San Diego Union*, Dec. 20, 1973). Commissioner Laufer followed on this point, saying, "Although it is not before us legally, I urge work to get it back before us as soon as possible" (*San Diego Union*, Dec. 20, 1973). Under the act, however, no legal means were available for reconsideration of the vote. Unless "a basic error" was found, the legal procedure called for resubmission of a revised application to the regional commission, which would initiate a new deliberation sequence. Since the political pressure made time critical, the commission and its attorney general liaison spent the bulk of December and part of January searching for a way to avoid this "circuitous wheel spinning process" (Bodovitz, Dec. 19, 1973).

At the January 9 regular commission meeting consideration of nuclear safety was proposed as the "error" that might be used to return the case for a revote. Although the attorney general liaison advised the commission not to "concede that there were errors," he argued that an agreement on this issue between the commission and the utilities might convince the court to intervene in the utility suit by stipulating that a revote be made without consideration of radiation safety (Bodovitz, Jan. 9, 1974b). An acrimonious discussion ensued with the Sierra Club claiming a violation of "due process" and several commissioners insisting their original votes had been without consideration of nuclear safety. A motion was finally approved to approach the court with the utilities and request resolution of the suit through this legal stipulation. Although ample evidence showed that both commission and staff members had followed the attorney general's instructions not to consider nuclear safety in the original deliberation process (Coastal Commission, Dec., 1973; Dec. 5, 1973), the San Diego Superior Court accepted the "technicality" and remanded the case for a revote. Representing those opposed to reconsideration without a revised application, Commissioner Farr termed the action "a legal gimmick" (*Los Angeles Times*, Jan. 10, 1974).

In anticipation of the revote, the staff started to work in late December on formulating detailed conditions to go with the eventual approval. Several meetings were held with the utilities in an attempt to determine modifications acceptable to the utilities and conforming to the coastal act. During these negotiations the staff argued for four changes: (1) relocation of the plant across the freeway; (2) public access to the 1,000 feet of beach originally planned to be closed during the six-year construction period; (3) a perpetual marine monitoring program combined with the requirement that the utilities remedy any harmful effects of the cooling system that appeared; and (4) the preservation intact of 0.3 mile of the remaining 0.85-mile bluffs for at least ten years. The utilities, which had been unwilling to entertain modification prior to the denial vote, resisted any major conditions, especially plant relocation, during the negotiations. According to Commissioner Laufer, they brought nothing positive to "the compromise table" (Bodovitz, Jan. 9, 1974b). Fearing legal reprisals by the utilities, the staff withdrew the plant relocation condition (Bodovitz, Jan., 1974) but held to the remaining modifications in an initial recommendation to the commission at the January 9 regular meeting (Bodovitz, Jan. 9, 1974a).

Several commission members, including some who had originally voted in favor of the project, remained skeptical of the "compromise" conditions and referred to them as "only cosmetic tinkering with the project" (Bodovitz, Jan. 9, 1974b). Concerned about public image and fulfilling the coastal act mandate, a group of commissioners led by Mendelsohn assumed command of the staff negotiations. The utilities, however, stood firm, vetoing any reconsideration of plant relocation and maintaining that they could not agree to the bluffs' preservation. According to SCE, acceptance of this condition would contract away their right to request further San Onofre expansion in the future (the SCE master plan called for additional units south of Units Two and Three where the bluffs were located). The impasse lasted all the way to an eleventh-hour effort during the night prior to the commission vote scheduled for February 20, 1974. The late-night negotiations took place in an upstairs suite of the Biltmore Hotel in Santa Barbara, the city selected for that month's regular meeting. Present in the suite were SCE lawyers led by Vice-President Fogarty, Commissioners Mendelsohn, Farr, and Laufer, and staff director Bodovitz (Broadhead, 1976). No environmentalists were allowed to participate, and at the insistence of SCE the commission staff coordinator for San Onofre was barred from the room. Although most of the points were worked out in the suite, no final commitments were made and no one knew for sure whether the utilities would accept the outcome at the morning public meeting.

The February 20 revote was preceded by a stormy two-hour discussion of the conditions worked out at the Biltmore suite. After distributing copies of the conditions, Bodovitz opened the discussion with an attempt to justify the staff's reversal of position. Being especially careful not to refer to the project as a new proposal, he said, "The point I cannot emphasize too strongly is that the difference in recommendations is because of a difference in the effect that the project would have" (Coastal Commission, Feb. 20, 1974, p. 6). Contradicting prior statements, he further said that denial now would cause a net adverse effect by requiring use of more air-polluting facilities along the coast. As Bodovitz finished, SCE's Fogarty rose and said, "The companies and the [commission] staff have worked for the last six weeks in developing the present proposal the staff has made. We are in agreement with those conditions and . . . will accept them" (Coastal Commission, Feb. 20, 1974, p. 12).

Environmentalist lawyer Sutherland followed with a blistering condemnation of the commission:

> . . . in return for playing the game openly . . . [we] have been rewarded by a well-placed knife in the back. . . . It is a sham to call these cosmetic conditions a . . . compromise, and if your commission follows this recommendation of the staff, you will have made a mockery of the law and a travesty of your commission. . . . If any of you Commissioners find that the pressure of your job is too great in order to enforce the law, I suggest you resign [applause]. [Coastal Commission, Feb. 20, 1974, pp. 14, 21, 22]

With disquiet in the audience, Bodovitz responded by saying that if disagreement in opinion was being equated with stabs in the back, "I am very concerned about the future of democratic government" (Coastal Commission, Feb. 20, 1974, p. 26). The discussion then moved to specifics of the conditions, and amendments offered by Mendelsohn and Wilson were approved. The revote followed and the project won its necessary two-thirds by a margin of ten to two.

An eight-page letter was sent to the utilities for confirmation (Bodovitz, Feb. 28, 1974), containing the following conditions:

1. The 1,000 feet of beach scheduled to be closed during the six-year construction period was to have a six-foot-wide public walkway to connect the north and south sections of the undisturbed state beach. This access, however, was limited to summer weekends and holidays.

2. A continuing study was required that would "result in the broadest possible consideration of the effects of Units 1, 2, and 3 on the entire marine environment in the vicinity of San Onofre." The utility-financed program was to be directed by a review committee consisting of three scientists, one chosen by the commission and the others by each of the two parties in the controversy. Semiannual reports were to be made by the committee, and any substantial adverse effects identified were to be corrected by the utilities immediately.

3. No cooling system diffuser port was to be within 1,900 feet of the area where the kelp bed was likely to expand.

4. The most scenic area of the bluffs, about 0.3 mile long, would be

preserved and left open to public access for the life of the utilities' site easement (until 2023). Excluding the possibility of technological innovation, this was also interpreted as precluding any future expansion of the San Onofre Nuclear Station.

5. The utilities were to establish "a reliability organization" at the vice-presidential level within SCE to oversee nuclear plant operating problems and solutions. Semiannual reports were to be filed by the unit with the state PUC.

Reaction to the final decision was generally negative. Frautschy, the utilities' prime advocate on the commission, said, "I suspect that perhaps the [marine] study will be too narrow — being guided primarily by marine biologists . . . " (Frautschy, 1975). Claiming the approval conditions would add $100 million to the $1.3 billion project, SDG&E President Zitlau called the decision "a hollow victory. It brings an added burden to our rate payers" (*San Diego Union*, Feb. 21, 1974). Sutherland, representing the opposition, said, "There is a 90 percent chance the decision will be appealed. But we will have to move fast. The utilities probably already have the bulldozers warmed up" (*San Diego Union*, Feb. 21, 1974).

In the year following approval the environmentalists filed a suit in San Diego to reverse the outcome, but were finally defeated in September, 1974. In November the marine study review committee filed its first report, stating that it had organized itself around an initial study that would take five years (Connell, 1974). The most significant event, however, was the AEC's unilateral decision in 1975 to permanently close the beach in front of the nuclear station. Counter to both coastal commission intent and an original AEC pledge not to preclude postconstruction access (AEC, Oct. 15, 1973, p. 98), the federal agency made the decision without consulting outside agencies. Citing exclusive jurisdiction over nuclear safety, it claimed the beach had to be closed to recreational activities because the safety perimeter around the plant was not large enough (Kartalia, 1975). Although the AEC planned to provide an enclosed access through the restricted area, the coastal commission searched for ways to prevent exclusion to recreational use. In the end, it decided against confrontation and let stand the AEC order.

Construction of the new facilities started in late 1974 and were substantially completed in 1980. The marine impact study was presented to the coastal commission in November, 1979, and proposed no significant design changes to abate potential near-shore problems. Units Two and Three were scheduled for startup sometime in the early 1980s pending a license from the NRC.

CHAPTER 5

Kitsap County Government at Nettleton Lakes

"Here . . . is a case where the damage has not yet been done and where we can accomplish some of the national goal on this front . . . by *not* doing something rather than by reversing damage already done."

Walter W. Heller

NO STUDY of land use control would be complete without an examination of housing development. Among other reasons, a housing case holds significance because platting and construction review has been the special domain of local government. Although once representing nearly autonomous control, the power of local jurisdictions has been lessened over the last decade by the distribution of new authority to other government levels. With the inducements of federal planning grants, the Intergovernmental Personnel Act of 1968, and the proliferation of federal and state environmental laws, much of that unchecked authority has been incorporated in a larger system of intergovernmental relations with higher agencies. This case examines such a system where county government acted as principal authority for comprehensive review but was subject to mutual adjustment within a regional setting with specialized state and federal agencies.

The demand for new housing in the last two decades has been greatly influenced by the post-World War II baby boom as well as by increasing levels of affluence. In addition to the contiguous growth of suburbs, another segment of that increasing market has been rural recreational subdivisions. Promising an escape from urban pressures, such "second home" housing has precipitated overutilization of many substantially undisturbed natural resources outside urban areas. Led on by the belief that undeveloped open spaces were becoming scarce, much of the demand has come from the desire to save a piece of the "wilderness" for individual private use. However, excessive densities and subquality features built into these recreational projects have frequently resulted in desecration of large tracts of rural open space known for their exceptional esthetic values (Boschken, 1974).

By themselves, market transactions concerning land resource allocation do not adequately account for the variety of interests and values endemic to the use of undeveloped open space. Large rural housing developments are especially threatening because they restrict public access to and enjoyment of scenic areas of land and water. For public authorities this exclusive nature of private recreational communities causes dilemmas in public policy. What constitutes a politically acceptable balance between development and conservation of unique land resources? What level of development is appropriate without significantly diminishing the natural resource and profile of the area? Should emphasis be placed on preserving lesser developed localities for multiple-use recreation or on allowing greater development of rural areas to encourage employment advantages? With competition between local and regional priorities, can "winner take all" solutions be avoided? What policies are needed to minimize the external impacts created by such developments? Like the previous two cases, the locus of analytical interest is with the governmental form and process in resolving these sorts of questions.

The location of this case was the Puget Sound region of Washington state, an area known for its fine living conditions and exceptional natural surroundings. The central features of the region include its 2,500-square-mile system of inland salt waterways surrounded by rich forest lowlands and rugged mountain ranges. Proximity of these natural resources to urban areas has provided a base for economic development as well as spectacular recreational opportunities. Such proximity, however, also has created an intense interdependence among frequently conflicting interests competing for different uses of the land. For Washington public agencies control of land use goes far beyond the traditional zoning practices which separate tracts into different demand categories. Said one county official concerned with the case, "We had to determine whether or not our zoning regulations would allow us to protect the new awareness on environmental issues" (Barber, 1971). Many resource uses have an adverse impact on the profile of the region as a whole and have caused volatile confrontations among competing interests and agencies (Bish et al., 1975).

In this case public authorities were asked to approve the proposed development of a 6,000-acre high-density recreational community along Hood Canal in an undeveloped area of Kitsap County. Called Nettleton Lakes-on-the-Canal, this project raised a number of issues ranging from impacts on county services to potential pollution of the region's marine ecology. The significance of the case coincided with the environmental movement of the late 1960s and 1970s, as is seen in the state's identification of it as one of ten "areas of critical concern" (Slavin, 1971). At the local level one county planning commissioner said the county "went far beyond what we would do for any 50-acre planned unit development or 20-acre rezone" (Barber, 1971). In light of the complexity of issues and far-reaching impacts, the appropriateness of the public decisions was dependent upon both public decision rules and administrative structure.

Kitsap County and State Governments

Since the size and diversity of Puget Sound have produced considerable social, economic, and political differences, few common perceptions or unified identities exist for governing the region. Compounding this is the fact that various resource uses differ in such a way that no single jurisdictional boundary is able to internalize all the influences and consequences of major issues. Consequently no single government is "responsible" for Puget Sound. Instead, public authority is divided among several administrative units at the local, state, and federal levels. In the case of Nettleton Lakes this federalist web represented a system of concurrent jurisdictions where coordination mechanisms emerged as a result of on-going intergovernmental relations (see Table 7).

For land use and natural resource administration in Washington, local government continues to provide the major arenas for public decision making and represents the "workhorse" of the system (Avery, 1973). In this case the local jurisdiction was Kitsap County,[1] which had authority to plan for local public needs, regulate construction by zoning and permit approvals, and provide public services conjunctive with development. According to one county official, the Nettleton Lakes proposal raised a number of questions to which the county had to respond: "Is it a good and proper land use that doesn't adversely affect their neighbors? . . . Would there be proper services" provided by the developer (Rylander, 1971)? Determination of these questions was based on the county's intent "to protect property values . . . by ensuring the location of buildings in good taste, proper proportion and in harmony with their surroundings and to secure the best and most appropriate use of land" (Kitsap County, June, 1969, p. 41).

The county is governed by an elected three-member board of county commissioners who make the final decisions and are responsible for maintaining public access to the local decision process. During the Nettleton Lakes controversy the board was composed of three Kitsap businessmen who held leadership roles in local service organizations (e.g., Chamber of Commerce, Kiwanis) and were active members in the

---

[1]Mason County, adjoining Kitsap at the location of the project, would also have been a central approving local agency if the proposal had not been tabled by the developer. It consequently provided only an advisory role through its initial review efforts.

Table 7. Public Decision Authorities: Nettleton Lakes.

Project Impact	Public Agency	Certification Authority
Economic	Kitsap County Commission and Planning Commission	Management of urban growth; economic development; comprehensive planning; tax assessment
Public Services	Kitsap County Commission and Planning Commission	Dedication of public facilities; provision of water supply, sewerage, fire, police, and other services
Land Environment	Kitsap County Commission and Planning Commission	Platting and dedication of projects; control of density, lot size, and street arrangement
	SWPCC (state) Health (state)	Sewage system and water system approval; drainage systems; water quality enforcement
	DWR (state)	Freshwater rights, reservoir and dam construction, minimum stream flow requirements
	Fisheries (state)	Regulation and management of anadromous fish; use of surface water
	Game (state)	Regulation and management of freshwater game fish, game, animals and waterfowl
Marine Environment	U.S. Army Corps of Engineers	Flood control; marina dredging permit
	DNR (state)	Tidelands leases; dredging approval
	Fisheries (state)	Regulation and management of saltwater and anadromous food, game, and shellfish resources

Abbreviations: SWPCC — State Water Pollution Control Commission
                DWR — State Department of Water Resources
                DNR — State Department of Natural Resources

regional association of governments. One was a major figure in the state Democratic party, and another had previously held several elected positions in local government. All considered themselves development-oriented and referred to various environmentalists as a "Joker from California" and "Minnie Mouse" who provided "no practical information" (Lobe, Randall, and Mahan, 1971). None were college graduates.

Although having original jurisdiction, the county commissioners delegated the responsibility of land use policy to an appointed nine-member Planning Commission. While state law limits planning commissions to an advisory function, such quasi-legislative units are allowed to hold hearings, collect the bulk of public information, and create the primary reports in support of their recommendations (Washington State Laws, 1969). In Kitsap the Planning Commission was the main focus in land use decisions, with the County Commission entering deliberations primarily on appeal. During the Nettleton Lakes case the Planning Commission was composed of part-time lay persons with a variety of backgrounds, including among others a nuclear engineer, a local restaurant owner, and a housewife. While one was new to the area and had few community ties, most were indigenous, and a few were central figures in community organizations and local party politics. Although some were viewed by environmentalists as "pompous asses" with "a sneering attitude" (Masley, 1971), the Planning Commission seemed to represent a broader spectrum of interests than did the elected County Commission.

Regarding the land use question at Nettleton Lakes, the county legislative process was determined by three factors: the requirements of state law, the administrative resources of county departments, and the use of comprehensive planning. In 1969 the state replaced its 1937 law on local land use regulation with one imposing more specific criteria on local decision making (Washington State Laws, 1969). Through this new law the state instructed the local legislative body to "inquire into the public use and interest proposed to be served . . . [and] determine if appropriate provisions are made . . . for . . . drainage ways, streets . . . water supplies, sanitary wastes . . . " (Washington State Laws, 1969). In order to avoid adverse impacts on the local community, the state also allowed local government to impose restrictions, condition project approvals, and require performance bonds.

Second, to administratively reinforce the legislative bodies, the county maintained the usual departmental specialties including health and sanitation, parks, engineering, building inspection, sheriff, fire, county prosecutor, tax assessment, and planning. The departments, however, were primarily one-to-three-person operations staffed by a less professional mix than their metropolitan counterparts. Some officials held second jobs, for example, the director of public health who was also a real estate agent. As a result, the administration was considered to have neither broad resources for research and evaluation nor the enforcement capabilities to contend with urban pressures. One partial exception to this condition was the planning department, which was responsible for collecting and coordinating information on the Nettleton Lakes proposal. Although operating with only a clerk and a secretary, the director had a strong professional background in public planning, including a master's degree in urban planning from the University of Washington.

Third, the legislative process was determined by the establishment of a comprehensive plan which was used as "the basic source of reference" in land use decisions. The process of local land use planning usually involves first the development of a master plan with appropriate zoning maps and then the adoption of zoning ordinances that correspond to the comprehensive plan. Like most remote counties, Kitsap was prodded into land use planning by the threat of urban development interests eyeing its semiwilderness state. Its first master planning effort in 1964 was precipitated by a court ruling which struck down the county's zoning ordinances because it had no master plan map. The county hastily complied by making a map which, in particular, designated the semiwilderness site of the proposed Nettleton project as high-density residential use. One county planning commissioner explained that "in 1964, we felt that waterfront property should be used by as many as possible, so we made it R-7.5" (*Bremerton Sun*, July 30, 1969).

Owing to intensified developer interest in the area, in 1968 the county commissioned Harstad and Associates, Seattle planning consultants, to create a new comprehensive plan replacing the one of 1964. This master planning process had several relationships to the timing of the Nettleton project. First, with the rise of environmentalism and local demand for publicly accessible open space, the Kitsap community had become sensitive to the growth of large-scale developments along Hood Canal. This precipitated a request in 1969 for an interim rezone of the canal area including the Nettleton property. The intent was to establish a development moratorium until the new comprehensive plan was approved. The County Commission approved the rezone in February, 1970 (one month before it was to consider the Nettleton Lakes proposal), and placed the land in a forestry and agricultural zone restricting development to one dwelling unit per five acres. A Planning Commission statement explained the action: "The Commission . . . does not intend to convey its approval of an indefinite suspension of either private or public development [on Hood Canal], but only a desire to prevent de facto zoning, while the Commission moves forward . . . toward the adoption of a comprehensive plan . . . " (*Bremerton Sun*, Jan. 29, 1970).

A second timing factor was the county's adoption in June, 1969, of a set of planning policies developed as an element of the new comprehensive plan. Two aspects of the policies are of particular interest. First, under its "residential development policy," special allowance was made for recreational communities, such that "improvements may be less than those required for urban-type developments" (Kitsap County, Sept. 30, 1969, p. 17). Second, with regard to minimum lot sizes in undeveloped areas, the 1964 plan had allowed a maximum of one dwelling unit per five acres. But the new policies made exception for planned unit developments (PUDs) in rural areas, allowing for recreational plats to have up to three units per acre, with a minimum lot size of 12,500 square feet (one-third acre). In effect, this special provision for recreation platting encouraged creation of PUD communities in remote areas of the county. Special status for PUDs was based on the assumption that such private planning would "produce an integrated and balanced development of mutually supporting uses that might otherwise be inharmonious . . . " (Kitsap County, June, 1969, p. 31).

A final timing factor related to the new plan itself, most of which had not been formally approved by the county prior to the Nettleton Lakes case. To account for different land characteristics and different public demands, the plan was broken down into north, central, and south study areas. The Nettleton property was located along the western edge of the Central Kitsap Study Area (CKSA), which represented the county's most undeveloped section. The plan was completed and presented for deliberation before the Planning Commission in June, 1969. Besides the planning policies element, two aspects are also pertinent to the case. First is the plan's future population projections for the CKSA. For Holly (the hamlet adjacent to the proposed development), the plan anticipated a 25 percent population growth rate in the central area and would give the Holly area a population of only 200 residents by 1990. Following an "urban centers" concept for future development, the plan was inclined against growth in the western section, saying, " . . . the existing urban centers can easily accommodate projected urban residential land demand [including second home] with only small increases in dwelling unit densities, and . . . no new area need be added to the centers before 1990" (Harstad and Associates, 1969, p. 18).

The second aspect is the consultants' recommendation for controlling future growth. Recognizing a need to protect the wilderness reserves from encroaching urban influences, the plan asserted: " . . . Kitsap County is still largely undeveloped. If most new population is accommodated in already existing urban centers, as is the principal recommendation of this plan, this rural character will not appreciably diminish by 1990. Of real concern, however, is the significant and increasing trend in the platting and sale of vacation and recreation homesites" (Harstad and Associates, 1969, p. 27). Concerned with scatter de-

velopments along the canal, the county sought "to encourage intensive urban development" in the eastern portions of the county near
Bremerton and the Sound (Kitsap County, Sept. 30, 1969).

In addition to local government, various state agencies representing
specialized jurisdictions were involved in the decision process. State
government was the level most immediately responsible for the content
and administration of public policies concerning the Sound as a whole.
Owing to the strength and influence of special-interest groups in Washington, state authorities tended to be defined and distributed according
to segments of affected constituencies. To the extent that several impacts from the project had regionwide implications, six state agencies
were drawn into the public process with direct authority to regulate
development. These included the departments of Natural Resources
(DNR), Water Resources (DWR), Fisheries, Game, Health, and the
State Water Pollution Control Commission (SWPCC).[2]

The DNR, which represented environmental concerns and commercial resource harvesters in the case, held control over use of tidelands
and maintained authority over the Nettleton proposal because the project was to include the construction of a marina in a small river delta
along Hood Canal known as Anderson Cove. In past leases of the cove
the DNR had restricted use to oyster harvesting, and any other use
would have required new decisions by the agency.

The DWR, which represented environmental concerns of project impact, maintained authority over the allocation of freshwater rights, applications for reservoir and dam construction, and setting minimum
stream flow requirements. The agency was drawn into the decision process by the developer's intent to construct a number of artificial lakes
which would have impounded runoff to two rivers traversing the property. In addition, requests were made for the rights to establish wells for
the project. The DWR had to establish whether water quality would be
maintained by lake impoundment and to determine the minimum
downstream flow necessary to maintain stream ecology.

The Fisheries and Game departments worked closely together to protect the interest of commercial fishermen and sportsmen. In addition to
the management and regulation of fish, animal, and waterfowl resources, the two agencies cooperated in controlling the effects of stream
alteration and siltation on the surrounding ecology. Fisheries and Game
exercised authority over the Nettleton proposal because the project area

[2]In 1971 a governmental reorganization took effect that consolidated among others the
DWR, Shoreline Management, and the SWPCC into a single Department of Ecology
(DOE). Since it came toward the end of Nettleton deliberations, little mention will be
made of this change in land and natural resource administration, but others have evaluated
the impact of consolidation (Haskell and Price, 1973).

supported significant populations of fish, shellfish, game animals, and waterfowl. The potential environmental impact on fish and wildlife also extended beyond area boundaries because of the possibility of large amounts of siltation and other nonpoint-source pollution.

The state Health Department, which represented public health and safety concerns, and the SWPCC, which represented environmental interests, held similar authority over project approval. These included certification of a sewage collection and treatment system, a water supply system of such size to guarantee sufficient high-quality water, and a runoff drainage system to minimize erosion. For the Nettleton case, both agencies were governed by state water quality standards approved by the federal government.

In addition to the direct authorities held by the county and six state agencies, several local and regional agencies played advisory roles. These included the Puget Sound Governmental Conference (the regional COG), the Hood Canal Advisory Council (a state-sponsored citizens' planning group), the Marine Resources Advisory Committee (a state-sponsored professional advising unit), and the State Planning and Community Affairs Agency (responsible for statewide comprehensive planning and interagency clearinghouse activities). These governmental and quasi-governmental units acted primarily as data gatherers and information suppliers to instrumental decision makers.

Besides the diffuse structure of multiple authorities, a second important feature of Puget Sound government was the methods of intergovernmental coordination. Both the complexity of potential impacts and interest represented by various governmental units raised the possibility of interagency conflict. Nevertheless, the task of coordination was facilitated by past relationships among most agencies which had worked together on previous land use decisions.

Three methods of cooperation were evident. First, numerous formal and informal exchanges of information and recommendations took place. Through these exchanges interaction among agency experts provided a means for assessing the variety of considerations that had to be integrated into the approval process. This was further augmented by the State Planning and Community Affairs Agency and the Puget Sound Governmental Conference, which acted as information clearinghouses. Second, a number of agencies, including Kitsap County, the DNR, and the DWR, initiated interagency coordination meetings where issues that overlapped different jurisdictions were mutually worked out. In some cases these included the developer for purposes of clarifying points of intention and fact. Third, state agencies were actively involved in the county public hearing process. The effect of this was to give the county an early awareness of state concerns and to let state agencies observe points of contention in different public arenas.

Just as there was no single hierarchy of government in Puget Sound, there was no single decision criterion common to agency jurisdictions. The formal organizational units and their rules for decision making were sufficiently different to provide access for conflicting parties seeking to maintain or change the distribution, rate, and type of resource use. In lieu of a monolithic welfare function, the state established different rules for each of its specialized agencies such that the separate collectives of expertise were responsible for representing public welfare from the perspective of different constituent interests. This extended to county government as well, where state law provided that local rules be made to "determine whether the public interest will be served . . . If it finds that the plat makes appropriate provisions for the public health, safety and general welfare . . . then it shall be approved" (Washington State Laws, 1969). Kitsap County operationalized its statutory requirement by defining a decision rule that apportioned the costs of land use changes according to those who benefited from them. Zoning policies provided for changes in use only if they were "necessary for the preservation and enjoyment of any substantial property right of the [developer] and not materially detrimental to the public welfare nor the property of other persons located in the vicinity . . . " (Kitsap County, June, 1969, p. 42).

The Kitsap Environment

Puget Sound is one of a few places where urbanization and development are closely tied to natural areas of water, forests, and mountains. Although the region is less than a fourth of the state's area, it contains about two-thirds of Washington's population and economic activity. The Sound's 1970 population was 2.2 million, of which 82 percent lived within the metropolitan areas of Seattle, Tacoma, and Everett (U.S. Bureau of the Census, 1971).

Kitsap County is located in the middle of the region on a peninsula surrounded by Hood Canal on the west, the Sound on the north and east, and Mason County on the south (see Figure 10). Although the county is only about fifteen miles across the Sound from Seattle, access is difficult and isolation over the years has kept it rural. The county is irregularly shaped and consists of 252,160 acres or about 393 square miles of land (Kitsap County Planning Department, 1972). Topography varies from steeply sloping shoreline and river gorge terrain to gently rolling hills, and the contour varies from sea level to a high of 1,761 feet. No significant mountain range traverses the county and most of the terrain is within 500 feet of sea level (Harstad and Associates, 1969, p. 14).

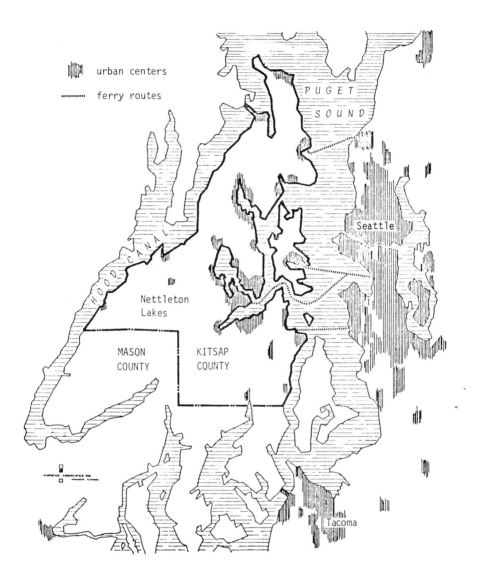

Figure 10. Kitsap County and the Puget Sound Region.

Foliage varies somewhat as well. The western half along the canal, which gets seventy to eighty inches of rain annually, is characterized by a heavy growth of timber, lush underbrush, and many swamps and ponds; in the eastern half, where annual rainfall is only about thirty-five inches, the forests are not as dense and fewer lakes are evident. The primary tree growth is Douglas fir.

The people of Kitsap are diverse in many ways and include wealthy executives, middle-class commuters to Seattle, retirees, small farmers, local businessmen, and an element of the military. Yet a very significant portion of the population does seem to share a desire for natural undeveloped open space, isolated serenity, and dispersed low-density living conditions. The county had a population of 101,732 at the 1970 census, with over 50 percent of those concentrated in the Bremerton/Dyes Inlet area along the Sound (Kitsap County Planning Department, 1972; Harstad and Associates, 1969, p. 3). With Bremerton/Dyes Inlet the only urban area, the dispersion leaves the county with a rural environment that is striking when compared with predominantely urban counties in the Sound. While the three major urban counties had "percent urban populations" that clustered around 80 percent, Kitsap's was under 45 percent.

Finally, employment in the county in 1970 was about 50 percent military, with the remaining jobs being in retail trade, small-scale construction, and forest production. In addition, income levels were among the lowest in the state and shared slower growth during the 1960s than either the Puget Sound four-county (King, Pierce, Kitsap, Snohomish) average or the state average (Harstad and Associates, 1969, p. 11).

The immediate location of the Nettleton project was to have been along Hood Canal in the much more isolated western section of the county, designated the CKSA. Encompassing 81,580 acres (35 percent of total Kitsap), the CKSA contained a 1970 population of only 11,400 (11 percent of total Kitsap). This population had fluctuated very little in the preceding twenty-year period. As a condition of the subarea's rural nature, the CKSA had no urban centers and only a few "population areas," the largest having 1,270 people. Furthermore, less than 10 percent of the land was "developed" in the broad sense that it had been improved in any way. The consequence was a diffuse environment with a density ratio of 0.04 dwelling units per acre. The comparable figure for total Kitsap was 0.14, while that of King County (Seattle) was 0.45 (U.S. Bureau of the Census, 1972). This isolated condition in the CKSA was reinforced both by poor road access and by the Sound, which acts as a natural barrier from Seattle. Access to the Nettleton project area was achieved either by an out-of-the-way two and one-half hour drive via Tacoma and the Narrows Bridge or by a two-hour route starting with a ferry across the Sound (1970 ferry cost: $3.90 one way for a family of four).

Industry in the county was almost nonexistent except for the naval facilities, and in the CKSA none existed at all. However, in most of the subarea forestry was a major crop. In 1968 Christmas tree and evergreen brush production reached combined sales of $2.75 million (Harstad and Associates, 1969, p. 11). Furthermore, whether for Christmas trees or for longer-term primary lumber production, the potential for forest production in this area was great. The Kitsap County topography, weather, and soil conditions are characteristic of the Puget Sound lowlands, which are "among the three or four best places to grow forests" (*University of Washington Magazine*, 1970, p. 5; Hidy, Hill, and Nevins, 1963, p. 224).

In addition to the rural population and forestry characteristics, the immediate project area was unique in many other ways. The largest landmark of the area is Hood Canal, which runs over sixty-five miles from Admiralty Point in north Kitsap to Lynch Cove in the south in Mason County. Being glacially formed, it is barely two miles wide at most places. As a result of its confined boundaries, the canal is especially susceptible to pollution. Although tidal action occurs as it does in Puget Sound, the narrow channel greatly impedes complete flushing. Estimates on complete turnover in the canal range up to two years, while complete flushing in the Sound takes only a few weeks (Ray, 1970). The marine ecology and shoreline life of this unique body of water, however, have environmental implications that extend far beyond the immediate circumstances of the canal itself. For example, eel grass, which is at the base of the Puget Sound food chain, grows only in areas of minimal tidal action such as estuarian waters and is extremely sensitive to pollution (Taylor, 1970). Consequently, it is found almost exclusively along Hood Canal. Another example is that of waterfowl. Anderson Cove, the location of the proposed marina, was, in addition to being a marine nursery and feeding area, one of the most significant bird sanctuaries in the canal region. According to the state game director, "Anderson Cove waterfowl use is approximately 2.5 times greater than that of our regular census areas [along the Canal]" (Biggs, 1970).

By substantially all measures, Kitsap County was considered a rural and remote area, reflecting only a minimal interdependence with the urban environment. Consequently this countryside had neither the extensive needs nor the pressures of the urban milieu, and Kitsap provided only a minimal level of public goods and services. The 127-square-mile CKSA in 1968 had only eight schools, one branch library, seven fire stations, and one county park (Harstad and Associates, 1969, p. 29). These are shown in Figure 11. No county facilities existed at all in the vicinity

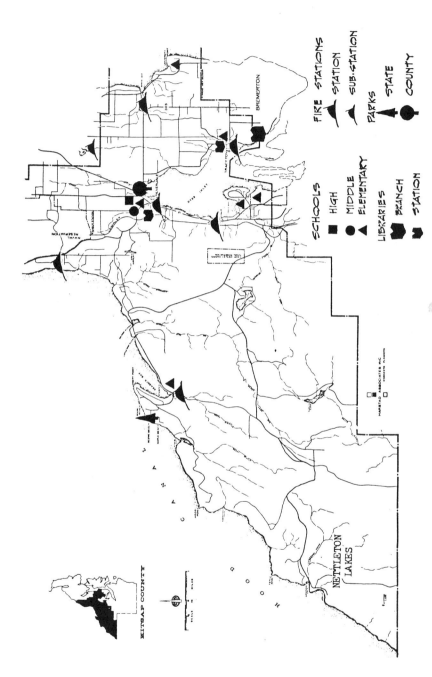

Figure 11. Central Kitsap Study Area: Existing Community Facilities.

of the proposed project, the nearest being twelve miles to the north at Seabeck.

The Nettleton Lakes Proposal

By contrast to the pastoral setting, the proposed recreation community was to be a large-scale commercial venture for urban customers. With rising middle-class affluence during the post–World War II period, the idea of having a private retreat intrigued a great many people who previously did not have the means to indulge. Consequently during the 1960s recreation community developments proliferated. This growth did not necessarily indicate a substantial increase in effective demand for second homes, however, and actual demand usually occurred for vacant lots only (Boschken, 1974). In contrast to the proliferation of vacant lots, only about 1.7 million households (3 percent of total U.S. families) owned second homes in 1967 (U.S. Bureau of the Census, 1969, p. 2). Further, the actual number of second homes built during the 1960s increased only at an annual rate of between 3 and 6 percent. In contrast, and exemplifying the impact of promotional influence, recreation community lot sales increased by several hundred percent. Because of the low buildout and use rates, public officials sometimes referred to these developments as "premature subdivisions" (Taylor, 1970; Berliner, 1970).

With the unique natural resources of Puget Sound, places like Hood Canal were especially desirable for second-home ownership. In 1970 just over 6 percent of the residents in the Puget Sound region owned second homes (U.S. Bureau of the Census, 1971). Excluding recreational vacant lots, an additional unknown number of out-of-region residents also owned second homes in the Sound area (Boschken, 1974). Hence, while recreational second homes were not new to Kitsap and the region, the size of Nettleton and its emphasis on vacant lot sales were.

Of even greater significance, however, was the size of the developer. It was the Boise Cascade Corporation, a conglomerate ranked as the sixty-fifth largest U.S. industrial company in 1969 (*Fortune*, 1971). Having grown from a small timber company in 1957 to a huge diversified organization in 1969, the corporation amassed enormous economic and political influence in its areas of operation. Besides impressive financial statements, it enjoyed the image of a sophisticated technology-oriented enterprise (see Table 8). With over $1.7 billion in annual sales, the firm derived about 12 percent of this figure from recreation community revenues. Clearing a 33 percent pre-tax profit, this activity was a lucrative cash flow source which some Boise officials referred to as "the great earnings faucet in the sky" (*Newsweek*, Mar. 13, 1972).

Table 8. Size Indicators: Boise Cascade (1969 Data).

Assets (in millions)	$1,333.5
Net Sales (in millions)	1,725.8
Net Income (in millions)	84.0
Employees (in thousands)	59.9
Recreation Communities as Percent of Total Sales	12%

Source: Boise Cascade (1970).

Boise had gotten into recreational communities through mergers in 1967. By the Nettleton controversy in 1970, the firm had become involved in thirty projects in tracts of between 700 and 31,000 acres, distributed over ten states coast to coast (Boise Cascade Credit Corporation, May 5, 1970, p. 11). The physical layout and size of these projects were comparable with those of master-planned urban residential development (Boschken, 1974). The firm came to the Pacific Northwest in the summer of 1968 intending to enter the recreational lot market of the greater Puget Sound region. At that time Boise owned no timber or recreational lands west of the Cascades, within easy driving distance of Seattle or Tacoma. Based on inexpensive price (about $200 to $300 per acre), the company settled on the Nettleton property in August, 1969. Such factors as lack of highway access, severe slope on over 25 percent of the acreage, and poor weather conditions were not seen as large enough problems to offset the financial bargain.

The development phase of the project commenced in August, 1969, when Boise retained Harstad and Associates (the same planning consultants being used by Kitsap County) to carry out engineering feasibility studies and develop a master plan providing for platted lots, urban improvements, and recreational amenities. The only criterion given by Boise was minimal project cost; according to one Harstad official, this was done by balancing the mix of urban improvements and amenities with the number of projected individual lots. The type and quality of salable project features were determined by a formula that transformed the investment in these improvements into a cost-per-lot figure. To make the effort more precise, Boise utilized computer models to scrutinize improvement combinations and lot shapes to minimize the per-lot figures (Smith, 1972).

Harstad, in conjunction with several subconsultants, carried out soil and percolation tests, topographical studies, and inventories of the canal and creeks. By October, 1969, Boise had found the work satisfactory and made the financial commitment to introduce the project for sale by mid-1970. Harstad was given instructions to make initial contact with the necessary public agencies for project approval. The project characteristics detailed below represent the level of refinement of the initial proposal submitted to the DNR and Kitsap County in February, 1970.

Boise officials believed that the PUD offered the greatest freedom from public intervention (total planning was more appealing to county officials than "patchwork") and the most flexibility in arranging and balancing lots with salable improvements (Kitsap County Planning Commission, Apr. 28, 1970, p. 10; hereafter cited as Planning Commission). Further, the PUD technique had been used in almost all of Boise's previous recreation communities, and hence Nettleton Lakes would be nearly identical to previous efforts. Boise defined a pastoral image for the project that involved providing "a recreational opportunity in an environment conducive to relaxation and restoration. . . . [It] is specifically not intended to be a city" (Kitsap County Commission, Sept. 9, 1970b, pp. 32–33; hereafter cited as County Commission). The Boise master plan is shown in Figure 12.

Although about 25 percent of the project area lay in Mason County, all of the major amenities were located within Kitsap. Most of the land was gently sloping terrain covered by dense forest and numerous marshes and ponds. Approximately 25 percent of the land had severe slopes, but most of them were located on the west side adjacent to the canal (366 acres). They formed a semicircle tapering from a higher plateau. Because of the extreme difficulty of building in this steep area, Boise devoted this acreage to undeveloped "open space." The remaining open-space areas were located primarily in smaller severe slope areas throughout the project.

From the canal the land rises rapidly to a ridge of 600 feet and then gently drops off into a flat plateau averaging 400 feet in altitude. Most of the proposed lots and amenities were to be located in this gently rolling area. The surrounding crest, on the west and north, isolated the bulk of the project from view of the canal.

The overall project size was to be a total of 6,295 acres, of which 4,017 acres were in Kitsap and 2,278 acres were in Mason. The project was about four and one-half miles long from north to south and about three miles wide at its widest point (Boise Cascade, Apr. 6, 1970). The project was developed in two sections, a north park and a south park. The north section had a marina at Anderson Cove, about two miles of beach area, and a golf course. The south park included several artificial lakes (County Commission, Sept. 9, 1970a, p. 53).

The project was to contain a total of 6,478 dwelling units situated on 4,898 lots. Available lot sizes ranged from one-third of an acre (12,500 square feet) to ten acres, but the one-third-acre lots accounted for over 70 percent of the total. The project was planned primarily for single-family dwelling units, and 3,368 (about 70 percent of the total) were so

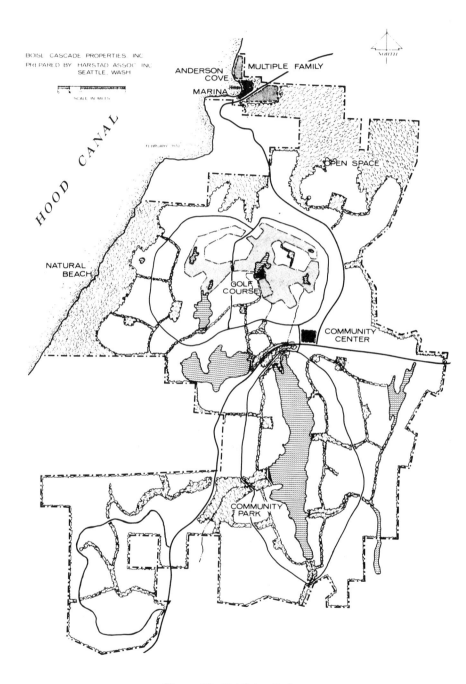

ANDERSON
COVE

MULTIPLE FAMILY

MARINA

HOOD CANAL

OPEN SPACE

NATURAL
BEACH

GOLF
COURSE

COMMUNITY
CENTER

COMMUNITY
PARK

NORTH

Figure 12. Nettleton Lakes.

designated (Boise Cascade, Apr. 6, 1970). Although the Boise project was to consist of lot sales only (Planning Commission, Mar. 31, 1970, p. 38), certain stipulations were established in the "protective covenants" that limited the range of housing unit variance. For example, no mobile homes or trailers were to be allowed, and all single-family dwelling units were to have fully enclosed floor areas (exclusive of porches and carports). The minimum allowed floor space was small to encourage cabin-type structures, but no maximum area was specified. Without special approval, all were to be single story (not exceeding thirty-five feet in height) and were to be situated on the lot such that the unit was at least forty feet from a lakefront property line.

Besides single-family dwelling units, about 10 percent of the lots were zoned for multifamily use. These multifamily lots, platted to contain 1,665 dwelling units, were spread throughout the project with the intent of "keeping with the rural nature of what we're trying to promote here" and to avoid the "concentric ring theory of increasing densities toward the hubs of retail and commercial areas (Planning Commission, Apr. 28, 1970, p. 219). Boise established certain criteria concerning building specifications similar to those for single-family units, but they were more liberal. Structures were allowed to be either single or multiple story and either detached or joined by common walls. The lot, however, was not to contain more than a triplex unit and had to conform to the same setback requirements as single-family units (Boise Cascade, Apr. 6, 1970). In addition to the triplexes dispersed over 555 lots, Anderson Cove and the golf course were to have condominium apartments.

The project could have contained as many as 20,000 people at saturation. In terms of gross density this would yield a figure of 3.2 persons per acre, while dwelling-unit density would be 1.02 units per acre. However, since PUD projects typically cluster the lots and housing units in higher densities around various kinds of open space, the net residential density ratio is considerably higher. Project statistics indicated that of the 6,295 acres, only 3,064 acres were to be used for single- and multiple-family residences (including acreage for condominiums). Hence the net density ratios would be 6.53 persons per acre and 2.10 dwelling units per acre. A breakdown of land use is shown in Table 9.

The clustering of residential areas and the interspersing of open space and greenbelts were primary determinants in lot platting and configuration. According to a Harstad official, "Once we develop a model of the topographic system, we then tried to see what the run-off characteristics were. We plotted each one of these run-off streams and generally they are included in a green belt that is at least a hundred feet wide, in some cases more. We colored these green and put them up on a wall and then stood back and linked them together . . . the last step was plan-

Table 9. Summary of Land Use: Nettleton Lakes.

Land Use Category	Acres	Percent of Total
Single- and Multi-family Residential	3,064	48
Roads, Streets, and Parking	877	14
Parks and Open Space	1,798	28
Lakes	309	5
Marina and Boathouse	18	1
Golf Course	190	3
Commercial Reserve	39	1
Total	6,295	100

Source: Boise Cascade (Apr. 6, 1970).

ning the lots . . ." (County Commission, Sept. 9, 1970a, pp. 36–37). Boise noted that although most PUDs devoted only 10 percent to open space, the Nettleton project allowed over a third including lakes. The "excess" open space was due primarily to the more severe topography.

As in previous Boise recreational developments, residential areas were to have the appearance of urban platting, with winding arterials and many short collector streets augmented with cul-de-sacs (see Figure 13). The project was to contain seventy miles of roads and streets and most were to be paved, but none were to have conventional sidewalk curbing or urban drainage systems. Only minimal culverting was to be used. Major arterials were to be built to county standards for eventual dedication, and portions of existing county roads — Dewatto Bay Road, Elfendahl Pass Road, and Lost Highway — were to be relocated and rebuilt. The remaining bulk of roadway was to consist of sixty-three miles of secondary arterials and local access streets (Boise Cascade, Sept. 9, 1970b).

According to the developers, the project was designed "to limit the number of residential streets which would have traffic by them" (Planning Commission, Mar. 31, 1970, p. 12). In so doing, the plan first was to construct two major peripheral road loop systems, one in the north park area around the golf course and another in the south park area around the lakes. The secondary streets feeding into these loops were to be located along and within neighborhood boundaries and were designed to collect and distribute neighborhood traffic only. Finally, these minimum flow arterials were to be augmented by ninety-five cul-de-sacs (Planning Commission, Apr. 28, 1970, pp. 19–20). Except for the major arterials, the streets were to be private. To ensure "seclusion" for property owners, Boise anticipated some kind of security gate system (Planning Commission, Mar. 31, 1970, p. 28). The "protective covenants" restricted on-street parking, and cars were to be parked on the owner's lot

Figure 13. Partial Map: Platting and Street Configuration of Nettleton Lakes.

or in designated areas only. Public parking areas were to be located at the Anderson Cove boathouse, the golf course clubhouse, the commercial area, and the two condominium areas (Smith, 1970).

Along with the residential platting, another visible feature was a central shopping center. Boise stated that Nettleton Lakes was to be a recreational community and no industry was to be allowed which might encourage "full-time residential development" (Planning Commission, Apr. 28, 1970, p. 22). Only "neighborhood" business was to be permitted. Referring to this improvement as a "village square," Boise intended to set aside a thirty-nine acre "reserve" that would be independently developed by parties other than Boise (Planning Commission, Mar. 31, 1970, p. 39). Initially that "reserve" was also to contain the Boise sales facilities and other necessary ancillary equipment.

Although the visible physical improvements reflected a suburban residential appearance, the provision of conventional metropolitan services was substandard to absent. All power distribution and telephone service were to be by overhead wires, and narrow easements were reserved on each lot to "allow for lines, poles, guy wires, braces, and anchors" (Boise Cascade, Apr. 6, 1970). No underground installation of any part of the system, including transformer station, was planned. In the case of waste disposal, no central sewage treatment facility or garbage collection service and disposal areas were envisioned except for the marina and abutting cove condominiums. Disposal was to be on an individual basis, and sewerage was to consist of septic tanks, both for single- and multifamily dwellings and for the golf course condominiums, clubhouse, and the commercial-retail area. Water supply, on the other hand, was to be handled centrally. No permanent supply was guaranteed, however, and Boise was unsure of water sufficiency in the long run.

Other public services were generally absent except for fire protection and one or two security guards manning the gates. No hospital or medical facility, library, or schools were envisioned in the master plan. Fire protection was to include the necessary fire hydrants, small fire station, and one fire engine (Planning Commission, Mar. 31, 1970, p. 45).

Boise was prepared to provide a complement of recreational amenities. The cove's marina and condominium complex, besides being the most publicized, was also probably the most important of these salable amenities. The complex was to have consisted of a total of forty-two acres, of which eighteen were to contain the marina along the cove and twenty-four were to contain 244 condominium units along Anderson Creek. The cove itself was to be dredged and enclosed by a "rubble mound" breakwater to provide a protected home port for 375 boats up to thirty feet long. To prevent constant siltation of the marina, Anderson Creek was to be rechanneled north of the breakwater and the flow was to be directed outside and past the marina (Planning Commission, Mar. 31, 1970, pp. 20–22). In addition to the boat slips, the constructed amenity features were to include a public launching ramp, car and trailer parking, and a boathouse. The boathouse, to be about 2,000 square feet in area, would include a lounge and restaurant, restroom facilities, and boat services. The services would have included the sale of marine fuel to the general public and a receiving station for marina sewage-holding tanks (Planning Commission, Apr. 28, 1970, pp. 30–37).

The second major amenity was to have been the golf course, recreation center, and condominium complex. This complex was to have been situated on approximately 210 acres, of which 190 were for the course and clubhouse, thirteen were for 127 condominium units, and seven were for parking. The course was to have been a "championship" eighteen holes with a par seventy-two rating and a total length of 6,500 yards. It was to have been situated primarily on gently sloping terrain and along natural drainage ways. It was to have many water "hazards," with twelve of the eighteen holes containing at least one. The two largest of these were the eighteen-acre Bogey Lake adjacent to the eleventh and twelfth holes and the eight-acre Clubhouse Lake. Boise emphasized that the course upgraded the general environment of the area because its location was on acreage previously used for the "esthetically undesirable" Christmas tree production. In addition to the eighteen holes, the plan also called for a driving range adjacent to the clubhouse and first hole (Planning Commission, Mar. 31, 1970, pp. 14–16).

The 20,000-square-foot clubhouse was planned to contain a number of activities and be the hub of interest. Besides the pro shop and locker rooms, it was to include the principal dining room and restaurant facility, swimming pool and tennis courts, exercise area and saunas, and a teenage center consisting of a recreation room and a dance bandstand. Several covered porches surrounding the clubhouse were also envisioned to provide cover for golf carts on one side and outdoor lounging on the other side next to the lake. Proximity to the condominiums was made to establish a "total living environment" for the convenience-seeking apartment owners (Planning Commission, Mar. 31, 1970, pp. 16–18).

The more rustic amenity features of the project consisted of a trail-linked system of lakes, developed parks, a saltwater beach, and natural wilderness open space. A total of eighteen lakes designated for the project ranged in size from one to 154 acres. The largest, Nettleton Lake, was to have been one and one-half miles long and one-fourth mile wide, and would have been suitable for boating, fishing, and swimming. Most of the lakes would have been artificially created or enlarged in some way. A few, such as Lost Lake, existed as large swamps and were to have been cleared of decaying logs and silt. Others, like Nettleton Lake, would have been created by damming river gorges (Planning Commission, Mar. 31, 1970, pp. 24–26).

As part of the general open-space plan, numerous parks ranging in size from two to seventy-five acres were to be distributed throughout the project. The largest, designated as the community park, was to be seventy-five acres and contain a fish hatchery that Boise offered to ward off would-be environmentalists concerned about the dam proposal. Anticipated primarily as a "fisherman's paradise," this area was planned to accommodate camper vehicles, tents, and to be "for just going out and enjoying nature" (Planning Commission, Mar. 31, 1970, p. 24).

A final feature of the open-space plan was the setting aside of 1,560 undeveloped acres for permanent wilderness and greenbelt areas. A matrix consisting of thirty-two miles of hiking and riding trails was to be an integral part of this system. Designed to allow people to circulate throughout the project without having to resort to the road system, the trails were to provide a pleasurable means of linking the residential areas with the various lakes and parks, the saltwater beach, and the undeveloped open space (Planning Commission, Mar. 31, 1970, p. 13).

Most of the undeveloped open space was located in two large tracts referred to earlier as the Hood Canal bank area and the Anderson Creek gorge area. As part of the canal buffer strip, an isolated beach extended along the saltwater for 1.65 miles. Access was to be by two trails winding down the 1,500-foot-wide buffer that descended 600 feet to the canal shoreline below. The remaining open space consisted primarily of 644 acres of "greenbelt" areas dispersed throughout the residential neighborhoods.

Because of the project's comprehensiveness, Boise Cascade anticipated an above-average sales price for the individual lots. In developing the "optimal" plan that balanced the number of lots against project improvements, the Boise computers arrived at a price of $9,000 per lot. Although probably an underestimate, Boise figured average home prices would be about $15,000 excluding lot price (Turner, 1970, p. 16; County Commission, Oct. 29, 1970a, p. 26). The total potential lot sales value was estimated at $42 million.

The common improvements, including the urban services, roads, open spaces, and constructed recreational amenities, were to be dedicated by the firm to a home owners' association supported by monthly fees. Along with the home owners' association, Boise developed a set of protective covenants that essentially established the bylaws of the association and the administrative procedures for project maintenance and protection of the home owners' investments.

Because of the project's vast size, Boise expected to phase the development over a seven-year period and projected a total investment of about

$15 million (Boise Cascade, Apr. 6, 1970). For services rendered by Harstad and Associates and their subconsultants during the development phase, Boise Cascade paid $850,000 (Smith, 1971). Although not of unusual size to Boise, Nettleton Lakes would have been one of the largest urban PUD housing projects ever undertaken in the state of Washington.

Profitability was the central motive for proposing Nettleton Lakes, and Boise considered the pursuit of financial return as "the first social responsibility of business" (Fery, 1970). Nevertheless, corporate officials also stressed the welfare benefits that would accrue from providing this recreational community. According to the company president, "Profit made while satisfying human need is especially worthwhile because it is creating new values for people as well as for enterprise" (as quoted in Turner, 1970, p. 16). To show its "good neighbor" attitude, Boise indicated intentions that would satisfy national housing needs, the welfare of Kitsap, and environmental concerns simultaneously.

With regard to housing needs, the Boise project manager said its "recreational communities are deliberately designed for recreational living to satisfy a demonstrated demand as pointed out in a number of articles and research bulletins" (Planning Commission, Apr. 28, 1970, p. 6). Connecting the "demonstrated" need to Puget Sound, another Boise official argued, "The problem admittedly at the moment may not be Kitsap County. The problem is nationwide. People are crying out for some place to go to enjoy the kind of beauty that you have here. This is why we're here" (Planning Commission, Apr. 28, 1970, p. 268). Although the firm's previous record indicated that the developments were poorly designed for consumer demand (Boschken, 1974), the executive vice-president contended that "by properly planning these recreation communities we are fulfilling a need for a city-dwelling population which can't be met any other way" (Fery, 1970).

With regard to Kitsap County, the developer predicted the project would stimulate the county economy and contribute measurably to tax revenues. Boise said that the project "is going to mean new jobs and increased cash flow into the local economies of Kitsap County and the surrounding area" (Boise Cascade, Sept. 9, 1970c). For the first four years it estimated annual payrolls at $1.9 million and annual purchase of materials at $2.5 million (Boise Cascade, Sept. 9, 1970c). For a beneficial impact on the county budget, Boise officials promised that all open-space areas would remain on tax rolls and that services for the community would be provided by the private home owners' association. In addition, the project would generate significant net tax revenues, estimated over a twenty-year period to be $11.2 million (Pilkey, 1970). For Kitsap's welfare, the developer argued that the project "represents the achievement of the Kitsap County plan in one project" (Smith, 1971).

With regard to environmental concerns, Boise argued that it was especially determined to minimize pollution and improve air, land, and water quality (Boise Cascade, Sept. 9, 1970a). Maintaining that it spent "millions of dollars a year on antipollution" (Planning Commission, Apr. 28, 1970, p. 261), the firm said, "Boise Cascade strongly emphasizes the environmental planning and pollution control in its recreation home site projects, taking into consideration the recommendation and concerns of the local conservation groups" (Boise Cascade Credit Corporation, Mar. 10, 1970). Professional consultants and academicians from the University of Washington were retained to assure the project's environmental compatibility in areas such as water quality, fishery resources, erosion control, and soil permeability for sewage.

Boise argued that this environmentally oriented master planning would prevent pollution of any sort from both upland development and the marina complex. For example, to eliminate stagnation and algae growth in the impounded lakes, a water circulation system was proposed which would "pump water in and out of lakes within the residential core area. This circulation of water will also supplement the golf course irrigation system" (Boise Cascade, Sept. 9, 1970b). As for marina impact, plans called for relocation of Anderson Creek along the north side of the cove "to provide a good source of fresh water flow through the nearby eelgrass beds" (Lundin, 1970). Location of the marina in "the least productive area of the cove," one of the Boise consultants stated, would prevent "a problem of pollution" (Lundin, 1970).

The firm went on to argue that Nettleton Lakes would make large improvements on the property's existing condition. If Boise was not allowed to develop the PUD, it contended the land would either be desecrated by further Boise logging activity or become a patchwork of individual developments by sale to other parties (Boise Cascade, Apr. 6, 1970). The firm conceived of specific ways in which the PUD would "enhance" and protect the wilderness integrity of the area. For example, "by the use of the golf course, we are upgrading the general level of this Christmas tree area. . . " (Planning Commission, Mar. 31, 1970, p. 15). Another point involved the swamplike conditions characteristic of a substantial amount of the property. Feeling that nature had not maintained its ecological beauty, Boise said, "[The swamps] are full of downed logs, general forest litter and debris, and what we propose to do here would be to drain the ponds, to clean them and then to restore them. . . " (Planning Commission, Mar. 31, 1970, p. 18).

In short, the developer asserted, "It is our intent to enhance and not destroy the beauty of the Hood Canal area. We wish to work in cooperation with public bodies, our outstanding consultants and all interested parties to make this development a showcase to which we can all point with pride" (Planning Commission, Apr. 28, 1970, p. 7). Boise was supported in this effort by some state and local groups including the Washington State Research Council (a business lobbying group of which Boise was a chief sponsor), the Bremerton Chamber of Commerce, local real estate people, the contractors' association, and building trades union.

The Nettleton Opposition

Opposition to the development, on the other hand, was widespread and well organized. Interest groups in Washington have played a critical role in public decision making, especially at the regional level. They have acted as catalysts for raising public policy questions concerning land use, and have been influential in determining courses of action. During the year-long Nettleton Lakes battle in 1970, several groups and individuals found themselves in a sophisticated coordination of opposition that, from the beginning, assumed a national scope. Of this network, two local groups interested in Hood Canal preservation were responsible for the opposition's central effort.

The largest of these two was called the Hood Canal Environmental Council (HCEC) and was led by Philip Best, a relative newcomer and young lawyer from Bremerton. HCEC was founded prior to Boise's entrance into the area, and the group was involved in several other activities at the time of this controversy (HCEC, Summer, 1970; Turner, 1970, p. 17). Originally founded because of rumors of a large housing development eight miles north of the Nettleton site, the HCEC held its first public meeting on Sunday, July 4, 1969, at the Seabeck Fire Hall. On July 31, 1969, the group was incorporated as a nonprofit organization for the purpose of assuring "the highest standards of environment for Hood Canal and adjacent land areas for living, recreation, and preservation of open space for the indefinite future" (HCEC, Summer, 1970).

HCEC's original membership consisted of 240 families, with a fifteen-member board of directors. Many notable figures in Puget Sound as well as a few like Walter Heller, economic advisor to Kennedy and Johnson, were active members. In an attempt to build a powerful effort against the Boise proposal, the group developed links nationally with groups having knowledge of previous Boise activities. Contact was made with several state officials in Connecticut, New Hampshire, Hawaii, and California; with Harold Berliner, Nevada County (California) prosecutor who testified at HCEC expense about his knowledge of Boise's California operations; and with the Center for Environmental

Action, a religious-based California clearinghouse. Additional active support was gained from professors at the University of Washington and Dixy Lee Ray, then director of the Pacific Science Center in Seattle.

The other organization of major influence was the Committee for Holly Environment (COHOE) organized by Peter Pitell, a teacher at Ranier Beach High School (Seattle) who owned a beach cottage at Holly (Turner, p. 59). Unlike the regionwide membership of HCEC, COHOE came into existence solely in response to the Boise proposal and consisted primarily of Holly families. Representing the most immediate affected interest, the group was formed on December 7 and called "for affirming the basic rural residential and outdoor recreational nature of the Holly area and the curtailing of pollution that endangers the environment" (*Bremerton Sun*, Dec. 10, 1969). Being formed solely as a reaction to the Boise proposal, COHOE had not developed any public action expertise, as had HCEC. Nevertheless, in the first months of 1970 the group increased its membership to 136 families, established a sizable legal fund from member's contributions, hired the services of a prominent Seattle environmental attorney, gathered volumes of material for presentation at the public hearings, acquired 3,200 signatures on an antimarina petition, and solicited the aid of numerous scientists in the Puget Sound area (Pitell, 1971; *Bremerton Sun*, Feb. 19, 1970; Planning Commission, Mar. 31, 1970, p. 100).

Other opposition supporters in the regional environmental network included the Gillnetters Association (opposed to blocking salmon spawning areas with dams), the Hood Canal Advisory Council (opposed to large-scale development without comprehensive canal planning), the Sierra Club, the Seattle Audubon Society (opposed to marina impact on birds), the Washington Environmental Council (opposed to approval without more information on environmental impact on region), and other groups. The response nationally was equally strong. According to Best of HCEC, "We discovered there was an entire network of people around the country who are fed up with Boise Cascade" (Best, 1971).

The opposition's criticism centered on four major concerns, including the need for recreational housing on the canal, the environmental impact generated by the project's size, the socioeconomic effects on Kitsap County, and the developer's overshadowing political and economic influence.

Need for the 6,000-acre development was based on such factors as supply and demand, use of recreational property, and appropriate location (Boschken, 1974). To crystallize the impact of offering a large number of new lots for sale, an HCEC representative asked rhetorically, "Is there need now or in the foreseeable future for a city of twenty thousand in Kitsap County, and if there is, is the proposed location the best place for it to be?" (Planning Commission, Mar. 31, 1970, p. 62).

As in other areas, Kitsap County seemed to be glutted with available recreational lots. In the five years prior to the Nettleton controversy, Kitsap and Mason counties had annually approved about twice the number of subdivided lots as they had issued building permits. When adding the 6,295 Nettleton lots to the two-county oversupply, the number of vacant lots would exceed building demand by 17,745 units.

Moreover, ·Boise information from previous company projects reinforced concern over the glut by indicating that homes were constructed at a rate of less than 3 percent annually. The likely low buildout rate was further compounded by the project's remote location. "The intention is to create a city . . . where it doesn't belong," said one opposition member. "People have to live somewhere, but not in the last wilderness . . . (Planning Commission, Mar. 31, 1970, p. 49). The opposition believed that such a "premature subdivision" violated future demand projections of the county's new comprehensive plan, which anticipated growth primarily around the Bremerton urban center. A *Bremerton Sun* editorial summarized the concern for need: "Perhaps the weightiest argument against the Nettleton Lakes development is that there is no current need for recreation housing on Hood Canal at this time" (Dec. 23, 1970b).

The second area of concern was environmental impact. The opposition felt that the project would create a development bulge in a delicate pastoral wilderness area. Such fears were magnified both by the project's scale and the fact that Boise's consultants had not planned a development anywhere near its size before. Although Boise claimed its "developments are planned with emphasis on achieving a balance between the demands of people for leisure living and the desirability of preserving the natural environment" (Boise Cascade, 1970, p. 3), environmentalists were concerned that the urban-styled milieu would have intense, complex, and unpredictable impacts. HCEC queried, "Is the development adequately or insufficiently based on ecological considerations? Will it allow more people to enjoy a beautiful place, or will it impair and limit a public recreational amenity?" (HCEC, Oct. 30, 1970). Reviewing Boise's record of problems elsewhere, an opposition member warned the Planning Commission, "Don't think that your natural beauty here is so much tougher than other places. . . . It can be lost . . . " (Planning Commission, Mar. 31, 1970, p. 77).

The specific adverse impacts were viewed in two lights. The first was overcrowding. Boise's image was that "the recreation development concept . . . represents a place to get away from it all, a place of privacy or seclusion" (Planning Commission, Apr. 28, 1970, p. 8). In contrast, the opposition contended, "It's dense housing is what it is" (Planning Commission, Mar. 31, 1970, p. 111). Although the aggregate density of the project was about one dwelling unit per acre, density within the residential areas (excluding open space) was five dwelling units per acre. "Certainly," said HCEC, "it is not the rural-recreational environment which Boise . . . describes as preserving the natural aspect of the area. There are green belts on the fringes of the residential areas, but they do not provide low density recreational housing conditions to the 15,000 people who would be living back to back . . . " (Gardiner, 1970). The impact of overcrowding was seen to equally affect land use options for those who used the area for pastoral fulfillment. "The patterns of such use would be changed by the great density patterns. . . . [These] losses occur not only to people who live immediately around the area, but . . . by people from wide areas of Washington that come to enjoy the scenic [beauty]" (County Commission, Sept. 9, 1970b, p. 60).

The second context of environmental impact was pollution potential and ecological destruction. A number of project features raised concern. First, the use of individual septic tanks throughout the dense residential areas was seen as creating an enormous cumulative pollution impact on the pristine area. Although Boise claimed that "a very respectable school of thought" believed septic tanks to be the most environmentally sound means of waste disposal (Borgwardt, June 1, 1970), the impervious soil limited carrying capacity for that size and density of development. One opposition member commented, "It would appear that they are promising kind of a Calcutta for the Northwest" (Planning Commission, Mar. 31, 1970, p. 67). A second feature of equal concern was impoundment for the artificial lakes. Damming of streams and rivers causes water temperature increases, higher evaporation rates, and greater levels of siltation behind dams. The effect was seen as disastrous to spawning and the downstream ecology.

Perhaps the greatest concern, however, was with the proposed marina at Anderson Cove. The cove and surrounding area form an interwoven process that contains continuous flows of fresh water into a saltwater basin. Major features include the refurbishing of delta flats with sedimentation and nutrients, the harboring of major beds of eel grass, and the entrance to a significant spawning stream, especially for the imperiled chum salmon (Taylor, Feb. 18, 1970; Sternberg, 1970). Objections to the marina were made on the basis of extensive dredging and filling requirements, pollution from boats, and obstruction of the above-mentioned interwoven process. Writing for the opposition, Dixy Lee Ray said, "The physical factors clearly indicate that development of the kind proposed would destroy the area as it now exists, drastically modify the ecology of the immediate surroundings, and probably lead to an unstable beach condition for some time to come" (Ray, 1970). COHOE asserted, "It is the destruction of these abundant resources that we are objecting to" (County Commission, Oct. 29, 1970b, p. 69).

Summarizing the environmental concern, Pitell said in an editorial, "Those of us who oppose this gargantuan project do so because we enjoy the clean water and air, the fishing, the beautiful views, and the peaceful and serene feeling of being close to nature's handiwork. As it is now proposed, the Boise Cascade project will not bring those benefits to a greater number of people but simply deny those enjoyments to everyone" (*Bremerton Sun*, Oct. 22, 1970).

A third area of opposition concern was the socioeconomic effects on Kitsap County. Nettleton Lakes posed considerable implications for the local social structure, especially around the Holly area. Whenever a large development is created to accommodate people of a socially different origin who hold different interests from the existing community, the imposition is likely to create social divisiveness. Arguing that "outsiders" would increase such divisiveness, the Kitsap County prosecutor said, "This development had Southern California written all over it" (Brunton, 1971). A member of COHOE queried, "Where will we be served by this particular development? There is no one who is making any bit of concern for Holly. . . . It is our community that they are developing for us and . . . we will be directly affected (Planning Commission, Apr. 28, 1970, p. 200; County Commission, Sept. 9, 1970a, p. 21).

Regarding public expenditures, Boise promised that the Nettleton project would be completely private and the lot owners would take care of their own problems as well as pay their share of county taxes. The Boise opposition, however, raised a number of questions, saying, "It is hard to be fooled by such an argument really, but it is hard to turn it down because it sounds so hopeful" (Planning Commission, Mar. 31, 1970, p. 74). Even with little immediate need for public expenditures, they argued that basic services were necessary regardless of what Boise provided. Kitsap County had no public facilities within twelve miles of the project site, and the Boise proposal called for only one small firehouse and one school reserve that the local school board said was poorly located and inadequate in size (Huey, 1970). Further, even though Boise planned to use a private patrol for the project, opponents argued this would still have to be supplemented by the county sheriff. According to the Kitsap County sheriff, "The roads leading into the development would be county roads and would require greatly increased traffic control. The investigation of crimes would be the responsibility of the Kitsap County Sheriff's office. This would require a large increase of personnel and equipment, in order to provide adequate police protection . . . it would mean an expenditure of approximately $250,000 per year by the county" (Morken, 1970).

Other county costs not included in Boise estimates but of equal concern to opponents included road construction and maintenance, waste disposal, emergency medical facilities, and tax assessment. The inclusion of these and other county services would have tripled the expenditure estimates made by Boise (Boschken, 1974, pp. 152–59).

On the revenue side, opponents argued that taxes from assessed value of the project were grossly overstated. Other Boise projects had shown that the firm was able to sell lots at greatly inflated prices and that owner resales occurred at a fraction of the purchase price. Pointing to the disparity between estimated Nettleton prices and existing land values in the area, a HCEC representative said, "Unless values remain high in [this] development, all of the promised tax windfalls are jeopardized. Only real value sustains the promised tax increases to the county" (Planning Commission, Mar. 31, 1970, p. 69).

In addition to questionable net economies under successful conditions, concern was also voiced for the adverse impact from a home owners' association collapse. Such an occurrence was characteristic in the industry, and HCEC said, "Boise has not pointed out one area where a homeowner association has been able to provide governmental services for a protracted period of time" (HCEC, Oct. 30, 1970). Subsequent "dedication" of open space and common facilities to the county would have had a considerable effect on property values and public expenditures. Although Boise contended the county could refuse to assume the responsibilities, opponents argued that social and environmental costs would occur from neglect and result in a "wilderness slum" that the county would have no choice but to deal with. Said one HCEC lawyer, "I as a taxpayer am not going to get stuck for footing the bill for Boise Cascade's sloppiness in providing these people with essential services that they are going to demand . . . " (Planning Commission, Mar. 31, 1970, pp. 119–20).

The final area of major concern was Boise's overshadowing political and economic influence in state and local affairs. With their primary goal to protect the canal "from exploitation by a huge developer" (Best, 1971), opponents questioned, "How much is private about a corporation? The size, power, and effect of corporations are so far beyond those of individuals and small companies that they either dominate wherever their operations happen to be or force the people to protect their rights through government . . . " (Bergsagel, 1971). Boise's influence was seen in a number of activities, including the firm's community relations work and use of "expertise" to "neutralize" the political process. Opponents claimed all of these were subterfuges to avoid proper public scrutiny.

Past corporate behavior was not always exemplary. Contrary to the firm's claim that "you have before you one of the most responsible developers" (Planning Commission, Apr. 28, 1970, p. 270), the Nettleton opposition discovered a pattern of questionable occurrences, especially in

California. Regarding the market arena, the California attorney general's office wrote HCEC, "This firm has developed a number of subdivisions in California of a highly speculative nature which have received the attention of local authorities because of misrepresentations and lot owner dissatisfaction" (Mayer, 1970). Regarding deceptive practices before public agencies, the executive director of the Hawaii Land Use Commission wrote HCEC, " . . . This has been [Boise's] typical approach across the nation. . . . Team One appears on the scene and promises the world. Team Two replaces Team One with no knowledge of Team One's commitments, and proceeds with . . . getting the project under construction at the least cost to the developer" (Planning Commission, Apr. 28, 1970, p. 104). Fearing the review agencies would succumb to Boise's overshadowing effect, a HCEC member said, " . . . we are the people that have vested interest in this county, not them. We can't let someone come in and tell us that there are all these nice things that will go on and then take their word for it and let them . . . get the big fat money in their pockets and then walk right out. . . . It is not fair to us" (Planning Commission, Mar. 31, 1970, p. 131).

The four major concerns posed by the opposition were reinforced by an appeal to leave the property in its semiwilderness state. An opposition zoologist argued, "It is unfortunate that developers generally choose areas of unique scenic and ecological interest to modify for recreational use, missing the point that the same areas, if left alone, would furnish recreation in the form of sensory fulfillment for people who are more and more growing up in the city's environment . . . " (Paulson, 1970). Proposing that the area remain for the multiple uses of forestry and "ecologically sensitive recreation," HCEC requested the county to " . . . consider zoning the major portion of the semi-wilderness area . . . for forestry, and that it apply to state and federal agencies for funds to acquire and develop part of the area for low density non-urban, non-commercial, non-mechanical recreation" (HCEC, Oct. 30, 1970).

Multiple-Agency Deliberations

During the preliminary development phase Boise insisted on strict secrecy in hopes of preventing environmentalists from getting a head start on criticizing the plans. The problem of security, however, was compounded by the firm's engineering studies and use of helicopters for shuttling Boise officials to and from the project. From August to October, 1969, the area was alive with equipment and personnel. Well-drilling rigs, water percolation equipment, survey teams, helicopters, aerial photo planes, and the University of Washington research vessel

Commando were among the most obvious figments of this "spontaneous" activity (Smith, 1972). Public curiosity had grown to such a point that in November Harstad submitted some preliminary plans to the DNR against Boise wishes. This event in turn was reported to the press, and on November 19 the public gained its first knowledge of the project (*Bremerton Sun*, Nov. 19, 1969). Boise apprehension about early notification was apparently justified, for by the first public debate on February 18, 1970, before the DNR, the opposition had organized into a considerable force. The DNR hearing, however, was to be only the sounding gun.

Although several state agencies were involved in the project review process, the central focus was on Kitsap County, which held zoning jurisdiction over the site. Owing to the county's interim rezone in 1969, Boise had to request a special lifting of the zone to meet minimum residential standards. In so doing, the burden of proof was on the developer to show that the PUD proposal had superior merits to the land's existing multiple uses. The firm expected this request would take no more than thirty days to approve (Smith, 1972), but final county decisions did not come for twelve months.

County review of the proposal was initiated by the firm's submission of plans to the planning department on February 24, 1970. The department's role in county review involved the collection and technical evaluation of information provided by Boise, the opponents, and public agencies. According to the planning director, the department "didn't do too much research before the [first] public hearing . . . [but] as a result of the hearings, we sent out a monster amount of letters and had to have a lot of legal advice . . . " (Mitchell, 1971). During deliberations the department had up to a dozen "technical preparation" meetings with Boise and "less than half a dozen contacts" with HCEC, and the planning director participated in numerous meetings with state officials (Mitchell, 1971). In May the department formulated a memorandum of major issues and questions for consideration by the Planning Commission (Mitchell, May 15, 1970) and in June presented recommendations on "the more mechanical aspects of the decision" (Barber, 1971).

By state law, public hearings were required prior to any decision. Based on both the rezone and PUD approval requests, the county held four major hearings and several short public study sessions. Spanning seven months, two of the hearings were conducted by the Planning Commission on March 31 and April 28, and two on appeal by the County Commission on September 9 and October 29. While the Planning Commission sessions promoted maximum articulation of issues and allowed informal cross-examination, the County Commission restricted sessions to formal procedures. In total, the hearing process included a wide variety of inputs and extended outside the individual sessions, involving a complex of written exchanges on specific issues, the gathering of political support, and a running battle in the local newspaper, the *Bremerton Sun*. The controversy also gained the attention of the *Seattle Times*, the regional television affiliates, and some national news journals, including *Time*.

The first Planning Commission hearing, held at Port Orchard in the old two-story brick courthouse, ran over four hours. The hearing led off with Boise and Harstad officials giving a forty-minute, professional, mixed-media presentation of the proposed development. In general, the effort contrasted scenes of the property in its natural state with multicolored project plans. Many of the slides were aerial photos of heavily wooded terrain, and others were specifically inserted to create a mood or feeling of serenity of the wilderness: morning frost on the edge of ponds, vistas with Mount Rainier in the background, scenes of the Olympics looming beyond Hood Canal. The project's principal features were also discussed, and stress was placed on the comprehensive effort made on studies of environmental impact, engineering feasibility, and topographical constraints.

Upon Boise's completion, commission members asked a few innocuous questions and then yielded the floor to Philip Best, who acted as moderator for the opposition. As a keynote, he indicated that the occasion to approve such an enormous project was a first for Kitsap County and he emphasized certain questions: "What sort of project is this for the people who will live here? Who will buy these lots and what are the commitments and benefits and what obligations do you have to these people . . . What will the effect on fish and wildlife in the immediate surrounding area be? Are adequate provisions made for . . . necessary amenities and governmental services?" (Planning Commission, Mar. 31, 1970, p. 52).

The opposition testimony that followed was organized into a multiple-speaker presentation of views and factual material directed toward answering the moderator's questions and stressing the major concer.ns outlined earlier. In addition to local and regional speakers, Best also brought in several "outsiders." Most notable among them was District Attorney Berliner from California, who with significant knowledge of Boise activities pointed to evidence of major market and environmental drawbacks to project approval. This testimony was reinforced by several state agency officials from the DNR, DWR, and Department of Fisheries and by the reading of several letters from out-of-state public officials.

It was almost midnight when the opposition completed its presentation. Caught unprepared for such a sophisticated showing by its organizationally inferior opposition, Boise declined a rebuttal. One representative said, ". . . . we have seen more than three hours of what I think are misinformation colored by an extreme bias and a very emotional attitude by a lot of people. . . . I am not going to try to refute three hours of these charges. I think if we go forward . . . I am confident that Boise Cascade Properties can successfully meet each issue" (Planning Commission, Mar. 31, 1970, pp. 142–43).

In the interim month between the two Planning Commission hearings, significant activity occurred on both sides. Boise, concerned about its corporate image and equally surprised at the opposition's national scope, flew in its top officials to try to "set the record straight." Besides the public relations effort, the firm also made several proposal revisions in an attempt to stifle the opposition and reduce the mounting public concern that became apparent during and after the first hearing. Among others, they offered the guarantee of a permanent and adequate central water system and, if required, the provision of a complete sewer system. These and other alterations were presented in a revised application and verbally at the second hearing.

The opposition activity during the interim consisted principally of developing a greater public awareness of the project. HCEC, for example, solicited a total of 4,000 signatures from concerned citizens, 2,000 of which were from Kitsap County. In addition, Walter Heller, a canal cottage owner, wrote a letter to the commission saying, "It seems to me to be clearly in the long-range interest of Kitsap County and its land use planning to avoid . . . desecrating [this land] with a wholly inappropriate 'new town'" (Heller, 1970).

The second hearing, which was necessitated by a legal flaw in Boise's application, contained nearly identical testimony to the first and was substantially the same in mood and procedure. A major difference, however, was Boise's presentation, which, unlike its first appearance of forty minutes, took over two hours to deliver. Trying to re-establish its professional leverage, it brought forth top corporate officials and a number of its consultants to discuss charges and statements made by the opposition at the first hearing. Although conceding several past indiscretions by the firm, one representative contended that "like lots of other people and lots of other companies, we've made mistakes. . . . And I hope we have learned from these mistakes" (Planning Commission, Apr. 28, 1970, p. 82). The second hearing concluded like the first, with the opponents presenting much information that provided rather obvious contrasts to Boise's data and conclusions.

After three months of deliberation the Planning Commission recommended approval on July 28, 1970 (Planning Commission, July 28, 1970). However, based on county planning policies and zoning ordinances and an assessment of project impact, it also recommended twenty-three conditions including deletion of the marina complex and the requirement of a complete sewage treatment system at Boise's expense. Both sides appealed the recommendation to the County Commission.

The first County Commission hearing took place in September, and significant partisan activity occurred in the interim. Boise, in an effort to countervail local opposition, instructed its project manager to hold "housewarming" parties for those who had signed the anti-Nettleton petition and to intensify appearances before local service clubs. The opposition, on the other hand, carried out a mass media campaign involving the distribution of information pamphlets, position papers, and full-page spreads in the *Bremerton Sun*. Showing a map comparing the size of Nettleton with Bremerton, one newspaper statement opened: "Boise Cascade is one of the giant hard-sell 'recreational subdividers' that are carving up millions of acres of rural and semi-wilderness land. . . . For whose benefit? Boise's record . . . suggests that it is not, in the long run, for the state and people" (*Bremerton Sun*, Sept. 4, 1970).

The two County Commission hearings were similar to those of the Planning Commission and, although a great amount of testimony was heard, little new information emerged. Nevertheless, the controversy drew so much community interest that the proceedings were moved from the courthouse to the auditorium of a Port Orchard junior high school. Owing to the large amount of ambiguous and conflicting testimony, the county's decision was not delivered for two months after the October hearing. During this period the County Commission and the planning department sought the views of state agencies and out-of-state officials. Perhaps the single most important event was a commission trip to California and Nevada during mid-December to "authenticate the veracity of the information received by the Planning Commission" (Lobe, Randall, and Mahan, 1971). On this trip two of the three members plus a *Bremerton Sun* reporter visited four Boise developments and talked with several public officials concerning Boise activities.

In addition to county deliberations over local impacts, state agencies were concurrently involved in specialized reviews related to regional and statewide considerations. Probably the most visible of these was the DNR. Public discussion of the project started with the Anderson Cove marina, and the agency's authority over tidelands drew it in as the first public forum. DNR's first action was to hold an "informational hearing" in February, 1970, to assess the issues and public concern. While Boise presented nothing of substance, an unexpected highlight of the meeting was a powerful display of opposition organized by COHOE. Pitell presented a 3,000-signature "Stop the Marina" petition and orchestrated a parade of witnesses demanding marina denial. This effort culminated with a state legislator from Kitsap saying, "We're telling you . . . we don't want this kind of development here. We who live here don't want any large scale development." (*Bremerton Sun*, Feb. 19, 1970). Other state agencies reinforced this display of concern by testifying that considerably more information about the ecology of Hood Canal was necessary before proper decisions could be made.

While the other agencies outlined in Table 7 held specialized hearings and progressed through their individual evaluation procedures, the DNR and DWR tended to constitute the state's major effort. Acting as lead agencies, they initiated and organized several interagency coordination meetings and work sessions. Although most agency reviews advanced to preliminary decisions or suspensions caused by insufficient information, the concurrent process was curtailed by Boise's decision to postpone the project indefinitely in June, 1971. Nevertheless, as shown in Table 10, a number of important agency proposals and decisions were made along the review process.

Early in the process the SWPCC found the subdivision planning techniques inadequate and filed a statement with the Kitsap Planning Commission proposing that a complete sewer system be considered. In May the state Health Department raised concern over the lack of a long-term water supply. It notified all agencies and the developer that "an approval from this Department for a water system will not be granted until it has been demonstrated to our satisfaction that an ample quantity of water meeting our quality requirements is available" (Lane, 1970). Exasperated by Boise's lack of specificity, the Department of Fisheries resolved in July that "we are withholding final decisions on hydraulic applications made to our Department . . . until detailed answers can be furnished by Boise Cascade" (Tollefson, 1970). In November, arguing that alteration of Anderson Cove might adversely affect the future seafood industry in Puget Sound, the DNR ruled out the possibility of dredging the delta for marina construction (*Bremerton Sun*, Nov. 17, 1970). Finally, in 1971, the DWR took an unprecedented step and established minimum flow standards for the rivers that Boise wanted to dam. The ruling effectively prevented damming, given the existing technology, proposed lake size, and weather conditions.

Simultaneously with this stream of position statements and decisions, Kitsap County formulated its set of decisions. On January 5, 1971, the County Commission granted approval-in-concept to the overall proposal on the basis that the PUD would "enhance the best features of the subject property, and will result in harmonious and desirable development. . . . Planned and integrated development of such a large area is more desirable than piecemeal, small-tract zoning . . ." (County Commission, Jan. 5, 1971, p. 4). Nevertheless, the effect of the California trip and the concern expressed by state agencies and environmentalists led the county to impose thirty-four conditional provisions, including deletion of Anderson Cove marina and numerous en-

Table 10. Multiple-Agency Decisions: Nettleton Lakes.

Public Agency	Decision	Date
State Water Pollution Control Commission	Decisions withheld owing to inadequate PUD platting; sewer system proposed	4/13/70
Department of Health	Decision withheld owing to insufficient developer assurances	5/26/70
Department of Fisheries	Dam construction approval withheld indefinitely owing to lack of developer construction details	7/7/70
Department of Natural Resources	Dredging of Anderson Cove denied	11/16/70
Department of Water Resources	Lake construction approval with minimum streamflow requirements	11/71
Kitsap County	PUD approval with 34 conditions	1/5/71

vironmental, consumer, and construction safeguards. The logic behind the conditions was to assure a minimum of external effects on the environment and on county budgets. No condition short of project denial, however, would have mitigated the expected change in socioeconomic profile of the area. The County Commission concluded by reminding the developer that "this decision is predicated upon approval by all state, local and other agencies which have jurisdiction over any aspect of the development" (County Commission, Jan. 5, 1971, p. 8).

Publicly, neither party supported the county's decision. Postponing the project, Boise said only that "studies show that marketing of vacation home lots would be shaky in the area at this time" (*Bremerton Sun*, June 30, 1971). HCEC, on the other hand, viewed the decision with "apprehension," saying, "We oppose . . . permitting development because of the policy it represents of allowing premature sub-division of large remote areas. . . . We also oppose the high density allowed . . . and the inevitable adverse impact on the environment in spite of the conditions designed to protect it" (HCEC, 1971). Neither side, however, expressed an interest in appealing the matter to the courts. Eventually the property was resold to another lumber company, and continues to be used for forest production and recreation.

Part III | Comparative Analysis

CHAPTER 6

Environment and Administrative Structure

THE CASES outlined in the previous chapters are now history. To some, they pose implications ever relevant to the present. To others, changes in law and circumstance may seem to have obscured any lessons of relevance. For example, NEPA requirements were adopted at Mineral King and San Onofre but did not exist at the time of Nettleton Lakes. Mineral King and Nettleton would not be subject to the 1977 Clean Air Act amendments on nondegradation and nonattainment. San Onofre occurred prior to Three Mile Island and much of the antinuclear movement. Some planning procedures and public access requirements have been revised subsequent to all three cases.

While the dynamics of time suggest that the specific situations would unlikely recur today, one would err by concluding that the cases hold little usefulness as inferential studies of administration. Their relevance hinges not on the legal constraints and events of the early 1970s but on organizational processes and administrative politics of large-scale government that transcend time. The intent of this and ensuing chapters is not to recreate the past but to analyze history concerning those perennial questions about the consequences of administrative structure and organizational process.

For heuristic value, we are interested in the impacts of administrative structure on organizational process and the consequences they pose for people in the land use setting. We are suggesting a causal chain that starts with structural arrangements, and we are concerned about the compatibility of consequences to the contextual land use setting. Under conditions of task complexity, societal diversity, and environmental uncertainty, consequences caused by different administrative patterns may hold substantial implications.

The next four chapters examine segments of this contention. While Chapters 7, 8, and 9 focus on different organizational processes and their consequences, this chapter analyzes the land use setting and the characteristics of administrative structure in each case. The focus here will be on (1) the nature of the contextual setting, (2) the structural configuration of agencies, (3) mechanisms of intergovernmental coordination, and (4) the use of public participation in decision making. In making these assessments, it would be a gross oversimplification to suggest that the three patterns of control outlined in the second chapter are exact measures of reality. They are not being proposed as holistic types that operate accordingly only when all of their characteristics are present. They should be viewed only as devices that help clarify *central tendencies* in an otherwise disjointed reality of land use administration. In the analysis we will be addressing those general questions in Chapter 1 associated with land use setting and administrative structure (p. 15).

The Land Use Setting

The contextual setting associated with land use consists of two primary considerations. First, allocation of land among competing uses holds consequences for different individuals and the public at large. When those consequences are altered or increased by the nonmarket procedures of public agencies, the legitimacy of governmental involvement is always at issue. Second, land is interconnected in a way that causes uses on one parcel to have external impacts on others. The impacts may be socioeconomic or ecological, but all involve problems of common pool resources and environmental carrying capacity.

From a management standpoint, these two considerations may be perceived as constraints on and problems of administrative discretion and task. The observation of these contextual variables cannot be made with much scientific precision, and their outline here is drawn in part from the perceptions of different actors involved. The perceived context is, therefore, largely impressionistic. For the cases, these variables may be separated into three categories: (1) ecological complexity and factual uncertainty, (2) diversity of values and contentious publics, and (3) disproportionate power and corporate influence.

Ecological Complexity and Factual Uncertainty

The complex ecological interdependencies in each case were viewed in the form of highly uncertain and incomplete knowledge about circumstances and future scenarios. The substantial and far-reaching proposed changes suggested large and comprehensive impacts. Consequently, for each case, insufficiency of factual knowledge was a problem throughout the review processes. At Mineral King no substantial clarity was ever obtained even in the EIS. Erosion from ski runs and the road were contested issues as were the limits of carrying capacity for air pollution and sewage. Instead of resolution, the Forest Service expected to deal with these uncertainties during and after construction. At San Onofre the inability to resolve unknowns persisted past the deliberations. For example, in 1979 the marine review committee discovered in its monitoring that Unit One had been diffusing low levels of radiation into the near-shore waters through its cooling water return. The effect on marine life, however, was unknown. At Nettleton Lakes one Kitsap County commissioner reflected on the process, saying, "There was some doubt as to whether we had the capabilities in knowledge or statutory controls to render an ecologically sound decision" (Barber, 1971).

The ambiguities of knowledge came from three sources. First, there was a simple lack of data specific enough to the individual projects. Limited public funds and pressures not to hold up deliberations made comprehensive data collection and evaluation impossible within the decision time frames. The unique conditions and specifications of each project made previously acquired aggregate data on general area factors only marginally useful. General descriptions about soil, water quality, or air flow seldom can be used alone to determine whether particular sewerage, excavation, or air pollution abatement techniques would adequately internalize problems.

At Mineral King the Park Service and other agencies argued that (1) no specific knowledge existed on potential parkland impacts from the road and resort, and (2) general data could not determine the extent of any potential damage. The state coastal commission concluded in its original recommendation on San Onofre that not enough information on major impacts was available to make any judgment of findings. At Nettleton Lakes a DWR engineer commented that "the information given so far is too preliminary . . ." (Planning Commission, Mar. 31, 1970, p. 148). With regard to marina construction at Nettleton, a Game Department official recognized that "substantial knowledge gaps" existed (Biggs, 1970). Regarding project platting and demand characteristics, a Kitsap official highlighted his unmet need for a "comprehensive report of what exists in terms of trade-offs" (Barber, 1971).

Second, ecological complexity and uncertain project features compounded the lack of data. At Mineral King and Nettleton air pollution was a persistent possibility owing to changeable air flow and uncertain vehicular traffic in confined air basins. While conventional air pollution was not at issue at San Onofre, the possibility of a nuclear accident represented a much larger air-borne hazard for a greater number of people. Moreover, because of the nature of generating facilities, the state coastal commission staff declared that "the addition of Units 2 and 3 at San Onofre would have an impact on all 3 parts of man's physical environment — air, land, and water" (Bodovitz, Feb. 28, 1974).

Regarding land resources, the forest ecology at Mineral King and Nettleton composed an undisturbed and intricate web of animal, plant, insect, and soil interdependencies. Concerning water resources, the pollution potential at San Onofre was uncertain, but at Mineral King and Nettleton the limited carrying capacity left little question as to project impacts on water quality. At Nettleton's Anderson Cove a state health official said it is "very difficult if not impossible to control the quality of water near marinas" (*Bremerton Sun*, Feb. 19, 1970). To this was added the elusive question: ". . . how many tidal flats can we alter and still maintain the integrity of the ecology of Hood Canal?" (Taylor, Feb. 18, 1970).

Ecological intricacies in each of the cases were further compounded by project size and the potential transboundary ecological impacts. Disney had been noted for restoring the popularity of amusement parks on a grand scale, and San Onofre was to be the largest nuclear facility in the world. Of Nettleton, Boise's chief consultant said, "We have never designed a recreational development of this size. I don't know of anyone else who has as a matter of fact" (Planning Commission, Mar. 31, 1970, p. 43). Owing to such sizes, the scale of external effects could have far-reaching implications for distant but interconnected places.

Third, the preponderance of biased information by the developers concerning methods and intentions contributed to the condition of insufficiency. Substantially all businesses act in their own self-interest when providing information, but the size of financial resources gave the firms a near monopoly over the creation and interpretation of data. Mountains of facts and equations were used that frequently obscured more fundamental issues and lent appearance of objectivity to corporate expertise. At Nettleton and San Onofre this approach was augmented by the hiring of consultants who, even though paid by the developers, claimed to be offering expert and objective opinions. In short, in a world of large-scale professional institutions where quantitative techniques are coveted but where environmental variables are frequently intangible, such bias often results in information viewed as objective instead of unknown reliability. One Nettleton opponent concluded that it is "a lot easier to bring up statistical support of long range economic benefits than long range ecological damage" (Pitell, 1971).

Diversity of Values and Contentious Publics

Land use settings of far-reaching magnitude usually foster a milieu of overlapping societal spheres where actors are not often confined by clear geographical and political boundaries. At Mineral King and San Onofre proximity to the project sites had little to do with identifying those parties who perceived themselves as affected. At Nettleton Lakes most participants were local, but several including the developer had no

primary residence in the area. For example, an HCEC spokesman concerned about the traditional notion of territorial representation conditioned his presence, saying, "I realize I am an outsider; I come like Boise
from California . . . " (Planning Commission, Mar. 31, 1970, p. 62).
Another nonresident user of the area asserted, "I may be considered
. . . an interloper. However, I feel that the canal belongs to me as
much as it does to the residents . . ." (County Commission, Sept. 9,
1970b, p. 1). For deliberating agencies, such amorphous conditions cause
uncertainty as to who are the relevant constituents or publics.

This is compounded by a setting where contentious partisans struggle
to attain different values over land use. Diversity measured as conflicts
in values is not easily perceived unless broken down into component
pieces. Although not completely separable, three sets of contentious
values were operative in the cases.

First, the significant conflict of development versus preservation was
present. At Mineral King Disney claimed, ". . . our efforts now and in
the future will be dedicated to making Mineral King grow to meet the
ever-increasing public need. I guess you might say that it won't ever be
finished" (Walt Disney Productions, 1967). The environmental opposition countered by saying such development violated the integrity of the
valley and surrounding wilderness.

At San Onofre energy growth was juxtaposed to esthetic coastal
values and public safety. An SCE vice-president asserted that the
utilities "have been responsive to environmental concern. We now urge
this Commission to show a similar responsiveness to energy needs"
(Coastal Commission, Dec. 5, 1973, p. 27). On the other side, environmentalists argued that Proposition 20 did not allow balancing
with noncoastal considerations. The environmentalist lawyer contended that "development is permitted, but only where it is consistent with
the protection of the coast and not because development would be important to the economy or in this case to energy needs" (Coastal Commission, Oct. 18, 1973, p. 65). Neither side paid much homage to a
balanced decision and each sought a favorable winner-take-all solution.

At Nettleton the issue of development was juxtaposed to the
maintenance of a more rural profile of life. Boise argued that the highest
and best use of the land was economic and that the project "is going to
mean new jobs and increased cash flow into the local economies . . ."
(Boise Cascade, Sept. 9, 1970d). Opponents countered that ". . . land
and water cannot only be considered just mere property in an economic
sense, but must be looked at in terms of its esthetic qualities and other
environmental considerations" (Planning Commission, Apr. 28, 1970,
p. 163). Expressing a subordinate role for environmental interests, the
developer went on to submit that "while there will be some change [in
the area's profile], this change is a price that's well within the advan-

tages and the gains to be made economically" (Planning Commission, Apr. 28, 1970, p. 269).

The second area of conflict was over the urgency for development versus the need for time to consider its implications. At Mineral King the Forest Service mirrored skiers' contentions that a huge latent demand was going unfilled because of the Sierra Club's selfish political interests. At San Onofre SCE claimed that delays for further deliberation and new studies were increasing construction costs. At Nettleton Lakes Boise made application for project approval expecting the review process to reach a favorable decision in thirty days (Smith, 1972). By contrast, HCEC emphasized "the need for study so that the change that does come will be proper and . . . in the best interests of the public as a whole. . . . I suggest that . . . you postpone even making a preliminary decision for at least a year . . ." (Planning Commission, Apr. 28, 1970, pp. 240-41). Boise countered the advantage of further study, saying "the most effective way of killing anything is to study it" (Planning Commission, Apr. 28, 1970, p. 268).

The third area of conflicting values was over the legitimacy of corporate autonomy in planning the use of common pool resources for private or exclusive gain. Opponents in all three cases suspected that the overshadowing capabilities of the single-goal firms would destroy other public values if their actions and political maneuvers were left unimpeded. Perhaps the clearest expression of this was at Nettleton, where Boise was affronted by the opposition's attempt to politicize alternative uses of the land. Contending that evaluation of priorities was not useful or reasonable, the firm commented, ". . . we ask for assistance rather than antagonism. Anyone can find purpose and method in attacking, but attack very seldom solves problems. We hope we will have a spirit of cooperation in solving a problem. . . . We hope we will not meet blind opposition" (Borgwardt, June 1, 1970b). To this plea for unification around corporate leadership, the opposition responded: "Boise Cascade would like us to get enmeshed in the 'nitty gritty' of the technical detail rather than the overall question of whether there should be such a development at all. They have opened a large office at Kitsap Lake with a staff of six and a Xerox machine, hard at work selling the proposal as a fact with a few technical details left to be worked out. But it is important not to accept this 'fact' . . ." (Best, May 25, 1970). The conflict over autonomy was a reflection of the growing skepticism over the role of large corporations and their use of "professional" management.

Disproportionate Power and Corporate Influence

Acting in one's own self-interest is not an unusual expectation of partisans, but when one party holds large economic and organizational resources relative to others, disproportionate power becomes another variable to deal with. Environmental groups like the Sierra Club often command such resources, but more often than not the contest is between smaller, less-organized groups and a large corporation. In such situations corporate influence may obscure the difference between private planning and public policy making.

At Mineral King, for example, it became increasingly difficult to see a boundary between Forest Service decision making and that of Disney. At one point public perceptions of the project viewed the Forest Service as providing public legitimacy to a purely private venture. Disney statements frequently contributed to this image. There was considerable concern about who was setting parameters when Disney said, "The forward-looking thinking that is going into planning of Walt Disney World in Florida will be applied to Mineral King" (Walt Disney Productions, 1969). The influence of the Sierra Club was no less significant in this case, and it exercised considerable leverage with the Park Service.

At San Onofre and Nettleton opponents were not of comparable size to the firms. The combined economic resources of the utilities greatly outweighed the loosely organized opposition, and SCE had little problem with getting all but the state coastal commission to accept its position on issues. At Nettleton, where the use of corporate power was more directly visible than in the other cases, Boise attempted to maintain discretion over deliberations by fettering public scrutiny of its activities. Three methods were used.

First, Boise officials promoted an aura of expertise in scientific investigation and attempted to overpower the agencies with statistical data. By its use of professional consultants, university life-science scholars, and university research facilities, Boise claimed it was "eminently qualified as far as being able to judge environmental impact . . . " (County Commission, Sept. 9, 1970b, p. 60). The opposition argued to the contrary, saying that " . . . one of Boise Cascade's tactics is to monopolize expertise in the area" (Best, 1971), and that private control of such knowledge only obscured the issues. Although Boise maintained that "we don't go out and hire people to come before you to justify what we've planned" (Planning Commission, Apr. 28, 1970, p. 82), the opposition was able in one instance to point out the tenuous value of the developer's consultants. At one hearing a consultant from the University of Washington was asked by the opposition: if a graduate student submitted a paper similar to your report on such limited data, would he be conferred a degree for the effort? In fear of a diminished scholarly reputation, the consultant responded, "Let me say, absolutely not, on a short-term basis. . . . I mean mine is definitely temporary or preliminary in nature. . . . Obviously just a short-

term paper will not go" (Planning Commission, Apr. 28, 1970, p. 168).
Second, Boise acquired a reputation for corporate aloofness when dealing with public agencies and had a record of attempts to control public reviews of its projects by restricting release of pertinent information and creating conditions for public conflicts of interest (Boschken, 1974). Boise admitted at one point to its reticence, saying, ". . . our chief mistake [in the past] has been in failure and refusal to meet with public officials" (Planning Commission, Apr. 28, 1970, p. 78). But for Nettleton Boise asserted that ". . . we expect in the process of deliberation to meet with you, to work with individual requirements that you might have" (Planning Commission, Apr. 28, 1970, p. 27). Nevertheless, the concern of several agencies indicates Boise continued its past patterns. A Kitsap planning commissioner said, "Boise Cascade felt they were coming before little bumpkins [with their proposal]" (Eder, 1971). A state DWR official complained, "We have had such little communication with the property developers or engineers [that] we are still calling it the Big Ben project" (Planning Commission, Mar. 31, 1970, p. 144). The state Department of Fisheries found that even after "several meetings" with Boise, the firm would not provide "detailed answers" for "any specific items" of its procedure for dam construction, diversion, and impounding (Tollefson, 1970). These and other indications led the opposition to demand that the proposal be complete to "insure due process [and] fairness to all concerned" (Durning, 1970).

Third, Boise tried to create the image of being well-integrated citizens of the local Kitsap community. "We share your love for the area, we share your concern, and we come into this area with highest hopes that we can be a good neighbor . . ." (Borgwardt, June 1, 1970a). Shortly after the firm's public relations disaster at the first Planning Commission hearing, project officials moved into the Kitsap area and bought homes. When locating office space, they used a real estate person who was also the wife of a planning commissioner. As husband and wife teams the officals gave numerous social gatherings for local people. The wives promoted project approval as beauty salon patrons, and husbands spoke at professional luncheon clubs. During a community campaign fund-raising dinner for county commissioners and other local officials, Boise's project manager "crashed" the party without an invitation (Eder, 1971). During deliberations the developer gave a gala party for the Planning Commission and County Commission and invited all the prominent local political figures (Eder, 1971). These overtures carried a recurring theme: "We appreciate the beauty of the county. . . . We don't want to see you lose what you have. All we're asking is let us . . . come in too and enjoy it with you" (County Commission, Sept. 9, 1970b, p. 70).

In each of the cases one is left with the impression that the contextual setting was composed of a number of difficult factors that could not be routinely dealt with. Because of the size of the projects and their developers, the administrative task was perceived by most public officals as unique and requiring a highy sophisticated technical knowledge of multiple impacts. Because of contentious publics and disproportional power, adequate representation of diverse values provided no simple avenue of resolution. Because of the ecological intricacies making up the physical location, lack of sufficient information placed a premium on the judgmental capacities of public officials.

Structural Patterns

Complexity in each of the land use cases caused difficulties for the public decision makers in grounding their perceptions of the variables empirically. Common to the cases was the impression of uncertainty and disagreement over both fact and value. Administrative structure, on the other hand, varied considerably. The question emerges: were the evident patterns equally compatible or consistent with the demands of the complex setting?

Decision-making logic suggests that choosing appropriate patterns of administration is based in part on how flexible and responsive the subsequent organizational process needs to be. When cause-and-effect relationships in the external setting are obscure and where the impact of consequences is difficult to foresee, the setting calls for structural characteristics that augment organizational processes and strategies of learning, innovative judgment, and compromise, In this respect, each of the cases shows some important structural differences that affect the organizational processes.

Mineral King

From an intraorganizational viewpoint, the Forest Service represented a large decision-making hierarchy with many of the characteristics of bureaucracy. Through its multivolume procedures manual the agency tried to mold decision settings to fit standard rules and "preformed" decisions. Actions required review and approval from higher levels in San Francisco and Washington, D.C. In reference to various aspects of policy implementation and project planning, the Forest Service chief instructed the San Francisco regional office to "make no commitments as to formal hearings or future action without first clearing with us" (McArdle, 1953).

The unity of command also required members to view their responsibilities around the central goals of enterprise growth and organizational autonomy. Given the nature of incentives, the socialization process, and promotion procedures, the character of ambition was geared toward conformity, not critical review of agency positions. Demands for conformity were evident in the case to the extent that certain members who didn't assume the proper perspective risked being isolated as "lonely voices" of dissent.

Dissent arose in the divisions of Engineering, Range and Wildlife Management, and Watershed Management, and with the Sequoia forest supervisor. Nevertheless, all were handled in an informal manner by the project leader so as not to alter the direction of development. For example, the Sequoia forest supervisor, upon first reading of the agency's 1965 renewed plans, responded to a developer report supported by the regional director of recreation. He argued that ". . . these people feel they will have exculsive use and development opportunity for the whole basin with no concept of a multiple use approach. . . . The plan appears to be based on a complete preemption of Mineral King. . . . I also believe that a hurry up area plan is not satisfactory to meet this situation" (Whitfield, Jan. 20, 1965). At the bottom of the supervisor's letter the regional director of recreation handwrote the following: "Discussed with Whitfield on Jan. 21. Believe he is now more inclined to accept the concept of a major Mineral King development project than when the memo was written . . . W.D." (Whitfield, Jan. 20, 1965). According to Kaufman's analysis of the agency, "The dissenter, exposed, is apt to feel uneasy, embarrassed; the conformist, secure, reinforced, accepted" (1967, p. 220). Without an alternative avenue of support, the forest supervisor became a major spokesman for the project and Disney received exclusive rights to the area.

Such bureaucratic tendencies may be acceptable when tasks are routine, a broad consensus on policy is apparent, and consequences are predictable from prior experience. Policy, limited by incremental change, may be implementable with clearer direction and anticipated results. Mineral King, however, did not represent an incremental shift from prior practices. The broad impacts owing to size and complexity were not subject to routine solutions applicable to problems as they arose. The dysfunctional consequences that spanned thirty years in this case resulted from an inappropriate fit between administrative structure and the land use setting. Inertia of the command structure reduced the opportunities for learning about and making innovations with a project proposal that had no precedent.

As a result of the inertial impacts on process, the consequences were favorable only to a narrow set of interests, and checks on the validity of data were greatly reduced (these contentions are the subject matters of Chapters 7 and 8). Moreover, from the standpoint of administrative politics, the public role of the agency became indistinguishable from the private interests of Disney. At one point the Forest Service appeared to be promoting the resort more than were Disney and the industry. While the agency was stressing that Mineral King would satisfy *excess* demand, Disney and the industry knew that ski operators felt there was insufficient skiing to fill present industry capacity in the West. In 1966, for example, the Disney project manager circulated the Mineral King plans at a western ski convention where he found "the general attitude of [ski] operators was one of a little suspicion and resentment or fear of what Disney may do to them with a bigger and better ski development" (Hicks, 1966). It appeared that internalizing of a single private interest was more complete for the agency than for the industry.

From an interorganizational viewpoint, the Forest Service acted as if its relations with other agencies were center-peripheral. It perceived its mandate as superior and demanded compliance from other agencies as if their authorities were ancillary to its own. While the Forest Service precluded other agencies from exercising discretion over the forestland project, it openly dictated the terms and characteristics of the roadway across federal parkland at state expense. Resistance by the Park Service and some state officials notwithstanding, the mandate of exclusive authority over Mineral King gave considerable leverage to the Forest Service view. The Bureau of the Budget's resolution of the Udall-Freeman controversy lends further credibility to this point. As seen by its action, this central authority favored a winner-take-all outcome over a negotiated settlement.

Such a superior/subordinate relationship among agencies may be appropriate when consensus on interests and distinct alignment of roles around a unitary goal are possible. This case did not provide that uniformity of task perceptions. Except for the contentiousness of the Park Service, the inertial forces of the central command perpetuated a process where due deliberation was not one of the visible objectives. Tocqueville, more than a century ago, saw the risk in such monopoly behavior. "However, enlightened and skillful a central power may be, it cannot of itself embrace all the details. . . . And when it attempts unaided to create and set in motion so many complicated springs, it must submit to a very imperfect result, or exhaust itself in bootless efforts" (1956, p. 66). As a result of monopoly behavior, numerous adverse consequences were left unresolved. Moreover, Disney's capture of Forest Service deliberations also meant capture of other agencies' discretions through the center-periphery relationship.

San Onofre

From an intraorganizational viewpoint, this case provides a contrast of organizational processes. On the one hand, the Atomic Energy Commission tended to be highly bureaucratic with a process much like that of the Forest Service. Similar consequences from inertial behavior were also evident. The coastal commissions, on the other hand, tended to be more open to learning and innovation by virtue of their split-level jurisdictions.

Accounting for the advantages of both centralization and decentralization, Proposition 20 was drafted around the assumption that coastal resource uses were subject to transterritorial overlaps of local, regional, and statewide interests. The purpose in having a tiered system was to make the boundaries of jurisdiction correspond better to the combinations of overlapping interests and impacts, and thereby internalize different bases of representation (Boschken, 1982). The advantages of the regional commission were proximity and familiarity. Although regional review of San Onofre was marked by conflict of interest and the belief that the outcome woud be appealed to the state under any circumstances, regional deliberations served as a low-cost entry point for public involvement. Convenience of the local arena generated public visibility and communications that eventually crystallized into an organized and consolidated public effort at the state appeal. Owing to distance and the costs of participation, this would not as likely have happened with only a single arena remote from the locale.

The advantages of the state commission, on the other hand, stemmed from its role as watchdog over statewide interests and interregional impacts. The project was located in the San Diego region where development values heavily dominated politics, but a number of factors like interregional energy demands and state park use obscured purely local or regional boundaries. Resulting regional oversights were not corrected until the state commission reviewed the proposal from the statewide perspective. For example, the regional commission made no mention of and constructed no safeguard for the bluffs. Yet a central point of the controversy accepted by the state commission as germane to the public interest was bluffs protection. In sum, the problems seem to have been partially offset by the bi-level structure, and subsequent observers have agreed that the "broad-gauge nature of coastal planning . . . seems to demand a plural state body . . ." (Scott, 1975, p. 192).

From an interorganizational viewpoint, the agency's relationships are open to a variety of interpretations. The task-specific commission is a form of public control often used where contentious interests are likely to be dissatisfied with a bureaucratic solution of winner-take-all. As a Progressive alternative to the Federalist model, the commission is often set in a center-periphery structure where it is expected to provide an organizational process conducive to balancing at-large symbols of public interest.

Use of the commission system at San Onofre was viewed by all as part of a center-peripheral set of relationships.[1] Most saw this structure as causing an unsatisfactory outcome for coastal deliberations. Given its last-in-line position in the sequence, the coastal agency was unable to align deliberations concurrently with others, and reciprocal review by co-equals was not possible. At real dispute, however, was the center of power. Did the AEC as lead agency represent the center or did the coastal commission with its last-in-line veto power? Those who saw the coastal agency at the center perceived different consequences from those who saw the agency at the periphery.

Those who saw it at the periphery cited two reasons for this argument. First, the sequential process left the coastal commission at a disadvantage in representing the environmental perspective. The sequential process tends to be noninteractive and therefore minimizes mutual adjustment and integration of specialties in a system of overlapping jurisdictions. With its last-in-line status, the agency acquired a veto image when complex issues and interests were at stake. Without concurrent deliberations, the sequential process does not yield a condition of interagency equity. Instead, one gets an asymmetry of discretion based on the notion that prior decisions by others limit the flexibility of choice for those at the end. Those agencies at the beginning of the sequence have more discretion to make judgments and promote their interests because they have no prior approvals with which they must contend. Those agencies at the end of the sequence have the least relative discretion in a cooperating system because their approvals must be worked around prior approvals to avoid use of the veto. In the San Onofre case functional participation by the coastal commission was obstructed because the agency became "locked in" to a choice of either cooperating by submission to prior approvals or acting outside the system with a project denial. With its last-in-line status it was unable to negotiate changes in prior decisions, especially with the AEC, and thus contributed to the feeling of a winner-take-all outcome.

Second, the noninteracting nature of sequential deliberations obstructed the ability of agency experts to promote innovations and assess potential errors. Being last in line, the coastal commission left unresolved a number of issues it alone had identified. The state coastal commission staff encouraged interagency deliberations, but when no movement occurred toward reconsideration, the commission was left

[1]In other California coastal cases such as housing and residential development, the coastal commissions frequently were viewed as a unitary authority that expropriated the permit authority of local government. Some have argued that in this role the consequences of commission behavior were different from those at San Onofre, where multi-agency jurisdictions were present. Opponents of the agency, for example, argue that Proposition 20 only substituted one organizational process for another in maintaining zero-sum outcomes in the coastal housing sector.

with its denial as a last resort. Citing the lack of innovation as a major basis for the December 5 denial, the staff recommendation said, "Approval of the proposed project without utilizing available technology that would significantly minimize the environmental impact of the project would be inconsistent with the [Coastal Act]" (Coastal Commission, Dec., 1973, p. 14). Likewise, a number of errors were noted, but evaluation ended with the commission making "no finding as to the adequacy of the present proposal to meet the standards . . ." (Bodovitz, Feb. 28, 1974). The eventual "revote" was made without substantial resolution of these issues.

The problem of limited discretion of the coastal agency's last-in-line position was further compounded by the AEC's pre-emption of the nuclear safety question. Even though radiation has environmental impacts and carries significant implications for land use allocation, the AEC retained the right to act as both advocate and judge over nuclear safety issues.[2]

Narrowed by the sequential process, coastal commission decision making at times seemed directionless, uncommitted, and susceptible to the overshadowing of powerful partisan interests. During the San Onofre proceedings Commissioner Mendelsohn urged his colleagues not to be intimidated by the utilities' recalcitrance and threats, saying that SCE pressure "need not be binding on the Commission" (Coastal Commission, Dec. 5, 1973, p. 113). But Chairman Lane argued,

> In times past . . . there was more gained than lost by our doing what we thought was right, even though it was unpopular. I don't know if we can use that logic in this case. There are going to be a lot of whipping boys in this energy thing. . . . [W]hen we go to Sacramento a couple of years from now to sell a plan . . . those of us who worked for Proposition 20 might wish that we had taken a different move today. Now, whether that's compromising for big ones, I don't know. [Coastal Commission, Dec. 5, 1973, pp. 111-12]

In the end, as Lane's position prevailed, legal mandate gave way to short-term public emotionalism fostered by the utilities' political clout. The coastal commission, with its last-in-line position, was left no room for negotiation.

Those who viewed the coastal agency as the center of power probably were more visible than those who perceived it at the periphery. Fixating

[2]In California new siting mandates established for the state's energy commission have changed the sequential order somewhat. As seen by the commission's decision on the Sundesert project, the state can stop a project in siting stage before applications are reviewed by the Nuclear Regulatory Commission. Nevertheless, from a structural standpoint the sequential process of center-periphery remains the same. Only the level of pre-emption appears different.

on the agency's veto power and its last-in-line status, these interests perceived the commission as having the "final say" on coastline development, thus subordinating other agency discretion. A *San Diego Union* editorial said, for example, "The Coastline Commission stands as an arbiter of what is right and wrong for land use along the California Coast" (Dec. 4, 1973). Commenting on the coastal commission's December 5 veto, the AEC said, "It's very unfortunate that a needed additional source of power should be rejected after plans for the project have progressed so far . . ." (*San Diego Tribune*, Dec. 7, 1973).

The commission vote to deny represented the first time that an AEC approval had been countered by a state agency, and utility supporters argued that the coastal agency's biased advocacy was dysfunctional to "objective" judgment and good government. Following SCE's contention that the nuclear project *as proposed* was "required in the total public interest" (Coastal Commission, Dec. 5, 1973, p. 28), utility supporters maintained that the commission had "seriously disturbed [utility] planning in the midst of a nationwide energy crisis" (Durick, 1973). Holding the belief that the coastal commissions were simply an unnecessary "layer of government" that used its authority without external restraints, many argued for the agency to "compromise" with the utilities.

This view of the coastal agency-as-center may have caused some unfortunate consequences for due deliberations. The coastal commission might have enjoyed a greater long-run consensus of fairness had the agency not been saddled with its image as "the final authority" and had insisted on compromise with other participating agencies. Commission Vice-Chairman Harris asserted, for example, that the agency's unilateral attempt to balance energy and environmental needs "would not be a compromise, but a betrayal of the public trust" (Bodovitz, Jan. 9, 1974b, p. 5).

The two perspectives of the coastal commission's position in the center-peripheral structure are probably not reconcilable. Yet they do point out the ambiguities of role and dysfunctions of action that such a structure promotes. Moreover, the sequential process that sometimes emerges around a unitary value or dominant lead agency aggravates those possibilities of interagency negotiations that could provide symmetrical solutions. This notwithstanding, the fact that many more agencies held discretionary roles at San Onofre than was apparent in the Mineral King decision did seem to cause a more conscious and intense deliberation over societal issues and the adjudication of diverse interests. Throughout the coastal commission review stress was placed on the limited mandate of Proposition 20 and its relationship to other administrative codes. Hence, to some, the agency's environmental bias seemed to provide a functional role of representing discrete partisan interests long overlooked in California. Recognizing project denial in its limited capacity as an administrative last resort, the coastal commission represented not a "final authority" but a major access point in the larger system of public considerations.

If project approval had been the sole discretion of the AEC, as it had been with the Forest Service over Mineral King, several significant impacts on coastal resources and environment might have been overlooked. In October, 1973 (just prior to state coastal commission review), the AEC gave a sweeping and basically unconditioned endorsement to the utilities. In its decision the AEC said it had "reviewed the entire record and finds, on the basis of the information therein," that the utilities had accounted for all potential impacts with proper safeguards (AEC, Oct. 15, 1973). With this in hand and reinforced by other agency approvals, the utilities argued that the coastal commissions could provide no new insight of public expertise.

Bodovitz, however, vigorously resisted compliance to the utilities' viewpoint by pointing out that none of the approving agencies "were really charged with taking a comprehensive view . . . for making a rational decision. Each of those agencies was looking at a slice of the problem: safety, water quality, and so forth. No agency [except the coastal commission] was charged with looking at the effect on the land environment . . ." (Coastal Commission, Feb. 20, 1974, p. 10). By countering the centralized intergovernmental logic for conformity, Bodovitz supported the legitimacy of the coastal commission as a specialized review agency. Contrary to Lane's recommendation, resistance to the inertia of prior approvals on San Onofre would not have stymied the other agencies. The more likely effect would have been pressure on the agencies to hold a series of intergovernmental meetings to consider a more integrated and composite set of decisions. With no last-in-line positions, the concurrent review structure might have provided more direct points of adjustment and cooperation among the conflicting agencies.

Nettleton Lakes

From the intraorganizational view, structure did not seem to have much influence within most of the agencies. At Nettleton Kitsap County government was the primary focus of deliberations. Too small to have many structural characteristics, its administrative process seemed to be guided more by political figures than the impersonal imperatives of large-scale organization. Even though assessment of data was done by supporting departments and the Planning Commission, county infrastructure was highly personalized. Decision making ultimately rested with the county commissioners.

The personalized process was further accentuated by the nature of local responsibilities. In contrast to the larger network of agencies, the county had an expertise and purpose limited to local impacts and public service delivery. When the Nettleton project came along, Kitsap was in the middle of developing a new comprehensive plan for urban development. Existing policies were outdated, and the lack of an adopted replacement placed local review in a position of simultaneously establishing land use policies and assessing their consequences for a large development. Like coastal commission deliberations at San Onofre, this lack of established policy added a political dynamic to the internal process.

No one, however, suggested the local role was inappropriate or superseded other network responsibilities. Concerning local representation, most felt that state agencies had "no knowledge of our community" (Lobe, Randall, and Mahan, 1971) and agreed it was "easier to march down to Port Orchard than to bring citizens to [the state capitol]" (Best, 1971). To the extent that other network prerogatives were not preempted by Kitsap, HCEC said, "The County Commissions have left for other agencies the basic policy and technical questions [of environmental soundness]. . . . [We] will request hearings . . . where our efforts and resources can most effectively be used" (HCEC, 1971).

From an interorganizational viewpoint, this case contrasts with Mineral King and San Onofre. Instead of center-periphery relations, the intergovernmental structure reflected many characteristics of a network of concurrent jurisdictions. State agencies in Puget Sound consisted of an integrated nonhierarchical structure where the individual units held a large amount of separate authority over their specialized domains. For state/local relations, political tradition in the state recognized a parity with local prerogatives. To some degree, then, this was a case where a system of multiple government formed to encompass a range of participants, information, and values.

The advantage of a nonhierarchical network is that each agency is able to give priority to problems appropriate to its particular realm. With separate collectives of expertise, a low-priority issue in one context can be treated as a high-priority item in another. While the possibility remains for some interests to be excluded while a dominant interest prevails, the interdependent nature of concurrent jurisdictions reduces this risk. This was apparent at Nettleton for two reasons.

First, the diversity of forums provided concurrent deliberation points for highlighting individual concerns and issues. While the county dealt with questions of local land use profile and economic viability, the DWR and Fisheries concentrated on the various impacts of dam implacement, and so on. Such a disaggregation of perspectives into separate but concurrent deliberations tended to enhance awareness of individual issues instead of a single focus on a dominant interest. The less complicated atmosphere of the specialized units may also have made public participation more comfortable for a greater diversity of people than the comprehensive process of a comparable bureaucratic structure. The nature of the organizational process will be expanded in Chapters 7 and 8.

With regard to mitigating dominant interests, Boise's effort to capture the process was made more difficult by the multiple decisions that were made concurrently by specialists regarding individual aspects of the project. In contrast to the dominance of Disney and the utilities at Mineral King and San Onofre, the parity of overlapping authorities at Nettleton provided too many points for capture of the total system. Moreover, while the county was disposed toward the developer, the presence of several state and other local agencies made Kitsap more aware of competing perspectives and more careful about due process. Lamenting this reality, the Boise project manager of Nettleton said, "We feel that it's unfortunate that other higher authority becomes involved in these things before the county commissioners had an opportunity to act in the normal process of events" (*Bremerton Sun*, Nov. 17, 1970).

Second, the network structure also corresponded to the high levels of information uncertainty. Insufficiency of data was a problem in nearly all phases of the review. To compensate, differences of opinion and perspective among the agencies provided the basis for more open debates over factual discrepancies and uncertainties. For example, the county, which had no marine science experts, thought of the marina complex primarily in terms of economic and recreational value. This assessment of implications was broadened by the DWR, which showed that a state supreme court ruling partially precluded the proposed dredging, and by the Department of Fisheries, which demonstrated how cove and upstream development "could have a severe impact on the native runs of salmon in Anderson Creek" (Kauffman, 1970). This interaction among different perspectives was in particular contrast to Mineral King, where the smoothing over of "lonely voices" was caused by hierarchical command in the Forest Service.

Intergovernmental Coordination

Coordination of decision makers in a complex and uncertain setting is always a difficult and arbitrary task. Where information is insufficient, however, the lack of agreed upon criteria for deciphering fact mitigates the efficiency advantage that central coordination might have over interagency mutual adjustment (Lindblom, 1965, p. 188). Indeed, in those irreducible areas where "reason" runs out, the flexibility of negotiation and adjustment may provide the only satisfactory means for coordinating widely diverging opinions. As seen in the cases, no integration method was used exclusive of others, but dominance of one alternative over another tended to correspond to dominant structural type. Center-periphery relations at Mineral King and San Onofre relied heavily on central commands and formal communications of hierarchy, while concurrent government at Nettleton Lakes depended more on mutual adjustment mechanisms.

At Mineral King the Forest Service had defined the need to identify a clear and consistent general mandate for comprehensive planning. Where conflicts existed, prioritizing and subordination of interests occurred instead of negotiated trade-offs. This left little opportunity for interagency parity in deliberations. Even though some attributed the coordination problem to "a breakdown in communications" (Nienaber, 1973, p. 105), the actual reason stemmed from the lack of agreed boundaries of jurisdiction and the exclusivity of Forest Service behavior. The formal central authority muted negotiation attempts, as the agency used its leverage to smooth over differences with some and intimidate others.

For example, when the California Department of Fish and Game argued that the development would have a "considerable" impact on wildlife (Hart, 1968), the Forest Service as "lead agency" offered to jointly conduct a wildlife inventory study on area deer. The study would not deal with project impact. Intimidation became a character of interagency relations when the Department of Interior refused to relinquish its concurrent authority. Udall had commented that "neither the National Park Service nor the Department have at any time given a firm commitment for the construction of a new road through Sequoia National Park" (Udall, 1967). In response, Agriculture Secretary Freeman said, "This leaves us puzzled with respect to how we should interpret future agreements . . ." (Freeman, 1967). Interagency communications substantiate Udall's position and show considerable Park Service concern for road impact on park values. Nevertheless, on the basis of bureaucratic need, the Bureau of the Budget intervened at Mineral King as a higher authority. This means of coordination did not fit the land use setting because diverse considerations were left unsatisfied by the nonnegotiated solution.

At San Onofre similar consequences resulted from inadequate integration of overlapping jurisdictions. The effect of AEC's pre-emptive authority, combined with the sequential review, left the intergovernmental structure without a means to pull the process together. Coordination by sequencing assumed a superior/subordinate linkage of separate reviews and required that each successive review wait until the preceding review had been completed. Consequently project certifications were made with a minimum of interagency discussion and negotiation over critical issues of radiation safety, environmental impacts, and public need.

Until coastal commission involvement, interaction was limited for the most part to formal interagency notifications and acknowledgment of respective authorities. "Compromise" was seen not as a characteristic of intergovernmental coordination but as a function of each agency's role in cooperating with the utilities. In lieu of intergovernmental collaboration, each agency in the controversy was seen as having a turn at "compromising" with SCE. The veto problem arose when the coastal commission's "compromise" was contrary to those pro-development decisions that had come before. In the center-peripheral sequence, denying approval is often the primary negotiating leverage an agency has. Use of it represents not an agency dysfunction but a means of bringing the decision to a state of intergovernmental deliberation. Supporting the December 5 veto, Commissioner Mendelsohn said, "If I had felt that was the only possible way to build the new San Onofre units, I would have voted for it. But, it was obvious that modification could be made to protect some of the bluffs and the marine environment" (*San Diego Union*, Jan. 23, 1974).

The resulting delay and eventual redecision were frustrating and costly. Feeling caught in the middle of a noninteracting sequence of reviews, one SCE official complained that "the more we change [the project] to meet the coastal commission's desires, the greater the risk is that we would have to re-submit our plans to the other regulatory agencies" (*San Diego Union*, Dec. 20, 1973). Although the utilities were primarily interested in promoting trade-offs favorable to development, others also recognized that the sequential review extended delays and raised the potential for dysfunctional interagency conflict. Sobering to the state's right of reciprocal review, an AEC statement on the denial declared, "We believe that the action further emphasizes the need for a coordinated approach to power plant siting at the federal and state levels" (*Los Angeles Times*, Dec. 7, 1973). Arguing against fragmented decisions and frustrating delays at San Onofre, San Diego Mayor Wilson, a framer of Proposition 20, said he "would like to see the various permits . . . concurrent instead of sequential" (Scott, 1975, p. 54).

At Nettleton a number of integrative mechanisms were used including interagency correspondence and *ad hoc* meetings. In conjunction with these, however, the Kitsap public hearings evolved as the central forum for establishing and negotiating agency differences on project impact. While participation in hearings by outside agencies is not unusual, the purpose of attending may be. Instead of passively reviewing their individual roles, several state agencies used the local forum to

establish their individual stances and question others. A number of examples exist. With regard to the marina, the DNR (which controlled
tideland uses) used succeeding county hearings to update its position on
dredging and use of alternative sites. Viewing the interaction of the
DNR with others including Boise allowed the county to adjust its thinking on overall project considerations. In the case of septic tanks, the
state Health Department became "aware of some differences of
opinion" between Kitsap and Mason County sanitarians (Lane, 1970).
Instigating its own investigation, it submitted to the hearings its "long
standing policy" that a central sewer system had to be used "where urban density may be expected" (Lane, 1970). This declaration was reinforced at the hearings by the DWR and the SWPCC, which were concerned about soil absorption capacity and water contamination. A letter from the SWPCC, read at one hearing, stated that the project "does
not meet . . . requirements for sewer and water design criteria . . ."
(Planning Commission, Apr. 28, 1970, p. 166).

The motive for state agencies to use the Kitsap hearings as a coordination mechanism was apparently self-serving (Bish *et al.*, 1975, p. 134).
By participating as they did in the hearings, state officials were able to
have their views taken into account without being put in the politically
controversial position of refusing necessary permits for the project
which the county might otherwise approve without restriction. These
motives and behavior were in contrast to those evident at Mineral King
and San Onofre. Hence concurrent review represented a functional process avoiding a potential situation of dysfunctional political conflict.
Moreover, the outcome, as best evidenced in Kitsap County's decision
with thirty-four conditions, probably accounted for a broader number
of considerations than any single agency alone might have accomplished.

The functional aspects notwithstanding, coordination of this
nonhierarchical network occurred with some discord. For example, a
Kitsap County official was led to wonder ". . . which state agency
does in fact have control and responsibility over what? And how and
when is it exercised? . . . The state should put out a primer . . ."
(Barber, 1971). The Kitsap planning director suggested that in developing boundaries between overlapping authorities, ". . . the agency best
equipped technically to judge a subject should administer it. The state
needs to pin down regulation carefully . . ." (Mitchell, 1971). In addition to jurisdictional ambiguities, a Kitsap planning commissioner contended that the state occasionally hindered deliberations: ". . . you do
not get back definite statements from the state" (Eder, 1971). No one
suggested, however, that any agency was purposely uncooperative or
that the coordination problems were intolerable. Indeed, the few rough

spots in interagency relations were attributed to the newness of the network in environmental regulation.[3] Its recent origin left the network without sufficient formal agreement or historical understandings concerning their overlapping jurisdictions.

In each of the three cases cooperation among agencies to produce coordinated resolutions was also influenced by judicial review. Under this constitutional check either an aggrieved party or concurring agency may file suit on the basis that some agency in the process violated administrative law or exceeded its jurisdiction. Besides guaranteeing due process, this check sometimes acts as a latent coercive incentive for agencies to work out their differences without going to court. If a controversy is appealed to the court, focus on administrative right and wrong eliminates the potential for direct compromises and accentuates winner-take-all outcomes. Reluctance to resolve issues through the courts, then, stems from the uncertainty created for the agencies as to who will lose.

At Mineral King the intransigence of the Forest Service forced the Sierra Club to use the courts as a last resort. With due process measured by the ambiguous mandates of multiple use, the agency knew that any court test would have little ground to establish violations. Congress had granted the service the broadest possible discretion. On the other hand, the Sierra Club used the court as a rear-action offensive to gain time. By stalling development and using the suit to promote its position in the media, the club's conservation director argued, "the American system of courts will provide the answer to conservation problems of great importance to all" (McCloskey, 1969). Hence the latent incentive had little effect on behavior because the club felt it had everything to gain (even if it eventually lost) and the service was sure its autonomy would be sustained. Intervention of the court brought the latent authority into play as a central coordination mechanism.

At San Onofre and Nettleton Lakes, however, the courts remained latent. Reluctance to resort to court action ran high among the various participants because most felt there was more to gain by negotiation than by the uncertainties of a court-imposed winner-take-all decision.

---

[3]The questions of governmental efficiency and reduction of administrative costs were major interests in Washington state government. During the Nettleton controversy a program consolidation and streamlining of the executive branch occurred which merged several environmental agencies. The DWR and the SWPCC were consolidated with other units to form a single environmental bureaucracy called the Department of Ecology (DOE). Initially the DOE tried to eliminate administrative, budgetary, and job distinctions based on water pollution, water resources development, and other programs by replacing them with categories of planning, standards, etc. The objective was to give a total environmental approach, but both environmentalists and business interests feared the potential for arbitrary action by this concentration of authority. Moreover, the anticipated efficiencies of scale were not achieved and the organizational reform was partly reversed (Haskell and Price, 1973).

At San Onofre Commissioner Mendelsohn stressed this motive as the basis of the coastal commission's postdenial reconsideration: ". . . the project stands a much better chance of surviving court action" (*San Diego Union*, Jan. 23, 1974). The environmentalist suits that ensued were dismissed early on as having no merit. At Nettleton neither side filed suit, and the opposition contended that more could be gained by directing energies to other administrative arenas in the concurrent system.

Role of Public Participation

Another difference in structure among the three cases is reflected in the level and use of public participation. Interest groups, private developers, and others act as quasi-organizational units which span the boundary between the internal organizational process of deliberation and the external setting. Such units act as linkage so that administrative decision making is less remote from those publics affected by the consequences. Perhaps first expressed by Selznick (1949), "boundary spanning" is an important mechanism not only for inducing partisans to support public goals but also for identifying those external values and facts necessary to establish public policy. The effect of participation is to broaden awareness of issues and reduce the tendency for winner-take-all decisions. To the extent that boundary spanning is a structural characteristic of complex organizations, public participation is not a substitute for the administrative apparatus but a necessary component of it.

Given the complex settings in the three cases, the boundary-spanning nature of participation was an important feature — even when it wasn't used. At Mineral King the Forest Service perceived participation as dysfunctional to comprehensive planning and blocked its use. Noting the 1953 "hearing" sponsored by the Chamber of Commerce, the service argued that "to hold another public hearing [in 1965] would not be consistent with the long standing situation or current action . . ." (Connaughton, 1965). Thus the agency left differing public views unresolved. When partisan positions were stated in letters, the service responded: "It is obvious that you have strong and sincere convictions on this matter. However, there are others who just as sincerely do not agree with you" (Cliff, Nov. 12, 1965).

The decision not to provide public access and review resulted from concern over the opposition's desire to raise value considerations and the question of "should?" To the service, a public hearing was viewed not as an input of values and information but as a means of obscuring the agency's decision. Stating as early as 1953 that a hearing might set an "undesirable precedent" (Cliff, 1953), service officals argued as late as 1965 that "a hearing will not provide a sounding board" (Davis, Aug. 24, 1965). Viewing the public role solely as a means of expediting the implementation process and to rally support, the service favored controllable "group meetings" where it "would be able to gain viewpoints . . . in reaching a practical solution" (Wetzel, 1953). To this end, therefore, the 1953 "hearing," which was an invitational meeting, suited Forest Service objectives because it was used "to determine what could be done to expedite the development" (Cliff, July 27, 1965).

The service's disposition shunning public scrutiny dates back to the unit's 1905 origin and Pinchot's success in having the agency located in the Department of Agriculture where it was shielded from critics (Kaufman, 1967, p. 226). When it vigorously resisted public access over Mineral King, the agency was not departing from established patterns in protecting its circumference of authority. Throughout the thirty-year decision process, the agency maintained that it did "not see that a useful public purpose would . . . be served by holding a hearing on whether Mineral King should be developed or left as is. We feel that decision has already been made" (Cliff, Oct. 7, 1965).

The resistance to both administrative review and public participation in the Mineral King case subjected the Forest Service to much criticism and resulted in a rigid defensive posture. As a result, public involvement occurred anyway by blocking the decision process. Being neither a part of the governance system nor functionally represented by it, the opposition chose such methods as legal harassment to halt or postpone development. Without an administrative means to validate and legitimize land use policy, the unitary authority was helpless to escape the actions of a self-interested minority to block resolution of public needs for an indefinite future. The Sierra Club was able to hold up the decision for over ten years and in the process cause the Forest Service to lose its potential to develop without ever answering the question of whether Mineral King should be developed.

At San Onofre the AEC acted in a similar fashion to that of the Forest Service in trying to isolate participation and access efforts of the opposition. At the AEC deliberations those who questioned utility contentions and AEC findings were aggregated by the agency into a single group called the Consolidated Intervenors. In that group they included not only environmentalists and the Union of Concerned Scientists but also marine specialists from Scripps Institute of Oceanography and other agency dissidents such as the city manager of San Clemente, the Capistrano Unified School District (which was concerned about evacuation plans for San Clemente), and a representative of the California Department of Parks and Recreation. By doing this, opponents were neutralized by consolidating the diverse issues into a single theme where the aggregate image appeared as a hodge-podge of private concerns representing no one. Although the AEC acceded that the utilities "may not have adequately apprised the public of the nature and potential effects of the proposed new facilities" (AEC, Oct. 15, 1973, p. 15), the nuclear agency discounted the views of the intervenors as not substantial enough to merit consideration.

Such information from opposition experts did not come into public focus, then, until the coastal agency review with its separate basis for due deliberation. The coastal commissions served to break values and facts into component parts by giving light to coastal land use issues instead of nuclear development needs. Even here, though, the boundary-spanning function of participation was slow to rebound from the AEC's consolidation procedures to which most opponents had been subjected. At the regional level of coastal deliberations, public participation was unorganized and each affected party acted without much reference to others. This gave an unprofessional appearance to the opposition, with little continuity between speakers, redundancy, and "scattered" logic. This was overcome at the state review process when the opposition acquired the services of the Center for Law in the Public Interest. With the center attorney acting as leader and moderator, testimony and preparation of materials were given a professional delivery which included organized position papers, a slide presentation, and sequencing of speakers according to subject matter.

Consequently, at the state level public participation played a large role, including questioning conformity to the coastal act, highlighting the need for independent studies and "short dissertations" by outside consultants, and formulating questions and alternatives to the utilities' proposal. Even though the utilities expended much energy in countering opposition questions and suggestions, it was through public participation that the staff was able to formulate some alternatives, such as siting east of the freeway, use of an HTGR, the deep-water intake ports, and preservation of the bluffs. Moreover, the eleventh-hour negotiations at the Biltmore Hotel came about as a result of the opposition's protest of a "sellout" and demand for more stringent controls. At the revote Commissioner Mendelsohn said that opposition "suggestions have come to us over the past few days. . . . Therefore, we've had a few hours, some of those hours being late night hours . . . to see what . . . makes sense in terms of attempting to toughen up these staff recommendations" (Coastal Commission, Feb. 20, 1974, p. 42). Those additional considerations drawn into the approval included (1) moving the ten-year bluffs protection guarantee up to life of the nuclear station, (2) moving control of the marine study from the utilities to an independent review committee, and (3) enlarging the area covered under the bluffs protection agreement.

At Nettleton Lakes the structure of concurrent government allowed participation to be highly useful. The multiple arenas of smaller size provided sympathetic avenues for a greater variety of affected interests. Although some argued that the sole purpose of citizen involvement was "to stop this thing" (Barber, 1971), most agreed that encouraging partisan inputs served to achieve several boundary-spanning functions. For example, the structure of alternative forums was seen by many as a quasi-competitive arena of interests that established the means for different sets of public decision makers to more accurately perceive the range of values affected. How citizens felt about uses of the Nettleton property seemed to raise a number of useful questions, and several public officials recognized that the opponents developed "a number of issues that wouldn't have been brought out" had the corporation been the only articulator of values (Mitchell, 1971).

As another boundary spanning function, the partisans were important sources of information. According to one Kitsap commissioner, the opposition "brought in information we probably wouldn't have solicited ourselves" (Rylander, 1971). The provision of information took three forms. First, citizens raised a number of analytical questions that did not occur to certain public officials. With regard to damming cost and impact, HCEC asked about siltation and stream flow considerations, fiscal responsibility for maintenance of spawning enhancement programs, and other technically sophisticated problems (Best, May 25, 1970). As a result, the county solicited recommendations from DWR and the Department of Fisheries concerning stream alterations. With regard to police, an HCEC member queried, ". . . what is going to be the net effect when you have a burglary? Who is going to investigate, the private police department?" (Planning Commission, Mar. 31, 1970, p. 154). This raised enough concern for the Kitsap planning department that it asked the sheriff for his "reaction and assessment of public burden" (Mitchell, June 11, 1970). Finally, so many issues were raised by opponents concerning other Boise projects that the County Commission decided to take a trip to California, where they hoped ". . . the information we receive . . . will give us the answers we are seeking" (*Bremerton Sun*, Dec. 1, 1970).

Second, by working with several involved agencies simultaneously, partisans were able to aid in the interagency transfer of information. For example, in promoting the need for its marina proposal, Boise testified at the Kitsap hearings that a Puget Sound pleasure boat study carried out by the state Parks and Recreation Commission and the Corps of Engineers provided ". . . a strong indication . . . of the desirability of the amenity features such as we have planned for the Cove" (Planning Commission, Apr. 28, 1970, p. 17). Although neither of the agencies making the study was actively involved in the Nettleton controversy, project opponents contacted them to see what the study's applicability was to Anderson Cove. Among other points, the agencies indicated that although recommendations for future marinas were not made on the basis of environmental criteria, they should not be located in areas like the cove where a shellfish culture was apparent (Puget Sound Task Force of Pacific Northwest River Basins Commission, 1968). Pointing out further that Hood Canal had the least demand for moorages in Puget Sound, the Corps of Engineers said ". . . Anderson Cove is not included in the [study's] Early Action Program," which called for development before the year 2000 (McConnell, 1970). No one can say whether this information would have been eventually discovered by public officials, but Boise opponents expedited its early transfer to the review process.

Third, partisans gathered an enormous amount of outside materials comparable to that of Boise. Although the firm argued that the information represented "attacks made by people whom I dare say know very little about the corporation and who base most of what they're saying on some scandal sheets" (Planning Commission, Apr. 28, 1970, p. 261), opponents solicited and presented data from out-of-state public officials on recreational lot oversupply and Boise's deceptive practices and environmental problems. According to HCEC, "This company's activities elsewhere are important, because their cavalier attitude toward regulatory agencies is a pattern" (Best, May 25, 1970). Likewise for Nettleton, outside experts and analysis were submitted on a variety of impacts in substantial contrast to Boise contentions. The effect of these partisan inputs was apparent in the deliberation process. On the subject of sewerage, for example, the Kitsap planning director wrote to Boise: "Having reviewed the testimony . . . we have acquired many misgivings. We feel that in the long run, sewage treatment facilities should be used . . ." (Mitchell, June 15, 1970).

Trade-offs

This chapter has been concerned with the relationship of appropriate administrative structure to tasks promulgated by the land use setting. While the cases had similar complex settings, the structure and consequences varied considerably. None of the administrative patterns were completely bad or good, and none represented cost-free alternatives. At Mineral King and San Onofre some observers felt that few substantial benefits had been achieved for the administrative costs and delays that were incurred. At Nettleton Lakes a number of important policies were made by concurring agencies, and the developer waited for a decision that took considerably less time than the other two cases.

Viewed in the context of trade-offs, the consequences can be assessed in terms of the breadth of representation, the manner in which information was addressed, and the extent to which administrative errors contributed to the uncertainty of adverse external effects. The purpose of the next two chapters is to compare the organizational processes in the cases and examine their consequences more closely. Chapter 7 deals with the impact of decision rules on who is represented. Chapter 8 deals with the impact of experts on information evaluation and error mitigation.

CHAPTER 7

Decision Rules and Representation

A CENTRAL THEME in land use control is to assure that the administrative process provides public policies suitable for the allocation needs of competing interests. As mentioned earlier, there is no single best way to both augment freedoms and provide sufficient control to protect other rights. Indeed, if by solution we mean a cost-free process, then there are no solutions. The real due process and policy questions are phrased in the context of trade-offs. In the largest sense, should we be concerned more with how efficiently (in the least-cost sense) our land use agencies operate or more with how effectively they help allocate benefits and costs among affected interests?

Ths answer to such concerns is seldom unequivocal. Any discussion and interpretation of due process and appropriate consequences are largely impressionistic and dependent on one's biases. For example, protecting a "status quo" is a topic in public policy that generates serious ideological differences. How one views its source and meaning partly determines which decision rules and policy outcomes a person accepts as appropriate. If one attributes status quo to "watered down" decisions made through interagency accords, he is probably also inclined to believe that progress is achieved by single-goal agencies promoting fundamental change. Few situations are such that nonviolent policy creates comprehensive change without significant interests losing out. Zero-sum outcomes can provide fundamental change, but positive-sum outcomes from mutual accords are too "compromised" to represent such change. Hence, to dominant interests seeking policy changes that promise big payoffs for them, a positive-sum rule is inappropriate because it protects other interests by spreading benefits more widely.

On the other hand, if one attributes status quo to the ability of dominant interests to continually gain the bulk of advantage from public policy, one is likely to believe that a decision rule which distributes political power more evenly is the primary means of progress for a broader spectrum of interests. A "watered down" outcome here means that dominant factions were prevented from maintaining their status quo advantage and had to share the benefits of public policy with others. Clearly, decision rules can simply promote one status quo over another, but a more optimistic view is that government can provide decisions that promote improvements in which many can share.

The problem of bias notwithstanding, decision rules are reflections of how the administrative process is structured. In an earlier section this study associated use of welfare at large with the unitary bureaucracy, intuitionism with the task-specific commission, and fairness with concurrent government. While these models seldom reflect reality exactly, the causal sequence of administrative structure, the behavioral process, and policy consequences is seen to some extent in the use of decision rules. The type of rules employed will skew consequences in certain directions.

The welfare-at-large rule tends to accentuate demands for streamlined decision making around a single pinnacle goal. As a result, variant interests are more likely to be prioritized out of sharing the benefits. Intuitionism frequently generates a protean process with unconnected outcomes. With its *ad hoc* basis of decision making, political influence over the long run is likely to drive the commission away from intuitive balancing and toward the firmer ground of welfare at large. Institutional fairness, on the other hand, tends to accentuate due process of an interagency network and broaden the horizon of relevant interests. Here mitigating adverse effects for some and spreading the benefits of allocation become the policy guides alongside the need for efficiency.

Analysis in this chapter, then, will focus on (1) decision rules and the results they produce, (2) the custodial strategy of welfare at large, (3) the protean strategy of intuitionism, (4) the management of conflict under fairness, and (5) the role of NEPA and the courts. Those questions in Chapter 1 concerning decision rules and representation (p. 16) are used to structure the analysis.

Impact of Decision Rules

As different bases of representation, decision rules are used to identify relevant publics and determine policy choices. Implicitly or explicitly articulated by public officials, they are ingrained in the organizational culture and provide logic and structure for the administrative process. Each of the cases involved different rules which are shown to have fostered different processes and outcomes.

Mineral King

The Forest Service was clear and consistent in embracing the welfare-at-large rule. "In the development of National Forest areas for public use we must make our decisions on the basis of service to the maximum number of people" (Cliff, Nov. 9, 1965). In order for many *interests* to be accommodated, however, they would have had to be consistent with or part of the service's primary value. Variant or inconsistent values tended to be ignored because decision makers in the unified bureaucracy needed to identify a clear mandate for comprehensive policy and synoptic planning. Where conflicts among values existed at Mineral King, prioritizing and subordination occurred instead of negotiated settlements. According to one forester, "The wishes of the minority must be subordinated" (Norris, 1965). With the agency's exclusive jurisdiction, other agencies had only limited means of negotiating a parity among affected interests through intergovernmental review. Once it was decided by the service that "Mineral King should . . . be managed to provide the greatest benefit to the overall public need" (Davis, June 1, 1965), then questions of partisan representation or market choice were moot.

The results of this were evident in several instances, but one example was the manner in which the agency approached the issue of identifying market demand. Although Forest Service public statements emphasized a "desperate" need and a vast excess demand for Mineral King development (Forest Service, Feb., 1969), the effect of the resort may have been to foster or "seed" still greater demand. The theory of markets suggests that as the cost of a product declines or the commodity becomes more readily available, customers along the market periphery will be drawn in. By providing a large increase in ski resort availability, the service was not only satisfying existing demand but unilaterally inducing market changes as well. Instead of allowing markets to incrementally adjust to competing demand and supply for forest resources, the service would have seeded ski demand at the expense of other natural resource uses. The agency eventually acknowledged this seeding effect, saying, "The proposed plan affords greatly increased winter use opportunity levels. . . . This may also give an added impetus to the rising popularity of snow skiing, generating in and of itself an increased demand for ski facilities" (Forest Service, 1974, pp. 189-90).

Yet to *assure* seeding a demand spiral, the agency plan also anticipated large expenditures for promotion. Creating artificial images was Disney's recognized expertise, and a major consideration in choosing the firm, according to the Forest Service chief, was Disney's heavy emphasis on attracting "large numbers by actively promoting to do so" (Cliff, Oct. 7, 1965).

Neither seeding nor creating demands is in and of itself inappropriate for a public agency to engage in. However, public planning is by nature a mechanism that alters or supersedes the market process in order to "better" allocate resources. It substitutes administrative fiat in the political arena for individual choice in the marketplace. Without such agency intervention, competing demands would adjust to market equilibrium forces by either accepting the cost/benefit profile of skiing or finding substitutes. With the intervention, market equilibrium for all competing resource uses should have been a major consideration. Existing supply and demand for the area's resources were based on certain trade-offs, namely the cost of difficult access versus the benefit of pastoral experience. In equilibrium, "the ecology of the area has been maintained by inaccessibility in winter and reasonable use in the summer" (Bergren, 1965). Although the Forest Service's "principal planning guideline . . . is to protect the resource while developing it . . ." (Forest Service, Feb., 1969, p. 10), the changes in access and provision of modern conveniences affect the trade-offs not only in an environmental sense but also with regard to who benefits.

In the case of Mineral King, then,

1. Was it legitimate for the Forest Service through a private concessionaire to actively entice summer and winter recreationists and conventioneers away from other resort facilities?

2. Was it the proper role of the service to stimulate one industry at the expense of another?

3. Was it appropriate to trade off a pastoral experience in semi-wilderness for skiing and mountain convention facilities?

4. What considerations of resource demand and supply should the Forest Service have viewed as critical to the decision?

5. If demand exceeds supply, was it more appropriate to achieve equilibrium by comprehensive public action or by allowing smaller adjustment through the market mechanism?

6. If public action was appropriate, how should external effects have been treated?

The Multiple Use Act gave no adequate hints as to how these questions should be answered, and policy was essentially determined unilaterally based on a single image of welfare at large.

Besides the rule's unitary solutions, the fact that no interest at Mineral King represented a majority (Lamb, 1976) may also have made the at-large rule inappropriate. Although skiing has been a highly organized and visible sport, its enthusiasts in Southern California amount to only about 6 percent of the population (2 percent on a nationwide basis). Those who might be interested in Mineral King summer activities would probably not exceed 10 percent of the Los Angeles settlement. Consequently, the controversy that developed over policy did not involve a majority or even a significant minority but occurred instead over competing specialized interests. The welfare rule cannot decipher policy under these conditions.

With Forest Service support for a partisan minority based on a welfare-at-large doctrine, the Mineral King environmental factions saw no just consideration of their interests and consequently came to view their plight as like that of American Indians, "who were delegated by treaty to the lands which no one else wanted" (Park Service, 1966, p. 96). The Supreme Court in the Mineral King case seemed to have sympathized with the opposition, saying that "aesthetic and environmental well-being, like economic well-being, are important ingredients of the quality of life . . ." (*Sierra Club v. Morton,* 1972). Justice Douglas tried to relate this argument to public decision-making rules: "The standards given those agencies are usually expressed in terms of the 'public interest.' Yet 'public interest' has so many differing shades of meaning as to be quite meaningless on the environmental front" (*Sierra Club v. Morton,* 1972). Hence the high court seems to have argued against the at-large interpretation of welfare in the formation of public policy.

San Onofre

In this case competing decision rules obscured a clear basis of how to judge. The commission system is normally charged to act by an intuitionist rule, but when this pattern overlaps with other agency jurisdictions, the rule places the commission in an ambiguous situation. Every agency cannot be charged with the responsibility for creating comprehensive, separately balanced decisions. The AEC avoided the problem by exercising pre-emptive authority in the name of general welfare, but the coastal commissions did not have such exclusive rights to accomplish at-large "balancing." Moreover, their newness to the scene prevented role clarity in the intergovernmental network. Since no prior understanding of roles in coastal siting was achieved among participating agencies, unilateral choice of one rule over another was problematic. The state coastal commission's two San Onofre "decisions" reflect this confusion.

In the process that led to the December 5 decision, most coastal agency people saw Proposition 20 as the decision guide. That mandate, however, specified not a balancing of at-large interests but an advocacy role in protecting "common pool" resources along the coast. In attaching the San Onofre marine impacts to this logic, the San Diego regional staff emphasized that "those using waters from the ocean for cooling purposes are capturing a resource of economic value to them but which belongs to all the people of the state and nation" (San Diego Coast Regional Commission, Sept. 4, 1973, p. 3). In a decision sustaining the coastal commissions' advocacy role, a state court said, ". . . the impact of an activity which in times past has been purely local, may under changed circumstances transcend municipal boundaries. . . .

Where the activity, whether municipal or private, is one that can affect persons outside the city, the State is empowered to prohibit or regulate the externalities" (Coastal Commission, 1975, p. 13).

Instead of seeing the coastal law as broadening the basis of representation for an intergovernmental system, the temptation of many, however, has been to view the advocative authority as "a definite policy bias" against economic interests (Sabatier, 1975, p. 9). The implication is that one value has been substituted for another in government decision making. Opponents of Proposition 20 took the law as a fresh sign of government's pre-emption of the right to develop property. This interpretation of bias is inaccurate for two reasons.

First, the coastal act did not replace other laws and agencies governing coastal use. Instead, it recognized the coastal agency as an *incomplete* authority of government existing within a system of other jurisdictions. The act "does not provide for a balancing of interests" (Coastal Commission, Oct. 18, 1973, p. 64) but acts, rather, as one of several land use laws to better ensure fair access to the public policy process. According to the agency, evidence of this was clear. With a 96 percent approval rate for permits, "the Coastal Act has *not* halted construction in the coastal zone. Instead, it has allowed construction to proceed, provided building is consistent with the Act" (Coastal Commissions, 1973, p. 7).

In this light, the act may be construed as part of the fairness doctrine for a larger governmental network of agencies. The coastal act offsets the disproportional bias for construction and development that existed prior to Proposition 20. Calling on the other overlapping jurisdictions to engage in a collaborative effort, Bodovitz affirmed this, saying that San Onofre "is an opportunity to do a kind of planning that . . . use[s] a limited supply of land along the coast for multiple purposes" (Coastal Commission, Dec. 5, 1973, p. 19). To this the agency staff added as a preface to its recommendation for denial that those multiple purposes "should be both enough energy *and* a healthy environment" (Coastal Commission, Dec., 1973).

Second, the act does not simply wedge in a new bias for environmental interests. It more accurately deals with short- and long-term tradeoffs. The law has to do with making judgments, for example, about the immediate economic use of coastal resources for nuclear energy and the potential cumulative hazard for other economic uses of the resource such as near-shore aquaculture and fisheries. The coastal agency denied approval on December 5 because the other agencies' decisions left insufficient latitude for the agency to properly represent the coastal act interests.

The uproar that ensued promised a clouded future for the agency. SCE threatened political and legal consequences, saying, ". . . the

Commission disregarded approvals of the project by nine other . . . agencies. . . . Because . . . the overall public interest demands that these nuclear units be built, we . . . will investigate all avenues to accomplish this purpose, including possible reconsideration by the Commission and legal action, if necessary" (Horton, 1973). Rather than risk the political cost, the commission backed off toward a decision rule of intuitive balancing. Developer interests pressed for this because the ambiguity of intuition and loss of concrete criteria made the agency more vulnerable to those demands for political flexibility and "compromise" with the utilities.

The shift from one decision rule to the other created the appearance of an *ad hoc* or protean deliberation process. The adverse facets of this were several. For example, the agency's resort to intuitive judgment caused confusion as to what "publics" were being represented. The open-endedness of intuitive decision making left no firm basis for interlocking agency responsibilities with others. If an agency working within an *advocative* administrative network attempts to provide comprehensive balanced decisions on its own, it loses its ability to integrate the interest it represents into the network's concert of policies. By deciding to compromise with the utilities and balance its own decision around coastal as well as energy and noncoastal issues, the coastal agency stepped outside its more predictable legal role and acted as a "philosopher-king."

The intuitionist balance left little basis for public accountability, and the "redecision" appeared to some as a "sellout" and to others as "window dressing." Whose interests were balanced was equally unclear for agency officials. The state staff guarded its "redecision" recommendation, saying, "In this proposal, as in all compromises, no one is entirely pleased; no one obtains all he wishes" (Bodovitz, Jan. 9, 1974a). Commissioner Frautschy believed the final decision was fair but admitted "it is a decision that nobody is happy with . . ." (Frautschy, 1975). A San Diego regional commissioner was even more uncertain: "It is kind of hard to say what is fair . . . [but] the issue was diced as it had to be" (Keen, 1974).

Another adverse facet of the protean process was that intuitionism gave little defense against utility claims that the coastal agency had no constructive role. SCE contended that because of this "unnecessary added layer of government," the two companies were being forced to absorb "very substantial cost penalties of nearly one and one-half million dollars per week" for delays (Coastal Commission, Oct. 18, 1973, p. 60). Advocating a "one-stop" procedure, SDG&E attributed its problems at San Onofre to "a delay caused by the burdensome procedures [and] seemingly endless regulatory review" (SDG&E, 1974, p. 10). Bodovitz was uncomfortable with the kind of statement that correlated waste with agency decision making. At one point he responded, "The question of delays I'm sure will come up more and more. It's tempting to say who's really responsible for the delays" (Coastal Commission, Dec. 5, 1973, p. 19). Later the state staff would argue further that "with unresolved questions of effect . . . it can come as no surprise that delays are encountered in gaining governmental approvals. . . . If more attention was initially spent in developing sites without environmental problems, the regulatory delays they claim to experience would be minimized" (Coastal Commission, Dec., 1973). Although the sequential process was the major cause of delay, the ambiguity of intuitionist decision making allowed the utilities to point a finger at the agency's aimless deliberations.

Nettleton Lakes

Like the previous two cases, the temptation to view the single agency as separate or autonomous from a network of overlapping jurisdictions was evident. Missing the point about interagency mutual adjustment and due process, Boise claimed the domain of compromise was between the individual agencies and the developer. "That's what this thing is all about: to allow the county to negotiate with the developer, to allow the developer to negotiate with the county" (Planning Commission, Apr. 28, 1970, p. 27).

Nevertheless, the question of institutional fairness usually has its reference point in the due process of concurrent government. In this case as a contrast to the other two, most participants in the controversy seemed to operate on the assumption that the intergovernmental process should result in a mutually beneficial outcome for affected parties. Establishing a fair outcome, though, was another matter, compounded by the conflicting parties seeking representation. On the one hand, the developer argued that as a property owner it had rights to use the land as it saw fit and that substantial governmental restrictions would constitute a "taking" of property without compensation. This position received some local support, including that of the *Bremerton Sun* editor, who said, ". . . there seems no legal way the commissioners can refuse permission for a reasonable and responsible development of private property" (Dec. 23, 1970b). On the other hand, opponents asserted that such a large development in a "wilderness type area" would destroy much of the satisfaction enjoyed by those who lived there. These local public pressures were reinforced by the interests of outsiders who maintained that "the only way you can be fair at the present state of knowledge . . . is to withhold your approval until the inadequate evidence has been impartially strengthened . . ." (Parkinson, 1970).

Consequently, under complexity and uncertainty of environmental limits, one could argue that fairness is related to how well public policy decisions mitigate long-run problems for affected interests without making needed development impossible. Notwithstanding the impact of administrative costs which may increase with the number of participating agencies, due deliberation of overlapping jurisdictions will tend to foster a higher assurance of long-run ecological stability and efficient allocation of resources.

The role of the county in achieving fairness revolved around both its specific authorities and its interaction with other agencies. The county seemed to recognize the need to assure a proportional relationship between who received the costs and who the benefits of the land use change. A member of the Planning Commission said, for example, that the county's overriding goal was ". . . a determination to have the county a better place for [local] people outside the development to live. We tried to do this through controls . . . on the development" (Barber, 1971). In countering the developer's argument of overrestrictive controls, another Planning Commission member asserted, ". . . if they want to do the job badly enough, they'll comply" (Eder, 1971). Many county officials favored developer interests as well, and the tenor of deliberations seemed to revolve around the question: ". . . how could [Boise] design a project to fit our policy" (Mitchell, 1971).

Although both the county and state agencies on the whole promoted cooperative and innovative solutions to accommodate the broadest number of interests, the question remains — were the Nettleton decisions fair? Those public officials involved in the decisions were unequivocal in answering this. The Kitsap County Planning Commission maintained that "this approval . . . is necessary for the enjoyment of a substantial property right of the petitioner and will not be materially detrimental to the public welfare nor to the property of other persons located in the vicinity . . ." (Planning Commission, July 28, 1970). No state agency publicly disagreed with this assessment or with the contention that concurrent deliberations as a whole were fair. This conclusion was reinforced by at least two indicators. First, the variety of specialized agencies seemed to provide ample public access to different sets of policy makers. Second, although the agencies tended to represent different constituent bases, they reached consensual agreements as semi-autonomous or quasi-competitive authorities. Relative to the other cases, the decisions on Nettleton were not left to a "final authority," an exclusive jurisdiction, or a dominant public value.

As might be expected, however, a lesser degree of consensus prevailed among the partisans. Project opponents seemed generally to view the outcome as accounting for their interests. Philip Best of HCEC, for example, used the marina issue in expressing his acceptance of the outcomes. Pointing to the work of the county and the DNR, he said, "Canceling the marina was a political compromise. It lets [Boise] develop the area, but shows you're protecting the environment" (Best, 1971). The developers, on the other hand, argued that major restrictions on agency approvals caused hidden costs: "We think we had some of those hidden costs imposed upon us . . ." (County Commission, Sept. 9, 1970b, p. 68).

Boise's characterization in this case, however, may not be a relevant argument against institutional fairness. Fairness in land use control has to do with allocation, that is, with changing from an existing condition to a new one. If an actor (in this case, a developer) makes a proposal for a land use change (a recreation community), a public decision that requires the developer to account for or mitigate external effects does not leave him worse off than his existing or original position. Property is a bounded physical unit. Its ownership conveys not open-ended freedoms of use but, rather, a set of property rights *and* prohibitions (Dales, 1968, ch. V). In acquiring the incentive and means to develop, the developer voluntarily made the necessary commitments knowing that risk was involved in obtaining public approval. Under the fairness rule, one is not entitled to unrestricted public approval because he has made an initial investment in the proposal. To make a proposal initiator worse off would require a condition where the developer was forced against his will to commit to the project. Where a public decision allows development so long as external effects are mitigated, the chance for widespread benefits is high and no one is made worse off by having to absorb disproportional costs.

While some see this as a "watered down" or status quo solution, it can also be seen as augmenting improvement in a positive-sum sense. Boise was granted approval on the project, but only so long as it was brought up to standard with residential equivalents in urban areas. Boise was also able to see early in the process what problems needed to be mitigated.

In the end, Boise tacitly accepted this logic, at least so far as the county was concerned. In a news release the company said, "Boise Cascade feels the decision by the . . . commissioners was the result of careful and complete consideration of the project" (*Bremerton Sun*, Jan. 21, 1971). Further evidence of partisan consensual agreement is demonstrated by the fact that although all sides had adequate resources, none appealed the various agencies' decisions to the courts. This is significant, because had a single bureaucracy made the decisions without the benefit of consensus from overlapping jurisdictions, a court fight more likely would have resulted. In Washington at the time of the controversy, public land use decisions were heavily dominated by environmental interests, and a single agency pursuing the "general welfare" probably would have denied development altogether. In the reverse, as occurred at Mineral King, nearly unrestricted approval might have resulted had the "majority view" been pro-development. At Nettleton the risk of favoring a dominant interest over others seemed to be mitigated by concurrent government.

The Strategy of Decision Rules

In forming public policy, agencies in each of the three cases had to address such questions as (1) what are the public needs and who is affected, (2) how are the benefits and costs to be distributed, and (3) how should values be accommodated and resources allocated? Decision rules guide the search for answers to these policy issues by structuring the kind of *strategy* the organization uses in pursuing tasks. Welfare at large, for example, connotes a symbol of majority interest that can be identified best by the professional management of an autonomous authority. This custodial approach, then, follows a strategy of achieving the greatest good for the greatest number. Intuitionism connotes an *ad hoc* approach that may be viewed as a nonstrategy. The rule encourages flexibility toward *situation-specific* circumstances but does not reduce control of the commission as professional custodian of public values. Institutional fairness, on the other hand, emphasizes due process considerations, thus connoting a "management of conflict" strategy. This section examines these strategies as to their processes and implications.

The Custodial Strategy of Welfare at Large

The unitary bureaucracy is not only an authority with a homogeneous goal structure but also one that enjoys a great amount of autonomy in decision making. In achieving welfare for society at large, it alone is in the pinnacle position of knowing what is best. Such discretion, acquired either by mandate or through administrative precedent, involves custodial behavior. It is a strategy that emerges from assumptions of monopoly power. Clients or customers do not have the wits to know what is good for them, and competition from other providers does not overlap significantly enough to contend with the exclusive authority. Accountability toward public values is protected by the professionalization of management where control and performance are deemed internal matters.

The problem with much of this logic has to do with incentives and motivation. The professional in the organization is viewed as apolitical but sensitive toward the welfare of society. Yet symbolic goals of betterment are always the most difficult to operationalize, and the autonomous bureaucracy provides few concrete measures for employees except those of career advancement. Often, then, the result is to forsake public goals in favor of those assuring maintenance of the organization.

All organizations, of course, pursue needs of "self-maintenance" (Selznick, 1949, p. 29), which promote the stability, integrity, and continuity of control over their public domains. How they do it, though, varies considerably. In an intergovernmental network agencies are kept "honest" by the influence of reciprocal review. To maintain legitimacy and prevent loss of support to other agencies, each unit in the quasi-competitive structure is obliged in the long run to make system or organizational goals compatible with public goals.

By contrast, the monopoly position of a unitary authority has reduced external checks, and its autonomy frequently produces a tendency to exclude those public goals that may obstruct ease of administration, organizational growth, and self-defined legitimacy. Without the competition for public support, few external influences exist to temper autonomous discretion and account for public goals. As a result, the custodial strategy frequently uses welfare at large as an umbrella to legitimize its pursuit of system maintenance.

As seen in the behavior of both the Forest Service at Mineral King and the AEC at San Onofre, the ramifications of custodial behavior are important. In each of these cases the hierarchies crystallized action around a "we versus the enemy" attitude which led to the protection of the organization against elements of the public they claimed to be representing. The *Federalist* predicted such occurrences, saying, " . . . there is in the nature of sovereign power an impatience of control that disposes those who are invested with the exercise of it to look with an evil eye upon all external attempts to restrain or direct its operations" (Hamilton, Madison, and Jay, 1961, p. 111).

The most visible example of protecting agency discretion from the "enemy" came from the Forest Service struggle with the Park Service and Sierra Club. Although recognizing as far back as 1945 that concurrent approval would be necessary (Gibson, 1945), the Forest Service vigorously protected its autonomy by sharing only with those who "gave us their blessing" (forester quote in Nienaber, 1973, p. 67). Communications with the Park Service were not even established until 1965 when development was imminent — twenty years after the initial decision was made (Davis, Feb. 5, 1965).

With its authority over road right-of-way, Park Service participation revolved initially around the establishment of wilderness boundaries along the existing Mineral King road. As public awareness developed, however, both the Park Service and Interior became actively involved. In its initial response to the Forest Service request for road approval, the Park Service raised its mandate for preservation values. "We are in sympathy with your proposal. Our only concern, and it is a vital one, is that any improvements to the . . . road . . . be accomplished in such manner as will not damage the giant Sequoia trees or other values for which the Park was established" (Hummel, 1965). Sensing Park Service concern, the Forest Service argued for closure, construing that the Park Service had relinquished review authority in this initial response (Cliff, 1967).

This attempt to short-circuit the review was further reinforced by the Forest Service contention that the project was past the review stage. The service reacted in a number of ways to those who viewed the development as if it were at a precommitment stage of deliberation. When the Park Service wrote a position paper on Mineral King during the interdepartmental fight in 1967, the Forest Service tried to have it rewritten, "not leaving any question as to whether or not Mineral King will actually be developed. . . . The possibility that your draft could be interpreted as implying that the development of Mineral King was still just a proposal was quite disturbing" (Cliff, 1967). Likewise, when partisans sought to question the project's value, the agency responded that their position "presents a distorted and misleading portrayal of this planned public recreation development. I had hoped the [Sierra] Club would consider the project more on facts and less on emotions" (Deinema, Aug. 15, 1969). The Forest Service claimed that the only logic for questioning the project as a fact was "on the basis of little information or misinformation" perpetrated by selfish political interests (Forest Service, Feb., 1969, p. 5).

When the Park Service refused to acquiesce, the struggle was elevated to the department level. Fearing that it would "be severely criticized" by environmentalists (Udall, 1967), Interior reaffirmed the Park Service intent "to make sure that those measures necessary to develop the area . . . are planned and carried out in such a way that they will not adversely affect important nearby National Park values" (Park Service, 1967). In support of this position Interior said, "The park and watershed values involved . . . are of sufficient importance to call for extreme care . . . and any decision . . . prior to full consideration of these values would be premature and ill-advised" (Luce, 1967).

This precipitated the confrontation between Udall and Freeman. In response to Udall's comment that his agency was "not trying to suggest how National Forest lands or resources should be developed and managed" (Udall, 1967), Agriculture Secretary Freeman said the facts did not bear this out: "Your department people . . . are clearly attempting to limit our activities and block National Forest development in ways that are not justified" (Freeman, 1967). The final outcome, which involved intervention by the Bureau of the Budget, resulted in unresolved issues and the elimination of possible review by the Park Service, representing a functionally different constituency. System maintenance succeeded at the expense of broad-based representation under the umbrella of welfare at large.

In addition to "we versus the enemy," a second ramification of the custodial strategy concerns the rightness of professional judgment. The monopoly authority vested in a unitary bureaucracy produces the situation where public officials must act as both advocate of a position and judge of its rightness. The professional knows best about social betterment. In the two cases of Mineral King and San Onofre, such exclusive authority had different origins but similar results.

For the AEC, Congress gave very specific pre-emptive rights to be both advocate of atomic energy and judge of nuclear safety. Even though radiation hazard involves impacts that carry significant implications for land use, the agency saw its protective role as secondary to its mandate to develop the resource. Because of the critical safety risk, many opponents were concerned over the AEC's autonomy in handling this dual role. Citing findings of AEC safety mismanagement, a Union of Concerned Scientists member asserted that " . . . agency arrogance, expert elitism and stacked-deck proceedings . . . are more the rule than the exception . . . " (Coastal Commission, Oct. 18, 1973, p. 108). Similarly, several state officials expressed anxiety over AEC's autonomy. After a conference with the atomic agency's chairman, coastal commission chairman Lane sensed that the AEC "thought they knew how to make it safe and we should trust them in doing so. . . . Frankly, I would like somebody who is sitting in a different chair to ask the hard questions that are separate from that promotional responsibility" (Coastal Commission, Dec. 5, 1973, p. 108).

For the Forest Service the logic for autonomous judgment was based on two considerations. First, the agency argued that experts provide an unbiased balancing of the public interest because they are neutral professionals augmenting the multiple-use mandate. The question of disguised values in the choice of alternatives was not real for the agency (Kaufman, 1967; McConnell, 1959). Second, the service believed that experts are coordinated by a common bureaucratic identity to efficiently administer technological complexity. Compared to the agency's collective expertise, those outside were viewed as neither qualified nor committed to achievement of a common purpose. The evidence of this logic was manifest in Secretary Freeman's support of the Forest Service when he stressed that "the collective expertise . . . in my Department is second to none. They have the experience, the know-how, and the motivation that is needed" (Freeman, 1967). Using this argument to spurn the Interior Department's bid for concurrent review, Freeman further added, "I urge you [Udall] to join me in placing your confidence in these men . . . " (Freeman, 1967).

The assumption of autonomous experts was expressed by agency behavior in a number of ways. For example, viewing its commitment to Mineral King as a "mission," the Sequoia forest supervisor stated that, "once having made the determination" to develop, little reason existed "to hesitate" (Whitfield, Feb. 15, 1965). Discounting the opportunity for external review, another forester emphasized that the agency had "the strongest moral obligation" to proceed without interference (Davis, Aug. 24, 1965). This approach confounds value questions with fact by making them implicit. In so doing, decision making in the public interest occurs by using "standards" which justify decisions "objectively." Although some Forest Service officials acknowledged conceptually the fallacy of administering values (Rupp, 1974), the persistent belief that agency professionals knew best was evident in two ways.

First, with measurability critical to objectification, those environmental considerations which were not easily quantifiable (i.e., the change in pastoral experience and the effect of mass intrusion on wilderness ecology) were not generally accounted for. Instead, Forest Service personnel resolved the issue by saying, " . . . you can be assured the Forest Service will only approve plans and administer construction activities that will cause the least impact on the aesthetics of this basin" (Davis, Sept. 20, 1965). The implicit value was that technology can be skillfully used to create the semblance of a natural condition where it no longer exists. "Our goal is to provide a needed public service . . . [and] to assure that the development can be accomplished without substantial impairment or permanent undesirable ecological impact. We are confident that these twin challenges have been faced in a creative and artistic fashion" (Forest Service, Jan. 27, 1969).

Such a contention, however, is not ascertainable in factual terms and is subject to a variety of interpretations. Juxtaposed to Forest Service confidence was the opposition belief that "we lose something with every new development, as well as gain something. . . . The quality of the environment is deteriorating because of a host of decisions to move ahead with more development, each of which can be rationalized as based on a proper individual balance between losses and gains" (McCloskey and Hill, 1971, pp. 6–7).

Second, the sense of "professionalism" pervasive in the custodial approach provides a basis for believing that experts objectively know what values "society" wants. That is, they can make the necessary interpersonal comparisons to produce appropriate public policy without involvement of partisans or other agencies. To the requests for partisan involvement the Forest Service responded, " . . . other important values are present at Mineral King. Our purpose here has been to strike a meaningful balance and to meet public need while still protecting the resource. Once having made the determination that the development of winter sports activities is desirable and a proper form of management, there seems to be little reason for the Forest Service to hesitate in its development" (Whitfield, Feb. 15, 1965). Rejecting the attempt of the Interior Department to raise questions of value, the Secretary of Agriculture reinforced the Forest Service, saying, " . . . the plan simply calls for replacing the existing, long-established, seasonal road with a standard two-lane road useable yearlong. I cannot construe this plan, or even understand it, in the terms and context of 'violation' that you use" (Freeman, 1967).

With regard to a policy stance, then, much of the reason the proposal became a controversy was due to the Forest Service's insistence on achieving cooperation around a certain set of implicit values that it was best qualified to promote and judge. To this end the San Francisco regional forester said, "We have invited the Club to consult with us constructively. . . . I am convinced such a course can do far more to attain our mutual objectives than can the Sierra Club's present 'adversary' stance . . . " (Deinema, Aug. 15, 1969). Juxtaposed to this argument, the opposition view was that, ". . . the Forest Service finds it difficult to satisfy conflicting interests, but here no conflict has been allowed to develop. . . . The real need for turning Mineral King over to skiers is open to serious question" (Bergren, 1965).

A third ramification of the custodial strategy was the manner in which public goals were subordinated to organizational autonomy. For both the Forest Service and the AEC, economic development was a crucial factor in fostering growth of agency domains and support for its legitimacy to act. Other values were treated as subservient or subversive depending on the nature of their contribution to the primary objective of organizational maintenance.

At Mineral King the agency's autonomy was partly related to its revenue-generating capacity. Consequently the economic motive, albeit couched in public welfare terms, was apparent as the primary concern. In justifying the project to the public, the service was assertive in detailing the economic benefits of retail sales, investments, expenditures, and a variety of tax revenues. Noting the existing economic stagnation of the area, one agency promotion piece stressed, "The economy of central California will be significantly improved" (Forest Service, Feb., 1969, p. 8). Behind this was the "maintenance" objective. In making the choice of Disney's proposal over Brandt's, the Forest Service listed two "swaying considerations": the size of the project and the hope that Disney would "bring in to the Government greater receipts . . . " (Cliff, Oct. 7, 1965). The service made little effort toward incorporating environmental and aesthetic considerations until the project became a public controversy of huge proportions.

In responding to the controversy, the Forest Service initially implied a fairness rule, saying, " . . . whatever the final decision regarding Mineral King may be, it will not be taken until the desires and needs of all those with an interest in the area have been most carefully considered" (Cliff, July 27, 1965). Nevertheless, agency actions suggest that little accommodation or adjustment to multiple interests was made. With regard to public scrutiny, partisan dissent was generally ignored. In response to opposition letters the agency said that " . . . in this instance the wishes of the minority must be subordinated" (Norris, 1965). On numerous occasions opponents asked to be "advised of any way in which we can be of assistance . . . " (Harper, 1965). Instead of seeking out such assistance, the agency shrouded itself in secrecy until the decision was made.

In the instance of public hearing requests, the Forest Service chief said, "We expect the Sierra Club to enter some form of protest. . . . In August, they asked for a public hearing. . . . We turned them down; but they do not give up easily" (Cliff, Oct. 7, 1965). When the agency denied requests for public hearings, the opposition argued that "all that the Sierra Club asks is that a fair procedure . . . be employed" (McCloskey, 1965). Forest Service response was that the "time for indecision in the Mineral King matter passed when the prospectus was issued" (Davis, Aug. 24, 1965).

The fact that political concern was intense seems to have been viewed by the service as irrelevant to the administrative process. Asserting that "the Mineral King area as an all-season recreation area will best serve the public interest," the agency responded to opposition letters by saying that although "[you] have strong and sincere convictions . . . there are others who just as sincerely do not agree with you" (Cliff, Nov. 12, 1965). Ultimately, public opinion came to view the project as outside the public interest. In responding to this, the San Francisco regional forester said, "We have noted some tendency to discuss the . . . development as a private facility. . . . The development is in every sense a public recreation area . . . " (Deinema, 1968).

The struggle over public goals versus organizational autonomy at San Onofre was similar to Mineral King, but involved more conflict over mandates. Most of AEC's opponents were angry over the pre-emptive rights to judge the safety issue. The basis of their contention in this case was that the coastal commission should have had concurrent jurisdiction to represent public values regarding nuclear safety. According to the act, the coastal commission is mandated "to promote the public safety, health and welfare, and to protect public and private property, wildlife, marine fisheries, and other ocean resources . . . " (Coastal Act, 1972).

Based on the "burden of proof" in demonstrating no substantial adverse effect, the question of uncertainty expressed by a variety of experts seemed to make safety a land use issue germane to coastal commission authority. Given the unknowns of ECCS reliability, earthquake considerations, nuclear waste disposal, and the outcome of a core meltdown, most citizens in surrounding communities felt they and their property were being subjected to an "experimental undertaking" of considerable risk. Emphasizing the lethal nature of radioactivity, an opposition member from San Clemente testified that "there are actually many thousands of persons too close to that plant to justify . . . its being there at all, but when they make it five times as big as it is now, we just can't see any excuse for being subjected to this kind of guinea pig arrangement . . . " (San Diego Coast Regional Commission, Aug. 10, 1973, p. 151).

One could argue, then, that safety was a land use issue dealing both with zoning questions and with irreversible damage to coastal resources. Moreover, considering safety as having an impact on land use provided a logic for an overlapping jurisdiction by the coastal agency that would not seem to violate the AEC's sole discretion over technical safety standards. The AEC held authority over procedures to assure safety (which it admitted was uncertain), while the coastal commission might be said to have held discretion over assessment of the impact of risk and uncertainty on the coastal zone.

Although the state coastal commission was not allowed to adopt this logic, many of its members and staff saw major dysfunctions arising from the AEC pre-emption rights. The state staff recommendations said, for example, that "the escape of radioactive materials at San Onofre could . . . endanger not only nearby beach users but, depending on wind conditions, the urban development, the open land, and the water of a large coastal area" (Coastal Commission, Dec., 1973, p. 2). The recommendation went on to argue that the pre-emption rights created "questions of coastal zone planning. What evacuation and emergency plans does the AEC have? How should these be integrated into coastal zone planning? . . . And should high-density residential development be encouraged in areas relatively close to San Onofre? (Coastal Commission, Dec., 1973). These land use questions were never resolved for San Onofre, and the 1979 marine review committee findings reaffirmed the unknowns (Fischer, 1979).

If the coastal commission had been granted the legal authority of reciprocal review over safety issues, the question of whether public goals would have been better represented remains open to speculation. The AEC spent considerable time in deliberating over safety and reached the conclusion that "realistic analysis" showed "that the environmental risks due to postulated radiological accidents are exceedingly small" (AEC, Mar., 1973, p. 7–5). The coast regional commission concurred:

"There is no firm evidence . . . that would lead the [regional] staff to the position of questioning the safety of the proposed development" (San Diego Coast Regional Commission, Sept. 4, 1973). Nevertheless, had the authority to judge safety been a shared responsibility, the statewide coastal agency would likely have been the arena for broader inclusion of represented interests. One indicator of this was the coastal agency's wish for the utilities to consider use of an HTGR generator, which does not pose a nuclear safety hazard. In arguing for concurrent jurisdiction over safety, Bodovitz said at the December 5 denial vote, "If in the light of the concern for energy, we turn our backs on the environment, it will be a sad day" (*San Diego Union*, Dec. 6, 1973). Chairman Lane was more categorical, saying, "I was concerned on safety. If we had a vote on safety, I would have opposed the [project]" (Lane, May 15, 1974).

The custodial strategy pursued by both the Forest Service and the AEC raises questions of accountability. Where autonomy grants the ability to act as both advocate and judge, whose values do the apolitical professional administrators reflect? What basis exists for validating the publicness of decisions? Can there be a test of representation beyond welfare at large? At San Onofre the AEC pre-empted all validity checks, and accountability did not gain its full meaning until the crisis of Three Mile Island seven years later. At Mineral King the primary reason project plans were modified was the tenacious efforts of the public opposition to halt development. Without the *cause célèbre* determination, few questions would have arisen until after the project was underway.

The Nonstrategy of Intuitionism

Using intuition about situation-specific variables does not lend itself well to the development of procedural standards and the structuring of deliberation strategies. Although commission integrity is at the base of such a decision rule, it is easily obscured by the protean process that results. At San Onofre the coastal commission was derailed by such side issues as "acceptance in Sacramento," the energy "crisis," the political careers of individual members, and the future of the commission as an organizational entity. Coastal commissioners, like all public servants, had their own unique personalities, beliefs, and value orientations. Some, of course, were motivated only by Proposition 20, but several held biases contrary to the coastal act's policy. For example, Commissioner Frautschy recognized that "it is a matter of what your values are as to whether [the project] is beneficial or detrimental" (Frautschy, 1975). He openly maintained a bias toward nuclear energy needs over competing environmental demands. Similarly, Chairman Lane expressed priority for legislative acceptance ahead of the act's requirements, saying, "I think in terms of procedures and commission's time and our ultimate acceptance in Sacramento" (Lane, May 15, 1974). In the San Onofre decision he admitted that "I voted for the project for pragmatic reasons [even though] there is no question in my mind that the project as designed was illegal under our enabling law . . . " (Lane, Jan. 4, 1974). As chairman, Lane also tended to show an impatience with environmentalists which was not displayed toward the utilities.

Some public officials are uniquely qualified to use intuition as a basis for decision consistency, but intuitionist assumptions of impartiality and stewardship are rarely attainable for the structure of commission decision making as a whole. A commission can give the deliberation process public visibility and participation, but the integrity of intuition for a panel of judges does not necessarily improve impartial representation.

This logic seems to account in part for the commission's public images of irrational behavior during the San Onofre deliberations. Nowhere was this nonstrategy more evident than during the state commission's postdecision interlude that culminated in the February 20 "redecision." Although the press referred to the approval conditions as "the strictest levied by any state agency on a nuclear power plant built in this country" (*Los Angeles Times*, Feb. 21, 1974), the process by which the final decision was reached was seen by many observers as arbitrary and incoherent. Three aspects, in particular, generated skepticism.

First, use of the safety issue as a "gimmick" to short-circuit re-evaluation by the regional commission had the appearance of violating due process. During the proceedings all parties including the utilities saw discussion of safety matters as legal and "entirely appropriate" to keep the commission informed (Coastal Commission, Oct. 18, 1973, p. 23). With regard to the voting requirement and the AEC's exclusive jurisdiction, the commission's extended discussion on safety jurisdiction moments before the December 5 vote indicated thorough awareness of the limits. Reflecting on the original decision, Chairman Lane asserted that "safety was not a consideration that we could include in our determination, and . . . none of us did" (Coastal Commission, Feb. 20, 1974, p. 4).

Second, although the ostensible reason for revoting was legality, the underlying motive appeared to be the overshadowing pressures of emotionalism. Contrary to the *Federalist* belief that government should act as "an anchor against popular fluctuations" (Hamilton, Madison, and Jay, 1961, p. 385), the commission gained a special sensitivity toward corporate interests and the energy "crisis" during the aftermath of its first decision. Cornered by the utilities' successful statewide lobbying effort and the public's fear of energy scarcity, the commission followed a line of least resistance. According to Lane, the decision "came at a bad time. . . . It hit right when the gas lines were longest. . . . So, I knew it was going to put us in dutch with Sacramento for meddling in their problems . . . " (Lane, May 15, 1974).

Third, the conditions worked out for the revote appeared to involve few concessions by the utilities. Indeed, utility spokesmen even referred to them as "environmental window-dressing" and "cosmetic alterations." Concerned over the image of a "sellout," Commissioner Laufer said, "The staff has acted nobly but what has Edison brought to the compromise table?" (Bodovitz, Jan. 9, 1974b, p. 4). The image of private deals was further accentuated by the closed-door sessions with utility executives. With claims of denying due process, environmentalist counsel Sutherland asserted strong objections to the secret meetings: "We were given no chance to be involved in those meetings, but instead . . . were presented with a fait accompli. . . . The question now becomes one of integrity of your Commission. . . . You have only to read the two staff recommendations that have been prepared to see how much has been sold for so little" (Coastal Commission, Feb. 20, 1974, pp. 14–15). Two months after the San Onofre revote the commission imposed a sanction against future secret or private meetings (*Los Angeles Times*, Apr. 18, 1974).

Public accountability was just as much at question here as it was for the custodial strategy of welfare at large.

The Management of Conflict Strategy

Fairness as a decision rule connotes the need for due process in deliberations. As a strategy, this means that where conflict arises between affected parties, the role of administration is to create an institutional process that can resolve the conflict in a way that broadens representation and spreads net benefits widely. The management of conflict allows partisans to mutually forge decisions through their representative agencies. Administrative units have advocative roles, but the judgment of rightness is a function of network integration through mutual adjustment.

At Nettleton Lakes the network of state and local agencies seemed to be motivated toward the management of conflict strategy. All agencies pursued advocative roles but were conscious that their individual decisions needed to mesh with others. Kitsap County, which probably had the most comprehensive discretion over project approvals, was reluctant to assert unilateral powers and made its decisions contingent on those of other jurisdictions. Public officials in all agencies seemed to want the public to see them as part of a larger intergovernmental network and to judge the legitimacy of their acts in that context. This relationship of administrative structure to fair deliberations was expressed by one state official who observed at the *beginning* of the controversy that "better techniques must be developed for evaluating all potential uses and combinations of uses for a given area in terms of their optimum long run social as well as economic benefits, including esthetic and recreational values" (Biggs, 1970).

The interest groups' view of legitimacy, however, was quite different. Accepting administrative units as separate and autonomous hierarchies of discretion, their expectations ran high for agencies to act apolitically and professionally. For example, many viewed Kitsap County in a balancing-of-interest role requiring impartial judgment. In requesting impartiality and openness, HCEC said, "Whether this particular applicant should be permitted to appropriate public resources for private use and profit, affect adjacent property values and real property taxes, and plan a potential city in this area valuable for its natural attributes, are questions which cast the county commissioners in the role of adjudicating between various public and private interests" (Best, Oct. 23, 1970).

Professionalism, however, seemed not to be the major influence securing the outcome that resulted. Indeed, a number of actions particularly at the county level raised public skepticism over the question of impartial custodial judgment. The county sanitation director's interests as a real estate salesman appeared to be the central motive for his public recommendation for septic tanks over central sewerage. Asserting that "experts know best," the director chastised an HCEC member with an M.D. and a public health background: "For amateurs to review reports by engineers and geologists and arrive at conclusions on details best left to engineers and sanitarians, is . . . wrong" (Weigel, 1970).

At the county Planning Commission and County Commission levels, similar bias was evident. In the Planning Commission the three members most concerned about adverse effects were from districts around the project site. One of those three maintained that "we should have the guts to say we don't want it out here. We represent the people and the people in that area were up in arms" (Eder, 1971). When selecting a time to vote on the proposal, a coalition of pro-development members chose a date when two of these three members had to be absent (Eder, 1971). In the County Commission all favored development, but prior to deliberation one of the three was known to be "gun-ho in favor" (Eder, 1971). Arguing that ". . . technology has stood us in good stead" and will solve all problems of adverse effect (Lobe, Randall, and Mahan, 1971), he took the role of promoting project approval. When HCEC requested that "Commissioner Frank Randall disqualify himself as having openly and publicly made statements evidencing a bias . . ." (Best, Oct. 23, 1970), the commission unanimously voted to deny the request.

Since local governments have traditional roots in territorial authority, the implied geographical limits on representation tend to skew public policy in favor of the most powerful *local* constituents, usually developers. Moreover, the bias toward economic interests is reinforced in part by the fact that most local public revenues in the United States are derived from local property and economic activity. As ordinary people with private beliefs and material desires, most public officials are no less susceptible to these influences than nonprofessionals. The Nettleton case illustrates how administrative "wisdom" and "objectivity" are conditioned by personal self-interest. Hence the expectation of "professionalism" may have been both unattainable and inappropriate in this complex land use controversy where accepted judgmental standards were absent. Moreover, as long as overlapping jurisdictions exist, can one really argue that local government is an inappropriate point in the system to stress representation of economic interests? Would a higher central authority, such as a state land use agency, have eliminated bias or only fostered it or other unitary values on a different level?

With this demonstrated agency bias, evidence in the case suggests that the public decisions showed an unusual amount of accommodation for opposing interests. Boise was allowed to develop the project, but only so long as certain adverse impacts were mitigated. In lieu of the professional custodial strategy as the basis for administering public values, one could argue that mutual adjustment was a major influence in fostering the broader inclusion of interests. The separation of advocacy roles from exclusive judgment via reciprocal review seemed to provide an acceptable process of conflict management where issues were satisfactorily resolved without a central authority or dominant public value. Judgments, in effect, were made in the network through mutual awareness of different agency opinions. While it was impossible for the county *acting alone* to establish and implement appropriate policy affecting regional or statewide matters, it did demonstrate a sensitivity toward its responsibilities within a larger intergovernmental system. According to Pitell of COHOE, the county was "cocking one ear" toward the state agencies during the review process (Pitell, 1971). The state agencies seemed to be doing the same.

Role of NEPA and the Courts

In the three cases the bulk of decision making was done through the administrative process. For the most part, representation of public interests was a function of organizational units mandated to make policy. Two exceptions to this circumstance intervened to differentiate the cases from each other.

First was the impact of the National Environmental Policy Act. When NEPA became law in 1970, many were optimistic that the required environmental impact statement would erode bureaucratic autonomy and open the decision process to review. As interpreted by the courts, however, the requirement only necessitated that an agency consider comprehensive impacts and alternatives, and did not provide administrative review capabilities for more objective study (Ferguson and Bryson, 1972, pp. 512, 518). As a result, the impact statement has frequently been used by a custodial authority in lieu of concurrent review and public participation.

The instrument encourages the soliciting of advisory data from other agencies and the public, but reserves the right of interpretation and decision to the individual agency initiating it. Because interpretation remains with the lead agency, many "agencies have found a way to comply with the letter of the Act, not its spirit" (Anderson, 1974, p. 411). While procedural compliance has shown improvement, a sufficient environmental perspective may or may not be present. "[A]gency decision making often appears to precede environmental impact analysis, which then becomes an after-the-fact rationalization" (Anderson, 1974, p. 411). In the end, an EIS may only serve to reinforce the already closed bureaucratic process.

At Mineral King the impact statement appears to have been used to retain and reinforce autonomy. The Forest Service stressed that although it was the lead agency, the effort represented the cooperation and consensus of a variety of state and federal agencies with its position (Forest Service, Dec., 1974). Likewise, when the service announced major modifications to the proposal in 1975, it used the impact statement to avoid public participation: "We plan no public hearings on the modified project as we believe the revised plan is responsive to the public comments received from review of the Draft Environmental Statement" (Wychoff, 1975).

At San Onofre the AEC created a similar aura of interagency consensus around its position. It used the EIS to mute contrary positions, then concluded that information showed no significant risk to people or the environment. Concentrating on why opposing views were inappropriate, the EIS became a substitute for open public debate and mutual adjustment with other agencies. The coastal commission, by contrast, developed an impact assessment which attempted to reveal the inadequacy of data and encourage the search for alternatives to the utilities' proposal. Because of the AEC's pre-emptive rights, the contrary findings of the two agencies were never resolved, and NEPA seemed only to aid the AEC's closure effort.

At Nettleton Lakes deliberations were completed without the use of NEPA or its state equivalent. Without any uniform or comprehensive requirements for environmental impact assessment, this case reveals a process by which information was probably more completely acquired and more widely assessed than in the other two cases. Representation of diverse interests seemed to have been served by the administrative arrangement, not a specialized procedural requirement.

The second intervening factor was involvement of the courts. The only court test of significance was that over Mineral King. The San Onofre suit was vacated without merit, and no suit was filed at Nettleton. At Mineral King the opposition led by the Sierra Club sought relief in the federal courts, believing the judicial system would provide "an opportunity for a hearing before an impartial tribunal" (McCloskey, 1969).

In instituting the suit, the opposition was assuming that through *legal* considerations the court could judiciously evaluate fact and value and arrive at a superior decision to that of the administrative review process. However, since court capabilities are supposed to be limited to review of agency action and not decision content, the administrative function is not well served by the judicial system. The courts gain jurisdiction over areas where an agency exceeds statutory limitations or violates due process. In the case of land use, where most agencies have been granted broad discretion by law (i.e., as in multiple-use management), the courts may have little basis for intervention. If the agency meets its minimum requirement, as most do, the usefulness of court action is minimal. Moreover, defining administrative law more specifically would not only restrict the agency's ability to adapt to change and respond to public need but also would seldom provide for the objective consideration of values.

While legal judgments clearly affect the formation and implementation of administrative policy, the trial court specifically noted its limitations in this case: "This court is not concerned with the controversy between so-called progressives and so-called conservationists. Our only function is to make sure that administrative action, even when taken in the name of progress, conforms to the letter and intent of the law as laid down by Congress . . ." (*Sierra Club v. Hickel*, 1969). The inadequacy of judicial review, then, lay in the fact that the court did not have the power to fashion a compromise suitable to both the Forest Service and its opposition. The political questions dealing with trade-offs and mutual adjustment are beyond the scope of jurisprudence (Krislov, 1965; Ferguson and Bryson, 1972). At Mineral King the court's decision granted one litigant's policy position over the other, but no evaluation of appropriateness was made. Active intervention by the courts created no superior outcome to the administrative process.

On the other hand, if the influence of judicial proceedings *indirectly* encourages administrators to be more conscious of representing multiple interests, this latent function may greatly advance due process.

"[T]here can be no escape from the legal requirement of 'due process' in regulatory proceedings . . . and if 'due process' is not afforded, reversal in the Supreme Court is an imminent possibility" (Morrissey, 1972). At San Onofre this awareness of the court's role in the administrative process was apparent. For example, in a discussion over procedure Commissioner Wilson argued that ". . . if there is lack of fairness, or for some reason an appellant does not feel the Commission acted wisely, it can use the Courts" (Bodovitz, Jan. 9, 1974b, p. 5). This latent authority thus seemed to have encouraged administrators to represent interests more widely.

CHAPTER 8

Experts and the Use of Information

IN ADDITION to the question of political representation, appropriate use of information is also a major concern of land use decision making. All of the cases represent rather complex and dynamic environmental settings, which generated substantial knowledge gaps and highly uncertain quality of data. Insufficient information is a problem under such circumstances because it contributes to miscalculation and raises the risk of oversight. The result is that project proposals, when tranformed into marketable goods and services, may produce substantial external effects.

External effects are misallocations of resources. When they take the form of *undesirable* effects imposed on individuals outside the contract of sale, they are borne as external costs. In this sense some individuals involuntarily subsidize the purchase of others who acquire the resources at less than full cost. Hence allocation is distorted in favor of those producers creating the misallocation, making it possible in land use to have too much commercial development and too little natural open space.

Correcting or preventing the market malfunction may require a public sector review process that provides sufficient expertise to perceive and assess a wide variety of potential problems. In this regard, predominant patterns of administration appear to be important factors in understanding how and why data are collected, analyzed, and interpreted in public review. Appropriate discretion, professional integrity, and coordination of expertise are for the most part a function of structural considerations. In associating the significance of structure to variances in professional behavior, the three cases demonstrate considerable differences in the meaning and limits of expertise and the approach to information, planning, and market intervention.

At Mineral King the Forest Service emphasized a cadre of apolitical generalists and cultivated a bureaucratic expertise through job rotation. The organization's approach to planning was toward a comprehensive process which seemed to supersede the market rather than offset its adverse effects. By contrast, the San Onofre case revolved around a sequence of agencies with specialized knowledge and limited discretionary mandates. Although tainted by circumstances surrounding the "redecision," the coastal commission appeared to be much more open and facilitative than the Forest Service. Recognition of overlapping jurisdictions was evident, and contributions of knowledge from other agencies and partisans were actively solicited and considered. Moreover, in regard to planning, the coastal commission adopted an incremental approach that augmented continuous public involvement and provided for adjustment around coastal intricacies and variations. At Nettleton the lack of a single source of expertise was even more pronounced. With numerous uncertainties and the absence of clear judgmental standards, the multi-agency network seemed to recognize data as tenuous and in need of recurring review. Considerable interagency collaboration resulted to develop information and reach mutually compatible solutions. Adequacy of data was hotly contested at times, but no single set of professional predilections or expert opinions was able to predominate overall.

The impact of structure on professional behavior and expertise can be seen in the differential levels of learning and the quality of innovations that emerged in each case. The evidence suggests that where a large bureaucracy holds nearly-exclusive jurisdiction, learning, adaptation, and innovation are reduced. At Mineral King the closed deliberations reinforced a "one best way" approach that generated much engineering feasibility data but little of an investigatory nature. Moreover, the offering of new alternatives and methods by partisans and other agencies was discounted as unrealistic. Substantially all changes which were made came as a result of the project opponents' tenacity in posing the case as a *cause celebre*. By contrast, more developmental learning and innovative proposals seem to have been evident at San Onofre and Nettleton Lakes.

The purpose of this chapter is to examine these conclusions in detail. Analytical focus will be on (1) bureaucratic use of information and the "one best way," and (2) the functional aspects of conflict among experts in assessing factual materials. Those questions in Chapter 1 concerning experts and the use of information (p. 16) are used to frame the analysis.

The Bureaucratic "One Best Way"

Through the hierarchy of control, the bureaucratic pattern promotes consensus on policy and operational procedures. To achieve such unity in perception and behavior, the symbol of welfare at large provides a context through which specific issues can be organized into clear and uncontentious images. Like the representation of public values, determinations of fact are viewed as the exclusive domain of organized experts, not that of conflicting advocates. For both the Forest Service and the AEC, the approach to research and evaluation tended to generate a "one best way." This is seen in the manner information and technology were used to make and implement policy.

Use of Information

Not conditioned by a system of shared powers, the unitary bureaucracy frequently becomes "locked in" to the rightness of its position and is unable to perceive potential trade-offs and dysfunctions. As the difference between its perception and that of "outsiders" widens, the single agency tends to separate and isolate itself from other agencies and the public. Sometimes viewed as in a defensive posture, it adopts strategies that protect a closed and synoptic decision process. Information gathering and interpretation are *post hoc* and used to justify established positions. Open investigation of benefits and trade-offs is reduced in favor of studies of technical feasibility.

At Mineral King the Forest Service pursued three methods that promoted its advocacy stance. First, collecting information on the proposal consisted mostly of after-the-fact studies that failed to address the question of "should?" or establish an open assessment of social trade-offs and impacts on ecological dynamics. Stressing its and Disney's research capabilities and the expenditure of $500,000 for research (Forest Service, Feb., 1969, p. 6), the agency said, "The resulting decision was based on exhaustive studies and planning" (Cliff, Nov. 12, 1965). These efforts, however, were channeled primarily into the determination of financial and engineering feasibility, master planning, and studies that would justify its position in the controversy. Contrary views within the agency were suppressed. For example, having no visible effect, the agency's regional range and wildlife section responded to the Disney proposal by saying it was "superficial," "sketchy," and "unacceptable": "The total basic concept of development appears badly biased in orientation toward a highly artificial, continued situation, without any real attention to ecological factors and needs to multiple use management" (Hall, 1967). The only period of open deliberation began and ended in 1947.

This was in contrast to persistent requests by the Park Service and partisan opposition for uncommitted studies that would not have a preconceived and self-confirming bias toward development. Implying the ability of multiple agencies to reach an innovative outcome, the Park Service argued that the combined research capability of several agencies rather than one was more likely to produce a "solution that will yield maximum future public and resource conservation benefits" (Holum, 1967). Rejecting this offer of collaborative planning, the Agriculture Secretary said, " . . . Mineral King is not the time or place [for] pioneering new methods" (Freeman, 1967).

Second, the Forest Service relied almost entirely on its structure of expertise as the discretionary source of knowledge. This left little avenue for review and resulted in a variety of decision discrepancies. In the case of interpretation, no method existed for validating agency assumptions and opinions of fact. For example, the opposition raised the question of whether the area could "accomodate the intensities of usage . . . without undue damage to the natural ecology . . . " (McCloskey, 1965). Contrary to other agencies' beliefs, the service answered: "We are confident that a Mineral King development will be compatible with ecologic values" (Davis, Aug. 24, 1965). In another instance the opposition questioned the project's compatibility with the valley's game refuge status. Agency response was that the "development . . . will not substantially conflict with the purposes for which the . . . Refuge was established" (Forest Service, 1974, p. 3). Likewise, when Park Service and highway department studies showed the possibility of destroying sequoia groves, the Forest Service responded categorically that the road would be constructed "without threat or damage to any Sequoia trees" (Forest Service, Jan. 27, 1969). With regard to avalanche and slide dangers, the service said, " . . . all situations of substantial geologic hazards which cannot be mitigated by design solutions will be avoided" (Forest Service, 1974, p. 129). No method, however, was operative within the single authority to determine the validity of these contentions. Although the Interior Department and other potential review agencies argued to the contrary (Udall, 1967), Forest Service experts felt they knew best and assured others that "semi-wilderness values can be retained while still providing basic outdoor recreation facilities . . . " (Davis, Sept. 20, 1965).

In the case of planning estimates, no significant procedure was evident for mitigating errors. Among the larger errors that resulted was the estimate for road costs. In 1965 the Forest Service estimated costs of $5 million. When other sources including a state senator set the figure at $25 million (Knight, 1965), the service responded that "road cost estimates made in recent years have never approached . . . $25 million to our knowledge. . . . Most run in the range of $5-$7 million" (Davis, Apr. 1, 1965). When the actual figure turned out to be nearly five times the Forest Service estimate, the agency explained, "We were using 1953 cost figures" (quoted in Hano, 1969, p. 66). In addition, a variety of other errors were revealed to which the Forest Service eventually acceded, including road impact and safety (Hartesveldt, 1966; Clarkson Engineering Co., 1967), the method of calculating ski demand (McCloskey, 1975, p. 13), and avalanche hazard (Brandt, Dec. 12, 1965; McCloskey, 1975). Further, the Forest Service attributed its 1975 project modification, which removed the project from the valley, to the large amount of "insufficient information" (Forest Service, 1975).

The third supporting method of the advocacy stance involved public relations. The service took it upon itself to be the major promoter of development. As far back as 1949 it sought publicity through the news media, ski associations, and chambers of commerce, saying, "We are anxious to get publicity on the deal . . . " (Gibson, 1949). The information supplied to the public, however, provided severely biased images that frequently appeared to be contrived and deceptive. Contrivances involved the organization of information in such a way that the uninformed reader would be left with no doubts that the agency position was correct. For example, in calculating the project's economic impact, the agency provided a series of data that included only the most favorable potential benefits (Forest Service, Feb., 1969). The cost side of the equation, which included the need for higher public service levels and large property tax increases in the "gateway" vicinity, was excluded until required by the environmental impact statement.

With regard to deceptions, a number of examples were apparent. First, the Forest Service attempted to make the project appear to the public as the result of continuous professional deliberation for two decades. In 1965, for example, the service chief wrote, "This development has been foremost in Forest Service planning since 1949 . . . " (Cliff, Oct. 29, 1965). Yet in 1959, when pressures for development were in a lull, the Washington office wrote a potential developer that " . . . there has been little if any discussion or consideration of the proposals since about 1953" (Sieker, 1959).

Second, the agency attempted to create the image that it had the developed expertise to control Disney and project impacts. In a 1969 promotional piece the agency rhetorically asked, *"Is the Forest Service Qualified to Make Such a Decision? Yes. Is this a Forest Service First? No."* (Forest Service, Feb., 1969, p. 9). Yet in an internal memorandum to Secretary Freeman the chief declared, "We lack a basis to challenge the Disney estimates of use. They are beyond Forest Service experience, as is his proposed development" (Cliff, Oct. 7, 1965).

Third, the service tried to tell the public that the area did not qualify for statutory wilderness: "It is not a wilderness — it would never meet Congressionally established wilderness standards" (Forest Service, Feb., 1969, p. 9). Yet, excluding the sparse cottage settlement at the valley entrance, one forester's internal memo said, " . . . the remaining roadless country there . . . certainly does [qualify] . . . " (Norris, 1965). The Forest Service later admitted that wilderness status was not considered because the agency believed the area had "higher value when allocated to intensive recreation" (Forest Service, 1974, p. 98).

Fourth, the service tried to mute partisan opposition by saying to the

public that the 1953 meeting sponsored by the Chamber of Commerce
to expedite development was an official public hearing and that "the
record of this hearing . . . discloses no opposition" (Connaughton,
1965). Although never admitting the private status of the "public hearing," the agency did finally modify its argument in the environmental
impact statement, conceding that "some opposition was voiced" (Forest
Service, 1974, p. 231).

Finally, with regard to interagency participation with the Park Service and Interior Department, the Forest Service told the public that
"initially, the Secretary of the Interior was dubious over the proposal . . . [but] in December 1967 he agreed to permit the road to be
built. . . . Substantial agreement has been reached" (Forest Service,
Feb., 1969, pp. 5–6). Actually the Bureau of the Budget had intervened
for the Forest Service, and Interior Secretary Udall refused to support
the unilateral decision.

All of these factors and others led the public and many of its representatives to be concerned about the apparent deceptions. Believing
they had come primarily from Disney, Congressman Waldie of California said that "as the administering agency for Mineral King, you have a
responsibility to prevent Disney Corporation from misleading the
public . . . " (Waldie, 1972). Apparently not recognizing the implications, the Forest Service responded: "Since the proposal complies with
conditions established by the Forest Service, there should be no inference that the Disney Corporation is attempting to mislead the
public . . . " (Leisz, 1972).

In actuality, the decision to develop Mineral King was handled
almost as a reflex reaction to ski promotion pressures. Although the Forest Service argued that "our decision to develop Mineral King was not a
spur-of-the-moment action" (Cliff, 1967), evidence shows the 1947
decision was made without much deliberation over its appropriateness.
The agency was "anxious to implement the development . . . "
(Sieker, 1948), and the only real question addressed was "how?" (Barnum, 1947). As this arbitrary decision became a public commitment in
1949, it formed the basis on which the Forest Service stood without reconsideration for the next twenty-five years. By issuing the second prospectus in 1965, the Forest Service reaffirmed its original 1947 decision
" . . . that Mineral King should be developed for recreation by private
enterprise. We now have the strongest moral obligation to accept the
best proposal that meets or exceeds our specifications" (Davis, Aug. 24,
1965).

In the case of AEC's use of information at San Onofre, similar behavior was evident. The agency went to great lengths to assure its autonomy
over nuclear power siting by ignoring a number of non-AEC experts on
critical issues and by persuading others that its EIS was the most objec-

tive and factual accumulation of information available on the project. In fact, much information from opposition experts did not surface until the coastal agency reviews. This was especially evident in the question of energy need. The AEC had made no attempt to seek out alternative methods to SCE's trendline approach to future projections and said only that its EIS "examined the need for power . . . [and] the staff concluded that the need for San Onofre Units 2 and 3 in the 1978–1979 time period was confirmed" (AEC, Mar., 1973, pp. 14–24). Arguing against opposition contentions, the AEC not only erred in using the wrong time period for San Onofre's on-line supply but also overlooked substantial studies such as the Rand Corporation reports, which estimated much lower demand projections. The Rand reports found major oversights in the utilities' trendline methodology caused by discounting such factors as market adaptability in dampening future demand (Doctor, 1973). The Rand studies used a methodology which included variables for market dynamics and concluded that sufficient generating capacity without Units Two and Three would be available through 1990. The years after 1973 have shown the Rand projections to be considerably more accurate than those accepted by the AEC.

Use of Technology

Exclusive jurisdiction reduces mutual adjustment with other agencies and in turn eliminates a source of limits or boundaries on behavior and policy. For professional experts this sometimes leads to an unlimited use of technology and the sense that large-scale intensive development is the best avenue for progress. As a source of reinforcement for the economic motive as well as pursuing welfare at large, the Forest Service argued that "there is now a far greater demand for recreation developments that can serve great numbers of people" (Davis, Oct. 26, 1965). Mineral King was selected because it "is the only remaining area where high quality, large scale winter sports opportunities can be provided . . . to Southern California" (Forest Service, 1974, p. 21). Even though the Forest Service recognized the area's "definitely limited carrying capacity" (Gibson, 1945), the agency maintained that alternatives were "in minor league compared to Mineral King. The public is entitled to the best available area" (Davis, Aug. 24, 1965, p. 14). The choice was in the general welfare because "in practical terms maximum benefit means the largest number of visitors to Mineral King . . . " (McArdle, 1953).

Disney was selected because the firm offered "a larger investment" (Cliff, Oct. 7, 1965), which represented half of all capital expenditures made for improvement on all public forestlands up to that time (U.S. Department of Justice, 1971, p. 14). In turn, Disney compared its investment at Mineral King with the Johnson administration's urgent mandate to spend $350 million in the ensuing decade for new recreation facilities on federal lands. Using the $35 million figure from the Mineral King proposal, the firm noted that "this amount represents 10 percent of the entire investment projected by President Johnson in 1967 . . . " (Tatum, 1968).

Beyond the question of project size, the unitary approach when tied to welfare at large seemed to promote a logic for unlimited development. Disney, for example, argued that "if we fail to develop selected areas, such as Mineral King, the 50 million people who will be in California before the end of this century will spill over . . . and ravage the Sierra with unplanned and undirected enthusiasm . . . " (Hicks, Jan., 1969). Encouraging this viewpoint and the value of technology in preserving the Mineral King area, the Forest Service further claimed that "if a better road is not built to Mineral King it will still be only a matter of years before the existing road would be heavy with cars and the basin crowded with people looking for the same serenity you have enjoyed in the past" (Davis, Sept. 20, 1965). Both Disney and the Forest Service agreed, therefore, that the Mineral King master plan would be "flexible" to accommodate added features such as a golf course, a small valley lake, and enlarged commercial facilities.

Noting Disney's intention that the project "won't ever be finished" (Walt Disney Productions, 1967), opponents argued further that master plan figures contained a number of discrepancies which suggested a concealed commitment to expand both the road and project facilities well beyond those proposed. Given the initial ski facility investment in twenty-two ski lifts, the opposition pointed to a gross underinvestment in overnight accommodations and access facilities. Discounting the possibility that large numbers would want to commute from the nonalpine "gateway" area, they drew the conclusion that such a bottleneck would be used later by the Forest Service to justify unlimited future development to access the slopes. The Park Service–commissioned study supported the likelihood of this conclusion as well (Clarkson Engineering Co., 1967, p. 17).

The idea of unlimited development places heavy reliance on technology and its ability to unobtrusively transform natural surroundings. The promise of technology is appealing because it can provide the means for enlarging the ecological carrying capacity of an area. However, if technology is not used in conjunction with nature's dynamic equilibrium, it may destroy environmental elements in the long run. Progressive logic for managing resources assumes that boundless mastery of resource utilization is possible if experts are left to apply technology without external restraint. The Forest Service seemed to have held this position, knowing the potential environmental consequences.

Although Disney argued that "we will prove once again that man and nature can work together to the benefit of both" (Walt Disney Produc-

tions, 1967), the construction requirements indicated a different conclusion. To accomplish the envisioned feat, technological necessity
called for a number of alterations including (1) extensive blasting and
bulldozing away rock formations and forested areas to accommodate ski
runs and the village; (2) "extensive grooming and manicuring" of most
slopes; (3) culverting Monarch Creek and the Kaweah River to minimize flooding at the village; (4) modifying terrain to prevent natural
debris problems; (5) constructing maintenance roads in the valley and
up the slopes; and (6) constructing the various facilities to accommodate
large crowds (Forest Service, 1974; Walt Disney Productions, 1965).
With respect to project trade-offs, the questions that were not addressed
had to do with compatibility with carrying capacity and environmental
character. Was the development misplaced? What mitigating factors
would prevent substantial ecological impairment? The service left the
Mineral King proposal incomplete and unsupported, asserting that the
organization exercised "far greater control over plan implementation
actions" than other agencies (Walters, 1974).

In 1945, before the commitment to develop was made, a preliminary
agency survey of the area concluded that "it is probable that any considerable increase in use would tend to destroy the peculiar values that
make Mineral King an attractive summer recreation spot" (Gibson,
1945). In 1969, however, the service approved the immense Disney
project, saying that "there will be no development at Mineral King
beyond, or out of harmony with, the natural ecological limits of the undeveloped valley . . . " (Forest Service, Feb., 1969, p. 10). To accomplish this degree of compatibility, one forester stressed that " . . .
ultimate development will be guided by aesthetic and ecological limitations, rather than market potential. The Disney master plan has been
designed with this consideration uppermost" (Forest Service, Jan. 27,
1969).

Nevertheless, confidence in the project's unobtrusive compatibility
was due less to environmental considerations and more to the desire for
commercial advantages accruable to welfare at large. For example, the
project was approved with agency *expectations* that (1) the summer
wildlife range (especially for deer) would be consumed by project facilities; (2) the "near-pristine" water of lakes and streams would likely
become contaminated with sedimentation, bacterial content, and other
organic matter; and (3) vegetation in the game refuge would be notice-
ably affected (Forest Service, 1974).

The questionable level of compatibility was also reflected by a
number of commercialized features which included (1) Disneyland-
type hay rides; (2) square and folk dancing areas; (3) an artificial "old
swimming hole"; (4) the potential for a valley golf course; (5) five-story
hotels that would give the "illusion of smallness"; (6) a theater, specialty

shops, and chapel; (7) a road to accommodate the arrival and departure of a car every six seconds at peak; and (8) promotion to encourage festivals and conventions (Walt Disney Productions, 1969).

In short, the level of compatibility apparently was established as an accepted fact in favor of development under a "one best way" approach. Ignoring the alternative views and favoring technological sophistication, the Forest Service was satisfied that compatibility would be accomplished because the project would "enable many more people to visit Mineral King and enjoy it in its somewhat man-modified state . . ." (Forest Service, 1974, p. 211).

Reciprocal Review and Innovation

The use of multiple agencies in a network of reciprocal review serves not only to adjudicate competing partisan values but also to more adequately decipher complex and often misleading factual information about social, economic, and political impacts. Because of data ambiguity and the complex interrelationships in ecological systems, most information on problems is presented in qualitative form. Having different collectives of expertise, then, provides a way to break large blocks of data into smaller and more manageable subparts for discrete analysis. The resulting variances in expert interpretation form a necessary incentive to think more broadly about validity of information and ways of dealing with the uncertainty of adverse impacts. Although such scrutiny of information may be more costly in time and money, the benefits of concurrent review have to do with mitigating error and oversight through learning and innovation. Each of the cases contained situations where the benefits of multiple review could be seen.

Mineral King

The Forest Service's exclusive authority greatly limited reciprocal review. Nevertheless, even with such mandated dominance, interagency reviews did occur with some marginal success. The Park Service, of course, was the most visible and, through its contentiousness over road approval, exposed Forest Service desires to avoid open review. When Interior Secretary Udall urged the formation of a "special study committee," Secretary Freeman responded that "this is out of the question. There have been studies aplenty in this case. . . . This Administration . . . is committed to development of Mineral King. . . . The project is needed, wanted, and feasible now" (Freeman, 1967).

Not satisfied with this, the Park Service went on to commission its own study of road impacts. Making a variety of structural engineering and soil tests, the study concluded that road cuts along the steeply sloping Kaweah Gorge would impair the ecology and natural aesthetics in this area of the park (Clarkson Engineering Co., 1967). In addition, the study (1) asserted that the proposed highway failed to conform to the latest engineering standards for environmental protection, (2) challenged highway department and Disney estimates of the new road capacity, (3) suggested that the Mineral King facility use public transportation over the road (an alternative which had not been considered), and (4) recommended modification *only* of the existing road "to preserve the Sequoias . . . [and] reduce the ultimate scar and disruption of plant life" (Clarkson Engineering Co., 1967, p. 7). In reporting these findings to the Forest Service, the Park Service suggested that the study's "recommendations on the use of additional bridges, tunnels, viaducts, cribbing, retaining walls and other methods be fully exploited" in the road design (Hummel, 1968).

Besides Park Service actions, another source of potential review was the California Division of Highways. Holding authority to finance and construct the new road, this agency did recommend route approval, but not without a process that raised some concern. First, the department engineer contended that construction of the road would come at the expense of other, more needed routes and suggested that funding the new access would be "very disruptive to previously approved planning and scheduling of projects in the Southern Counties Group" (Womack, 1968).

Second, because of public concern, the department reluctantly commissioned an independent study of the road's probable impact on parklands (Hartesveldt, 1966). The study concluded that because of extensive cuts on sloping terrain, drainage and erosion problems, and proximity of the road to small groves of giant sequoia, a substantial risk existed for environmental damage in the Kaweah Gorge. According to the study, the proposed road would threaten "one of the most unique communities of plants . . . in association with sequoias . . . [which is] of great beauty and scientific interest" (Hartesveldt, 1966, pp. 5–6). Although generally ignored in deliberations, this study and the highway engineer's concern over fiscal propriety served as useful stimulants for re-evaluation later on.

Indeed, these inputs and others did ultimately leave their marks on the Mineral King decision process, as a number of subsequent project modifications bore out. First, after continuous urging by the Park Service to consider the feasibility of less environmentally detrimental transportation systems, the Forest Service and the California highway department deleted the road across parklands. Despite its original claim that alternatives were not economically feasible, the Forest Service substituted a cog-assist railway in 1972. The change was attributed to delays caused by litigation (Davis, 1973), but the agency also indicated that "reconstructing the present road to an all-weather standard would be excessively destructive to the environment" (Davis, 1972).

Second, at the urging of a variety of groups and the Park Service, the overall sizes of the road and project were continuously scaled down between 1965 and 1978. In 1975 all proposed facilities were removed from the valley, the number of ski lifts was halved, and peak volume was reduced from 10,000 per day to 5,000 (Forest Service, 1975). In 1978 the village and reception complexes were moved two miles back from the valley at Silver City and ski facilities were further reduced.

Third, the two studies produced by Park Service and highway department consultants were instrumental in ultimately causing re-evaluation of road impacts on the Kaweah drainage ecology (California Division of Highways, 1967, p. 10).

These innovations and checks on information uncertainty, however, should not be overemphasized. The questions of whether the project should be constructed at Mineral King and the trade-offs of development were never explored enough to provide a means for negotiated solutions. Instead, an indirect relationship existed between expressed concerns of the public and other agencies on the one hand and reactionary interpretation and adjustment by the Forest Service on the other. The decision process, therefore, rested primarily on a *de facto* ability of the Forest Service to learn and adjust on its own. In the end, most issues remained unresolved, the proposed project was left without its developer, and jurisdiction over the valley passed to the Park Service.

San Onofre

Like the Forest Service at Mineral King, the exclusive authority of the AEC to some extent overshadowed attempts at reciprocal review. Nevertheless, with the coastal commission's vigorous efforts, evidence of success in concurrent deliberations may be seen in two areas.

First was the coastal agency's attempt to minimize project impact by innovation. Interagency interest in formulating project innovations and alternative technologies was not generally apparent until the state coastal commission entered the deliberations with its perspective of preserving coastal resources. Although several of the innovations suggested by the commission were eventually "compromised" away, most had not been seriously considered by other agencies less interested in minimizing coastal impact. With Proposition 20's environmental incentive to pursue alternative possibilities, the state staff offered several impact-reducing strategies. These included relocating the project across the freeway, redesigning the cooling system by either the use of cooling towers or placement of discharge ports farther out at sea, expanding the marine monitoring program, and substituting an HTGR nuclear system for the PWR system.

The HTGR is a particularly interesting example because it was the state staff's concern over thermal and entrainment impact on near-shore organisms that led to the search for an alternative with less cooling water demand. Citing a 33 percent savings in water use, Bodovitz argued that the HTGR was "a type of power-generating facility that requires less cooling water and, therefore, less damage to the plankton in the ocean" (Coastal Commission, Dec. 5, 1973, p. 12). Unlike Mineral King, *alternative uses* of technology were visible factors in deliberations.

Second, the advantage of reciprocal review was seen in the use of information, especially in assessing marine impact. Prior to coastal agency review, most of the concern with data analysis had been with evaluating SCE's simulation models of cooling system impact on near-shore organisms. Little attempt to seek out alternative methods for comparison was made. Consequently, without the differing perspectives provided by the coastal commission's review, the inadequacy of knowledge on marine impacts might never have been established as a critical concern. The coastal commission was obligated to assess the degree of information uncertainty because of the coastal act's "burden of proof" clause. With this mandate, the state staff requested and got from SCE a sixty-day extension of the appeal period to clarify unresolved ambiguities of adverse impact. Bodovitz stated that "unless these findings can affirmatively be made, a permit must, under the Act, be denied" (Bodovitz, Oct. 24, 1973).

A major result of the coastal agency's extended review of information was the determination of need for a comprehensive marine study independent of SCE control. Probably because of the AEC's overshadowing effect on deliberations, none of the other review agencies were aware enough of their insufficient knowledge to demand clarity prior to construction. Nor did they recognize that the severity of the situation was caused by the fact that available data and interpretations came almost entirely from a single "vested interest" source — SCE. Yet, during coastal commission deliberations, many alternate sources came to light that suggested few conclusions could be drawn on the question of "substantial adverse effects."

One example of this problem had to do with the utilities' poor research methods and resistance to construction delays to establish more certain findings. SCE had spent much of its research energies in locating data to support its position, and it knew that giving up such discretion over scientific judgment to an independent research body meant jeopardizing its autonomy over the project. SCE's need to control was intensified when the coastal commission found that past SCE studies on Unit One were "superficial at best" (Coastal Commission, Dec., 1973, p. 7). One state commission expert said, "To expect that objective and accurate predictions be made on the basis of such a paltry effort is unreasonable . . ." (Coastal Commission, Dec., 1973, p. 7). Another official stated that "if this kind of research project . . . had been submitted to me by a graduate student, I would have given him a failing grade on it. It is poorly planned and badly executed research" (Coastal Commission, Dec., 1973, p. 8). Even the AEC finally agreed that utility data were "admittedly qualitative and subjective" (AEC, Oct. 15, 1973, p. 138).

To insulate itself from such public scrutiny, SCE refused in the beginning to consider either an independent study under coastal commission auspices or a study that would preclude construction until findings were established. Knowing the difficulty for a public agency to come back and impose changes after the start of construction, SCE insisted that "we would be opposed to a condition that would preclude construction prior to that study, but we would accept a condition which would say that we would make the study and we would implement any improvements that were obvious" (Coastal Commission, Dec. 5, 1973, p. 64). In the end, however, the "redecision" vote hinged on whether or not SCE would accede to marine research that would reduce information uncertainty and allow more objective evaluation. Although the utility never gave in to a study prior to the start of construction, it did accept an independent study and granted some negotiating powers to the coastal commission in determining postconstruction project changes.

A second source of evidence regarding inadequate information was the wide disparity in interpretations by the different agencies both generally and for specific issues. For example, the regional coastal commission hearings highlighted conflicting conclusions between two state agencies concerning the cooling system. While the San Diego Regional Water Quality Board argued that data on San Onofre Unit One "do not indicate any significant adverse impact . . . ," the state Department of Fish and Game disagreed, saying, "We believe the accumulated evidence to date does not validate any particular point of view" (San Diego Coast Regional Commission, Aug. 10, 1973, pp. 76, 82). Another contrast in expert opinions was apparent between the AEC and the state coastal commission. Using its environmental impact statement to fend off reciprocal review and create an aura of factual certainty, the AEC concluded that "no deterioration of water quality is anticipated to occur due to Units 2 and 3 effluents" (AEC, Mar., 1973, p. 9–11).

To this the state coastal commission staff argued that ". . . evidence before the commission indicates at least a possibility that the proposed San Onofre expansion could cause several square miles of coastal waters to become the equivalent of a marine desert" (Coastal Commission, Dec., 1973, p. 2). In 1979 the marine review committee's first report of findings presented evidence that Unit One effluent contained "radiological discharge." The report asserted the SCE marine monitoring program was "grossly inadequate" and "makes it impossible to determine with accuracy the amounts of radioactive material being released" as effluent into the near-shore waters (Fischer, 1979). The original cause for concern seemed to be partially justified by this subsequent discovery.

Disagreement among different collectives of experts was equally strong on more specific issues as well. For example, with regard to the impact of the reactors' cooling water diffusers on kelp, a number of disparities existed. With reams of computer output, SCE asserted that "the thermal plume is not expected to impact [the kelp]" (Coastal Commission, Oct. 18, 1973, p. 46). Discounting its own determination that SCE's simulation model for kelp was "unreliable," the AEC nevertheless agreed with the utility: ". . . the operation of San Onofre Units 2 and 3 will have no adverse effect on the present kelp beds" (AEC, Mar., 1973, pp. 3-42, 5-31). The state coastal staff, however, examined the information more closely and found that differing opinion on impact was due to different measurement techniques. The utilities had measured only the densest portion of the kelp bed, which not only left no margin for growth of the harvestable resource but also made the cooling diffusers appear more distant from them. A San Diego State University biologist, on the other hand, had measured the beds using their outer extremities as the boundary. This made the distance from the diffusers not 2,000 feet from the kelp, as claimed by the SCE, but only 600 feet. With this disparity, the coastal commission concluded that "until this matter is resolved by . . . an independent qualified source . . . no finding can be made as to whether there would be a substantial impact on the kelp bed" (Coastal Commission, Dec., 1973, p. 13).

Another disparity was over the actual temperature increases that would be induced into the marine water by the power plants. According to the State Water Resources Control Board, state and federal law "clearly requires that the maximum temperature of the waste discharge shall not exceed the natural temperature of the receiving water by more than $20°$ F" (Walsh, 1973). In response to this requirement, the AEC said that the water discharge of 1.66 million gallons per minute would be "$20°$ F above ambient ocean temperature" (AEC, Mar., 1973, pp. 3-5). The coastal agency, however, found an error in the calculations. Both SCE and the ACE had assumed the natural temperature of the ocean water at both the intake and diffuser points would be the same. Actually the intake ports, which were closer to shore, were to draw in ocean water that was $6°$ F warmer than the ocean water around the diffuser ports. Adding this to the 20° F increase created by the cooling system yielded a temperature in excess of state law. This represented a substantial variance and no one knew what impact it might have. Although the coastal commission's "redecision" did not specifically require alterations, it did conclude "that the proposed cooling system would not comply with Federal water quality standards . . ." (Bodovitz, Feb. 28, 1974).

These and other examples pointed to a great uncertainty about environmental impacts and the insufficiency of data to predict future outcomes. Because of this, most of the commission experts urged "a delay for more and better data, so we'll know the full scope of the probable environmental impact" (Coastal Commission, Oct. 18, 1973, p. 79). Although most of the state commissioners eventually voted in favor of the project, nearly all recognized the frail amount of supporting information. Indeed, the swing votes of Mendelsohn, Farr, and Laufer at the "redecision" occurred primarily because of SCE's agreement to an independent study combined with an adjudicating procedure for post construction project changes. Even Commissioner Frautschy, who was the utilities' major advocate, admitted "that with any major human intervention there are going to be environmental consequences and unfortunately we don't know how to evaluate these consequences right now" (Frautschy, 1975). The critical point about such revelations was that none of this concern for information uncertainty surfaced until the state coastal commission with its protection-oriented authority entered the deliberations.

A number of questions remained as to whether nuclear safety was a reasonable public concern, whether project innovations could have been made at reasonable cost, whether the generation of new energy was really needed, and whether the marine study and monitoring program would have any material effect without *pre-construction* findings and assessment. Nevertheless, to some extent the use of multiple public forums served to minimize the dominance of a single interpretation of fact and provided a structure of alternative avenues of access to the decision process. Arguing "that a win-all philosophy . . . is the surest path to legal, political and economic stagnation," state coastal commissioner Laufer said during the initial vote for denial that the state staff presented "options that would preserve power needs, environmental needs, and economic and job needs . . ." (Coastal Commission, Dec. 5, 1973, p. 102).

Nettleton Lakes

As in the other cases, insufficiency of information raised the possibility of an indefinite moratorium until independent comprehensive studies could be completed. At Nettleton the opposition and some state agencies argued for this approach. Nevertheless, decision postponement also implied costs, particularly the discouragement of future desirable development. Should all projects be tabled until all specific investigations are made? How much and what sorts of information are sufficient to meet such a requirement? Boise argued that ". . . if you appoint a big enough committee to study it, they'll never finish" (Planning Commission, Apr. 28, 1970, p. 268). The Kitsap planning director suggested that, in any event, such research requirements were "too expensive to do" (Mitchell, 1971).

In lieu of postponement, the limits of expertise were handled by "satisficing" (Simon, 1957). Recognizing that indefinite delays were costly and that waiting for further study might not yield more than incremental improvements in knowledge, the public agencies went ahead by examining the project proposal with the resources available. This did not mean that the agencies accepted the partisan data bases. In several instances Boise was forced to submit better and more complete information, and opposition data were subject to similar skepticism. Nevertheless, methods of reciprocal review seemed to emerge that allowed for initial judgments conditioned by the opportunity for public reconsideration later on. Satisficing through incremental judgments appeared as a functional process to a broader spectrum of considerations because positions were established by a composite of independent collectives of expertise representing different responsibilities.

While this does not argue that the single hierarchy cannot reach similar decision outcomes, it does suggest that certain advantages of flexibility may be gained by reciprocal review among different agencies that cannot always be matched by the unitary bureaucracy. Because of its generalist orientation, the single hierarchy usually does not contain within it the in-depth expertise to judge data of a highly specialized nature. While it can go outside to acquire it from private consultants, it still does not have the specialized expertise to evaluate the validity and quality of information developed by those consultants. In contrast, the noncentralized network provides an arrangement of *diverse* and *specific* sources of expertise within its administrative structure that come into play when certain mandated authorities are triggered by specific aspects of a proposal. Validity and quality, then, are judgments made in the process of interagency mutual adjustment.

At Mineral King most of the Forest Service proposal was justified on general statistics extracted from reports not specific to the project. Little information was developed concerning the particular characteristics of the valley ecology and demands for the resource until required to do so by NEPA. Even then a controversy developed over the adequacy of the EIS.

By contrast, the Puget Sound network of agencies recognized the marginal utility of general or aggregate data. General knowledge about Hood Canal, the adjacent land area, and the population profile was seen as insufficient for making decisions about the Nettleton proposal. While an inventory of areawide resources and a general knowledge of processes were useful in conceptualizing holistic boundaries, they did not provide the discrete insight on relationships between the project and the surrounding area. The wide disparity in partisan "facts" further compounded the review process and raised the need for separate professional perspectives. This need was partially fulfilled by the availability of a range of pertinent specialized agencies which provided alternative sources of information and scrutiny. While the county held the authority to assess the value of the overall project, the several state agencies contributed pieces of knowledge on individual areas of impact. This role of state agencies was highlighted by a Kitsap County commissioner who said, ". . . the state has assumed jurisdiction over certain areas and . . . has more resources and inputs" for gathering and scrutinizing specialized data (Lobe, Randall, and Mahan, 1971). In effect, no single agency had the intensive and extensive resources to understand all the implications of complex land use changes.

Moreover, the network structure of agencies usually facilitates data assessment. At Nettleton the differences of agency opinion in scrutinizing the proposal provided *open* debates over factual discrepancies and uncertainties that were not smoothed over by bureaucratic authority. In the case of sufficient water supply, the county initially accepted Boise's interpretations, saying, ". . . enough water will be developed for domestic use and fire fighting" (Weigel, 1970). But the state Health Department questioned ". . . the very limited success of the [Boise] test drilling program" and concluded that long-term availability was uncertain (Merry, 1970). A similar circumstance occurred with the safety of septic tanks. The Kitsap County Health Department surveyed the Boise data and recommended the firm's proposal as having no significant pollution potential (Weigel, 1970). Discrepancies emerged, however, when the Mason County Health Department and state Health both found in their independent studies that "soils in the project area are marginal at best for septic tank systems" (Lane, 1970).

When it came to developing and assessing information specific to individual aspects of the project, the intergovernmental network contained within it the necessary locus of specialized knowledge. For example, in assessing the boat marina's impact on "a very complex estuarine community" (Biggs, 1970), the county realized that the knowledge which was beyond the scope of its expertise was the forte of the departments of Fisheries, Game, and Natural Resources. The county was eventually compelled to delete the marina, in part by state environmental agencies which urged that ". . . we must manage estuarine areas conservatively, leaving adequate margins of safety for protection from miscalculation, emotional judgment, error, or extreme natural variations" (Biggs, 1970). In another example, errors in developer soil testing were identified by the Mason County sanitarian, who pointed out that federal and local standards had not been met and that other standards required ". . . at least four feet of permeable soil over any impermeable layer or ground water table in order to install a [septic tank]" (Planning Commission, Mar. 31, 1970, p. 93). A third example related to the uncertain purpose of Nettleton. Kitsap County was prepared to accept the project as ". . . a recreational subdivision because the general purpose as stated [by Boise] is to provide vacation and second homesites . . ." (Weigel, 1970). This assumption was questioned, however, by other agencies and partisans who were more familiar with other Boise projects and the industry. As a result, the county approval included requirements of a full-time permanent residential development.

In addition to judging the adequacy of specific information, the structure of concurrent expertise also was able to partially mitigate attempts by the developer to control the use and interpretation of information. Examples of the system's ability to contend with this influence were numerous, but the septic tank feasibility issue was probably the most comprehensive. Characteristic of Boise planning was a tendency to approach environmental impact analysis in a haphazard and hurried manner. Although the firm represented itself as having a special environmental expertise, it provided only four months for planning studies, most of which were spent on engineering, not environmental investigations. Yet the proposal represented a development that was similar to many large PUDs in America. With respect to septic tanks, Boise carried out a study to determine the depth of water-permeable soil. Although the resulting report concluded that no major risks were expected from septic tanks under existing soil conditions, the firm neglected to follow established procedure.

Overlooked by Kitsap County, these questionable methods were identified by two other agencies. According to the Thurston-Mason County sanitarian, ". . . the methods in which these tests were recorded, adjusted and presented raise questions as to their credibility" (Morigeau, 1970). This apparent falsification was also alluded to by the DWR, which testified at the Kitsap Planning Commission hearings:

> . . . on page four of the perc test report, it says in there the equipment used was a four wheel Jeep and a four wheel . . . Dodge power wagon. Then on page ten, it mentions some holes were not dug because they were "inaccessible." Last Thursday . . . we drove to every one of those with a common, ordinary two wheel pick-up and with low carriage, and the only thing we did find . . . were

springs. . . . The reason they were inaccessible is . . . they were under water. [Planning Commission, Mar. 31, 1970, pp. 147-48]

The "under water" condition was a sign of low soil permeability and indicated the inappropriateness of septic tanks. The DWR concluded that "the recommendations and opinions expressed [by Boise] in reference to the suitability of septic tanks is wholly inconsistent with similar reports [by others]" (Planning Commission, Mar. 31, 1970, p. 144). Kitsap County eventually required a central sewerage facility.

Numerous other examples of reciprocal review exist, but these are perhaps best aggregated and placed in the context of the county's thirty-four conditions on approval. These conditions resulted from numerous intergovernmental exchanges and represent to a great extent accords reached by the network as a whole. In addition to those aspects discussed above (marina deletion, sewerage and water requirements), two categories of examples are of interest.

The first concerns enforcement of public restrictions under uncertainty. Numerous agencies expressed concern for environmental impacts ranging from erosion and waste pollution to blockage of fish migration and spawning. Although the county did not deny such aspects as dam construction, numerous other environmental measures were inserted declaring that no one could dispose of untreated waste into any local bodies of water, cause siltation or heighten water turbidity, or carry out residential construction activities within seventy-five feet of major streams. In addition, Boise was required to install a complete urban erosion and storm drainage system. Since local environmental laws were inadequate for enforcement, the county further required Boise upon project completion to post a $1 million bond for a ten-year period to guarantee against environmental problems.

The second category concerns the incremental approach taken by network experts in dealing with insufficient information. Interagency consensus was reached by many agencies that information on some impacts was so incomplete as to preclude reasonable final decisions. These included consumer demand for second homes and need for public services (roads, schools, police, fire, etc.). The State Planning and Community Affairs Agency argued, for example, that the project would not be a second-home development at all and recommended that it "be designed at the same standards as for full-time residential occupancy" (Slavin, 1970). Hence, to the extent that uncertainty and continued public control over project specifications were commonly expressed interagency concerns, the county required that final approval occur incrementally on a plat division-by-division basis. Among other criteria, to qualify for final approval, each division was required to have all proposed and mandated improvements designed to serve the division installed. Further, an appopriate cash bond plus 15 percent was to be filed for each division with the county for potential problems. Before the opening of division one, all improvements designed for the total project were also to be completed and an appropriate bond posted. Specific requirements, including a complete fire station, regulation school reserve, and underground utilities, were made to assure adequate urban amenities.

The Nettleton case illustrates the functional side of conflict among different and independent collectives of public expertise. While conflict frequently causes delay and may increase allocation costs, these can be offset by the advantages of mitigating longer-term adverse effects. With regard to the county's role in this web of reciprocal review, most recognized the beneficial side. Although not pleased with the outcome, Boise acknowledged the thoroughness of the review. Likewise HCEC said, "We oppose the basic decision permitting the development. . . ." [But] we commend the County Commissioners and members of the Planning Commission for the study they have given this matter, and their work product represents an awareness of the need for adequate control, and environmental protection . . ." (HCEC, 1971).

CHAPTER 9

Some Larger Considerations

" . . . today government itself is the problem. . . . There
is serious doubt about efficacy and justice in the agencies of
government, the processes of policy-making, leadership
selection, and implementation of decisions."

Theodore J. Lowi

THE COMPARISONS are now complete. For the
three cases the analysis indicated important relationships among ad-
minstrative structure, behavior, and policy consequences. There is
enough evidence to raise serious concern over the use of hierarchy and
center-periphery relations in land use control. For those who do not find
themselves systematically advantaged by "the public interest" of
welfare at large, the unitary bureaucracy can be a repressive and deca-
dent form of governmental control. It can also foster serious errors of
judgment that go unmitigated because of pre-emptive rights of exclusive jurisdiction. Concurrent government is no panacea, but multiple arenas and reciprocal review did in these cases reduce some of the
problems of elitist representation and error oversight. In contrast to the
restricted learning of bureaucracy and the protean behavior of a last-in-
line commission, the policentric network had closer contact with those
affected and was more able to judge factual considerations from several
perspectives.

In a larger sense, though, the comparisons beg for a look at the
future. To the extent that pressures in land use and natural resources are
requiring public and private organizations to be accountable to a much
broader set of interests, administrative forms need to be more open,
flexible to change, and responsive to uncertainty. If our public institutions are to provide policies that encompass broader constituent acceptance and mitigate as many dysfunctions as possible, they will have to
be structured so as to concurrently deal with problems of representation
and expert judgment. The future will compound this as the political
economy becomes an even more interdependent matrix of scarce
resources and contentious transterritorial actors.

Yet evolution over the last hundred years is not encouraging. As the
number of technological and allocation variables grew and society

unified around material values, control and management were augmented by bigger and more unitary hierarchies. Beer has said that ". . . those ever larger and more complex networks of *interdependence* [cause] the background conditions for the continual trend of modern society toward greater *centralization*" (1974, p. 54). Over time, he notes, bureaucracy has become the instrumental means of making collective decisions.

With this evolutionary trend and its staggering implications, we have been flooded for nearly two decades with works attesting to a "crisis" in politics and administration. Among the first was Lowi (1969), who identified the "crisis" in terms of political philosophy, morality, and administrative discretion. Shortly thereafter a group led by Waldo (1971) and Marini (1971) assessed the "crisis" in terms of environmental turbulence and called for a "new public administration." A different perspective was added by Ostrom (1973), who asserted that the "crisis" was one of political economy. He contended that the situation will not improve until politicans and administrators are willing to rearrange governmental agencies according to discrete tasks, allocative functions, and political circumstances. More recently, Scott and Hart (1979) have argued that the "crisis" is due to the totalitarian nature of large organizations. Societal dependence on such institutions creates an "organizational imperative" that makes all aspects of one's life subservient to a deterministic system of control. "It is the *unexamined* determinism that grows out of the blind acceptance of the values of the organizational imperative that is at the root of our contemporary malaise" (Scott and Hart, 1979, p. 31).

Most causes of the "crisis," however, may be traced to larger sources of aggravation that have origins more than a century old. What we identify today as "crisis" is really a manifestation of the continuing transformation of a modern industrialized, urbanized, and bureaucratized society. Inherent in that transformation are a number of disturbing tendencies which confound the ability to augment governmental functions. Most of these tendencies revolve around the trade-off of certain freedoms for more administrative control. The federalists, for example, forged a new government based in part on the fear of concentrated authority and centralized control. Madison, who had read substantially all the treatises on government up to his time, was especially aware of this tendency and its outgrowth in the French Revolution.

Henry Adams, whose life spanned the latter half of the 1800s, saw the growth of large institutions, their impact on public philosophy, and their intervention in resource allocation (Adams, 1961). Watching society forsake "multiplicity" for "unity," Adams predicted that the subsequent imperative of control would unwittingly yield only greater "crisis." He thus proclaimed that "in the last synthesis, order and anarchy were one, but that the unity was chaos" (Adams, 1961, p. 406). The pragmatic need for total control meant suppression of diverse interests and the unrestrained utilization of natural resources for material development.

Feeding the spiraling demand for material enhancement was the growing separation of man from his environment, the loss of community, and a commensurate need for status identity. The rush for urban industrialization and abandonment of agrarian values raised the consciousness of individuals toward their social position in an emerging world of flux and upward mobility. As pointed out by Veblen (1899), the emulation of a leisure class through "conspicuous consumption" was manifest in the transformation from physical work in small communities to "honorific employment" and the struggle over materialistic security. With this came an enlarged middle class demanding a kind of orderliness that would provide at once upward mobility and social stability. Large-scale institutions promised these in the form of status through job advancement and planned futures through managerial control.

The real signs of the new institutional order go back before the Civil War, but the political philosophy and cultural setting were best articulated by the Progressive movement. Implicit in the logic was a redistribution of power and a reinterpretation of American political economy. The transformation involved the declining relevance of plural society envisioned by the *Federalist* and the emergence of a unitary order governed by giant organizations.

In plural society power is policentric. The handling of conflict among groups and the decision outcome occur through multiple access to government, and solutions emerge from politicizing alternative values, goals, and needs. Instead of unity, several measures of betterment form the basis of adequate policy. Instead of a "one best way," the contentiousness of many centers of power is meant to preserve the integrity of "intermediate associations" in the pursuit of multiple avenues of human accomplishment.

Although not always viewed in contrast to policentric philosophy, the logic of modern institutionalized society is quite different in character. Weber, for example, recognized that "bureaucratic organization has usually come into power on the basis of a leveling of economic and social difference. . . . Bureaucracy inevitably accompanies modern *mass democracy* in contrast to democratic self-government of small, homogeneous units" (Gerth and Mills, 1946, p. 224). Pre-industrial America gave way to functional specialization, nationally oriented industrial power, and conspicuous consumption.

The resultant image is a profile of centralized hierarchies and a distinct separation of society's decision-making capacity from the masses affected by the administrative process. Beyond this, the political process takes on the appearance of a "black box" of elite institutions. Since functionalism and bureaucratic efficiency were assumed to be superior to "directionless" federalism, the actual interworkings of this system frequently became unimportant in explaining how decisions occurred. The way of looking at "black box" performance was through *results* as measured by input-output analysis.

Institutional elitism was legitimized on the assumption of representative administration. Within the "black box," a number of functional blocs were to provide "countervailing powers" to each other and thus restrain the dominance of any one interest group. Viewed as Big Business, Big Labor, and Big Government, these aggregate blocs supposedly represented the major interests in society. Although portrayed as a sort of institutional Madisonian democracy, the real image is more of a "national managerial system [composed of] a vast complex of interlocking management systems, sharing a common set of values, which control modern organizations and which provide order and stability in our national life" (Scott and Hart, 1979, p. 5). In either case the object was for the "black box," through integrated efforts of its functional blocs, to develop policy and reach decisions that were in the public interest. The elitist behavior was legitimate as long as the system's output represented the wishes of society at large.

Coupled with unitary hierarchy and exclusive jurisdiction were the self-serving struggles of internal organizational politics. The inner workings of large-scale organization frequently have been envisioned as operating like parts of a well-oiled machine. The prevalent image of bureaucracy is that of a maze of automatons following succinct orders from supervisors, who also act as machines. Perhaps those most responsible for advancing this perception are the "systems analysts" who lay out the decision process as a rational matrix of interconnected decision "nodes" and "feedback loops." Being a fully functional and essentially nonpolitical structure of formal elements, the internal aspects of a large organization are seldom viewed as influenced by variant culture.

Scholars of the "humanist school" of organization theory as well as some in political science have recognized this as an oversimplification. Few, however, have explicitly seen the internal milieu as an intensely political environment of status-seeking employees. Struggle for upward mobility involves actors with aggressive personalities and a need for social, political, and economic achievement. Ambition to achieve in one's career involves primarily political considerations to succeed within the rising order of the superior-subordinate authority relationship.

Such a narrowed concept would not be as true, of course, if advancement were not defined in terms of wealth, status, and authority *or* if access to multiple alternatives were readily available "outside." Most bureaucratic situations, however, are viewed as providing a scarce commodity, and to quit prematurely very often means starting anew somewhere else. In short, large unitary bureaucracies create a form of advancement "monopoly" for many that requires subjugation of the subordinate to the authority structure — at least for a time. Limited-choice "markets" for job advancement mean that the internal political milieu can require the achieving personality to conform unilaterally to organizational need; in return he is granted a satisfying role, social status, and frequently great monetary reward.

Beyond this, the organizational achiever is also essentially "amoral." His efforts toward advancement within the entity seldom involve the consideration of values except those of duty in accomplishing acts that portray him as an ideal career type. Individual morality becomes synonymous with organizationally useful attitudes and behaviors. The implication is that individuals in bureaucracy act in accordance with internal goals that may require socially questionable and sometimes antisocial behavior.

To question the morality or consequences of bureaucratically defined goals or policy is seldom politically advantageous in the limited-choice advancement setting. Indeed, any direction-oriented bureaucracy that advances careers on the basis of performance is likely to select against the value-questioning mind. "[O]rganizational puzzle-solving is so engaging that serious concern about values is condemned within the management profession as a wasteful excursion into mysticism" (Scott and Hart, 1979, p. 39).

Consequently, organizational introspection, learning, and adaptiveness are reduced accordingly. The ability of bureaucracy to monitor external forces and infuse them as valuable opportunities and constraints on administrative behavior is in part dependent upon *awareness* of its cadre of top management. In the face of such bias against the value-sensitive mind, most iconoclasts would never reach a level in the bureaucracy where their entrepreneurial talents for perceiving the societal setting could be used.

In assessing the cases of this study, the historical trends toward unity and centralization appear to be clearly evident. There are far more cases involving center-periphery structures like those of Mineral King and San Onofre than the policentric network at Nettleton Lakes. There are, of course, signs that many people dislike the "organizational imperative" and are willing to fight in some cases. But how much of this expression of disenchantment is simply a catharsis for those unwilling to take their chance with another, more multiplistic order?

While history shows an increasing concentration of power in large institutions, those projecting a more complex future with a multiplicity of alternatives ought to be condemning the unitary means by which we are getting there. Some, like McConnell, suggest it is too late: the degree of complexity and contentious interests far exceeds an institutional solution. "There is simply no means of either administration or politics by which an ultimately acceptable solution . . . can be achieved" (McConnell, 1978).

This position, though, may be too pessimistic. It is clear that the tumultuous 1960s and 1970s brought on a proliferation of lifestyles, lack of consensus on land use policy, hidden consequences of urbanization and industrial development, and resource bottlenecks. But while they do not constitute conditions that are right for efficient and effective *central* administration, do they also mean the only solution is violent revolution? Instead of these alternatives, reciprocal review and mutual adjustment in a more *policentric* model would appear to augment greater acceptance from the multiplistic polity. Concurrent government may move more slowly, but it harbors more flexibility for change than bureaucracy and fewer uncertainties of sacrifice than revolution.

Contrary to Beer's projection, we are perhaps at a turning point where conditions are emerging similar to those surrounding development of Publius's compound republic. "[I]n a world of great diversity in wants, expectations and life styles, it is a way to obviate the necessity for too much uniformity—the kind that would be required if the body politic were to be treated as if it were one undifferentiated piece" (Elazar, 1974, p. 295). To the extent that a shift in the structure of government may be logical for the future, as network theory and noncentralized federalism might suggest, the most profound meaning of land use controversies like those of this study is that administration should not be a covert system of institutional control by "black box" elites. While the descriptions of Lowi, Galbraith, or Siedman may accurately connote the present, they obscure the source of that power by associating contemporary "pluralism" and "countervailing powers" with the network structure of concurrent government. The elitist connotations of bureaucratic control are much more a reflection of Progressive reforms than of *Federalist* origins.

The future is as yet still open, but the choices of governance that we make today will certainly mold those opportunities ahead. In speaking of solutions, the role of administration in land use control must be seen as highly political. When all the factual and technical information is gathered, the choices still require much discretionary judgment. This would seem to eliminate single-approach solutions. Decision costs notwithstanding, we are left with the possibility that several countervailing methods and organizational arrangements may be necessary. Central to this contingency logic is the idea of concurrent government for a future of complex options and uncertain resources. As the Nettleton

Lakes case shows, we need an explicit bargaining mandate in which agencies are given the discretion they need to work toward a consensual approach to land use policy and enforcement. The decision about *who* should be at the bargaining table, however, should not be in the agencies' hands, lest the most powerful of them arrange the rest on a center-periphery model. Until we make this commitment to due process, land use control and natural resource administration are likely to continue to be clouded with skepticism and mistrust.

References

Adams, Henry. 1961. *The Education of Henry Adams.* Boston: Houghton Mifflin.

Altshuler, Alan A. 1965. *The City Planning Process: A Political Analysis.* Ithaca, N.Y.: Cornell University Press.

American Law Institute. 1974. *A Model Land Development Code.* Philadelphia.

Anderson, Frederick R. 1973. *NEPA in the Courts.* Baltimore: Johns Hopkins University Press.

_____. 1974. "The National Environmental Policy Act." In Erica L. Dolgin and Thomas G. P. Guilbert (eds.), *Federal Environmental Law.* St. Paul: West Publishing Co., pp. 238–419.

Anderson, William. 1925. *American City Government.* New York: Henry Holt.

Andrews, Richard N. L. 1976. *Environmental Policy and Administrative Change.* Lexington, Mass.: Lexington Books.

Arrow, Kenneth. 1963. *Social Choice and Individual Values.* 3d ed. New York: John Wiley.

Atomic Energy Commission (AEC). Oct. 20, 1972. "Safety Evaluation of the San Onofre Nuclear Generating Station Units No. Two & Three," Docket Nos. 50–361, 50–362.

_____. Mar., 1973. "Final Environmental Statement Related to the Proposed San Onofre Nuclear Generating Station Units Two and Three," Docket Nos. 50–361, 50–362.

_____. Oct. 15, 1973. "Reporter's Transcript of Initial Decision in the Matter of SCE and SDG&E (San Onofre Nuclear Generating Station, Units Two and Three)," Docket Nos. 50–361, 50–362.

_____. Nov., 1973a. "The Energy Crisis," pamphlet.

_____. Nov., 1973b. "Radioactive Waste," pamphlet.

Avery, Mary W. 1973. *Government of Washington State.* Rev. ed. Seattle: University of Washington Press.

Babcock, Richard F. 1966. *The Zoning Game: Municipal Practices and Policies.* Madison: University of Wisconsin Press.

Barber, Jim. July 8, 1971. Member, Kitsap County Planning Commission, interview granted to Mitchell Moss.

Barlowe, Raleigh. 1972. *Land Resource Economics.* 2d ed. Englewood Cliffs, N.J.: Prentice-Hall.

Barnum, M. M. Aug. 21, 1945. Assistant regional forester, internal memorandum to forest supervisor, Sequoia National Forest.

_____. Aug. 7, 1947. Assistant regional forester, letter to Fay G. Lawrence.

_____. Jan. 7, 1948. Assistant regional forester, office memorandum to John Sieker, chief, Division of Recreation and Lands.

————. Aug. 30, 1949. Assistant regional forester, letter to William T. Eldred, publisher of *Ski Magazine.*

————. July 18, 1951. "Note to Sequoia," attached to letter by Clare Hendee, regional forester, to Harold G. Rainwater, Tulare County Chamber of Commerce.

————. Jan. 8, 1953. Assistant regional forester, letter to Harold G. Rainwater, Tulare County Chamber of Commerce.

————. Mar. 24, 1953. Regional forester, R-5, office memorandum to chief, Forest Service.

Baumol, William J. 1965. *Economic Theory and Operations Analysis.* 2d ed. Englewood Cliffs, N.J.: Prentice-Hall.

Beer, Samuel H. 1974. "The Modernization of American Federalism." In Daniel Elazar (ed.), *The Federal Polity.* New Brunswick, N.J.: Transaction Books, pp. 49–95.

Bell, Daniel. 1965. *The End of Ideology.* New York: Free Press.

Benson, J. Kenneth. 1975. "The Interorganizational Network as a Political Economy." *Administrative Science Quarterly* 20: 229–50.

Bentley, Arthur F. 1908. *The Process of Government.* Chicago: University of Chicago Press.

Bergren, William R. July 30, 1965. Letter to Charles A. Connaughton, regional forester, San Francisco.

Bergsagel, Daniel. Jan. 1, 1971. "Letter to the *Sun* Editor: Boise Cascade." *Bremerton Sun.*

Berliner, Harold. 1970. "Plague on the Land." *Cry California* (Summer).

Berry, David, and Gene Steiker. 1974. "The Concept of Justice in Regional Planning: Justice as Fairness." *Journal of the American Institute of Planners* 40, no. 6 (Nov.): 414–21.

Best, Philip. May 25, 1970. HCEC, letter to Kitsap County Planning Commission.

————. Oct. 23, 1970. HCEC, letter to Board of County Commissioners (Kitsap).

————. July 4, 1971. HCEC, interview granted to Mitchell Moss.

Beuscher, J. H. 1954. *Materials on Land Use Controls.* Madison, Wis.: College Printing and Typing.

Bieber, James. 1973. "Calvert Cliffs' Coordinating Committee vs. AEC." *Environmental Law* 3 (Summer): 316–33.

Biggs, John A. Feb. 18, 1970. Director, Department of Game, letter to Bert L. Cole, Department of Natural Resources.

Bish, Robert L. 1975. "Intergovernmental Relations: Cooperation or Collusion." Paper delivered at National Conference of American Society of Public Administration, Chicago, Apr. 1–4.

Bish, Robert L., and Hugh O. Nourse. 1975. *Urban Economics and Policy Analysis.* New York: McGraw-Hill.

Bish, Robert L., *et al.* 1975. Coastal Resource Use. Seattle: University of Washinton Press.

Bodovitz, Joseph E. Mar. 29, 1973. Executive director, statewide coastal commission (San Francisco), memorandum to state commission members.

————. June 14, 1973. Executive director, statewide coastal commission (San Francisco), memorandum to regional commission members, staffs, and general public.

————. Aug. 13, 1973. Executive director, California Coastal Zone Conservation Commission, interview in "Boards Forging Coastal Pattern," *Los Angeles Times,* p. 1.

_____. Oct. 24, 1973. Executive director, California Coastal Zone Conservation Commission, letter to David Fogarty, SCE.

_____. Nov. 17, 1973. Executive director, California Coastal Zone Conservation Commission (San Francisco), interview in "Coastal Agency Chairman Lists Changing Issues," *San Diego Union*, pp. 8–10.

_____. Dec. 19, 1973. Executive director, California Coastal Zone Conservation Commission, "Minutes of Commission Meeting."

_____. Jan., 1974. Executive director, California Coastal Zone Conservation Commission, intra-office memorandum to Frank Broadhead, staff coordinator of San Onofre case.

_____. Jan. 9, 1974a. Executive director, California Coastal Zone Conservation Commission, "Possible Conditions for Approving Expansion of San Onofre Nuclear Power Plant."

_____. Jan. 9, 1974b, Executive director, California Coastal Zone Conservation Commission, "Minutes of Commission Meeting."

_____. Feb. 28, 1974. Executive director, California Coastal Zone Conservation Commission, permit approval letter to SCE and SDG&E.

Boise Cascade. 1970. *Annual Report.*

_____. Apr. 6, 1970. "Nettleton Lakes on the Canal, Kitsap and Mason Counties, Washington: Revised Application for Planned Unit Development," submitted by Harstad and Associates to Kitsap County Planning Commission.

_____. Sept. 9, 1970a. "Boise Cascade on Environment," distributed at Kitsap County Commission hearing.

_____. Sept. 9, 1970b. "Information about Nettleton Lakes on the Canal: Roads, Water, and Sewers," distributed at Kitsap County Commission hearing.

_____. Sept. 9, 1970c. "Information about Nettleton Lakes on the Canal: Local Economic Benefits," distributed at Kitsap County Commission hearing.

_____. Sept. 9, 1970d. "Nettleton Lakes on the Canal: A Good Place to Live," distributed at Kitsap County Commission hearing.

Boise Cascade Credit Corporation. Mar. 10, 1970. "Preliminary Prospectus."

_____. May 5, 1970. "Prospectus."

Bolan, Richard S. 1967. "Emerging Views of Planning." *Journal of the American Institute of Planners* 33, no. 4 (July): 233–45.

Borgwardt, John P. June 1, 1970a. Boise Cascade, letter to Robert D. Sutton, HCEC.

_____. June 1, 1970b. Boise Cascade, letter to Harold A. Berliner, HCEC.

Boschken, Herman L. 1974. *Corporate Power and the Mismarketing of Urban Development.* New York: Praeger.

_____. 1976. "The Organizational Logic for Concurrent Government in Metropolitan Areas." *Academy of Management Review* 1, no. 1 (Jan.): 1–13.

_____. 1978. "Interorganizational Considerations in Coastal Management: The 1976 California Legislative Experience." *Coastal Zone Management Journal* 4, no. 1: 47–64.

_____. 1982. "Organization Theory and Federalism." *Organization Studies.* Forthcoming.

Bosselman, Fred, and David Callies. 1971. *The Quiet Revolution in Land Use Control.* Washington, D.C.: Government Printing Office.

Bosselman, Fred, David Callies, and John Banto. 1973. *The Taking Issue.* Washington, D.C.: Government Printing Office.

Bowen, William L. Oct., 1969. Regional director, Park Service, interview in Russ Leadabrand, "Mineral King: Go or No Go?" *American Forests* 75, no. 10: 44.

Brandt, Robert. Dec. 12, 1965. Mineral King Development Company, telegram to Jack Valenti, special assistant to President Johnson.

———. Dec. 30, 1965. President, Mineral King Development Company, letter to Orville L. Freeman, Secretary of Agriculture.

Bremerton Sun. July 30, 1969. "Planners Seeking Emergency Rezone for Hood Canal Area."

———. Nov. 19, 1969. "Developers Eye Hood Canal for Big Marina."

———. Dec. 10, 1969. "New Group Enters Hood Canal Scene."

———. Jan. 29, 1970. "Planners Adopt Hood Canal Interim Zone."

———. Feb. 19, 1970. "Hood Canal Plan Opposition Powerful."

———. Sept. 4, 1970. "A Subdivision Larger than Bremerton on Hood Canal??"

———. Oct. 22, 1970. "Letter to the *Sun* Editor: Boise Cascade."

———. Nov. 17, 1970. "Land Commissioner Rules out Dredging Anderson Cove Site."

———. Dec. 1, 1970. "Two Kitsap Commissioners to View Development Area."

———. Dec. 23, 1970a. "Incline Village Parallels Nettleton Lakes."

———. Dec. 23, 1970b. "Time for Decision on Boise Cascade."

———. Jan. 21, 1971. "Two Factions OK County's Nettleton Lakes Decision."

———. June 30, 1971. "Boise Cascade Reevaluating Plans for Hood Canal Project."

Broadhead, Frank. Feb. 14, 1976. San Onofre case coordinator, California Coastal Zone Conservation Commission, interview granted to author.

Brower, David R., and Richard H. Felter. 1948. "Surveying California's Ski Terrain." *Sierra Club Bulletin* 33, no. 3 (Mar.): 97–102.

Brunton, Bruce. Aug. 3, 1971. Kitsap County Prosecutor, interview granted to Mitchell Moss.

Buchanan, James M. 1959. "Positive Economics, Welfare Economics, and Political Economy." *Journal of Law and Economics* 2 (Oct.): 124–38.

Buchanan, James M., and Craig Stubblebine. 1962. "Externality." *Economica* 29 (Nov.): 371–84.

Buchanan, James M., and Gordon Tullock. 1965. *The Calculus of Consent.* Ann Arbor, Mich.: Ann Arbor Books.

Burns, Tom, and G. M. Stalker. 1961. *The Management of Innovation.* London: Tavistock Publications.

Burton, Phillip. July 8, 1969. Congressman from California, "What Is Mineral King?" In House of Representatives, *Congressional Record*, pp. E5673–74.

California Coastal Zone Conservation Act (Proposition 20). Nov. 7, 1972. California Public Resources Code, Sections 27000–27650.

California Coastal Zone Conservation Commission. Oct., 1973. "Regulations for California Coastal Zone Conservation Commission and Regional Commissions."

———. Oct. 15, 1973. "Appeal Summary," Appeal No. 183–73 (San Onofre).

———. Oct. 18, 1973. "Reporter's Transcript of Public Hearing on Appeal No. 183–73 (San Onofre) at San Diego."

———. Dec., 1973. "Staff Recommendation," Appeal No. 183–73.

———. Dec. 5, 1973. "Reporter's Transcript of Public Hearing on Appeal No. 183–73 (San Onofre), at Newport Beach."

———. Feb. 20, 1974. "Reporter's Transcript of Public Hearing on Appeal No. 183–73 (San Onofre), at Santa Barbara."

California Coastal Zone Conservation Commissions. 1973. *Annual Report.*

_____. 1974. *Annual Report.*

_____. 1975. *California Coastal Plan.* Sacramento: State Documents and Publications Branch.

California Division of Highways. Sept., 1967. "Report of Route Studies Relative to the Freeway Location of Route 276 in Tulare County between 0.6 Mile East of Salt Creek Near Route 198 and Mineral King."

California Office of Planning and Research. May, 1977. "Urban Development Strategy for California," review draft. Sacramento: Governor's Office.

California Resources Agency. Jan. 5, 1979. "News Release."

Cameron, J. 1928. *The Development of Governmental Forestry in the United States.* Baltimore: Johns Hopkins University Press.

Chandler, Alfred D., Jr. 1962. *Strategy and Structure: Chapters in the History of the American Industrial Enterprise.* Cambridge: MIT Press.

Chief of Recreation Division, Forest Service. May 17, 1968. Letter to editor of *Natural History.*

Clarkson Engineering Co. 1967. "Report on the Road to Mineral King in Sequoia National Park, Three Rivers, California 5," commissioned by Park Service.

Cliff, Edward P. Nov. 3, 1952. Assistant chief, Forest Service, office memorandum to Region 5 (San Francisco).

_____. Jan. 19, 1953. Assistant chief, Forest Service, office memorandum to Region 5 (San Francisco).

_____. July 27, 1965. Chief, Forest Service, letter to Thomas H. Kuchel, U.S. Senate.

_____. Oct. 7, 1965. Chief, Forest Service, office memorandum to Secretary Orville L. Freeman.

_____. Oct. 29, 1965. Chief, Forest Service, letter to Charles S. Gubser, U.S. House of Representatives.

_____. Nov. 9, 1965. Chief, Forest Service, letter to Tobert L. Leggett, U.S. House of Representatives.

_____. Nov. 12, 1965. Chief, Forest Service, letter to James Murphy.

_____. Jan. 6, 1967. Chief, Forest Service, letter to George Hartzog, director, Park Service.

Coase, R. H. 1960. "The Problem of Social Cost." *Journal of Law and Economics* 3 (Oct.): 1–82.

Coastal Zone Management Act. Oct. 27, 1972. Public Law 92–583, 92d Congress, S. 3507.

Comey, David Dinsmore. 1974. "Will Idle Capacity Kill Nuclear Power?" *Bulletin of the Atomic Scientists* 30, no. 9 (Nov.): 23–28.

Committee for Economic Development. 1966. *Modernizing Local Government.* New York.

Connaughton, Charles A. July 1, 1965. Regional forester, letter to William E. Siri, Sierra Club.

Connell, Joseph H. Nov. 10, 1974. Chairman, marine review committee, semiannual report to coastal commission.

Construction Industry Association of Sonoma County v. The City of Petaluma. Aug. 13, 1975. No. 74–2100, "Opinion," U.S. Court of Appeals, Ninth Circuit.

Cramton, Roger C., and Barry B. Boyer. 1972. "Citizens Suits in the Environmental Field: Peril or Promise?" *Ecology Law Quarterly* 2, no. 3 (Summer): 407–29.

Crandall, Thomas A. July 16, 1973. Staff director, San Diego Coast Regional Commission, memorandum to "all Commissioners."

_____. 1975. Executive director, San Diego Coast Regional Commission, interview in Stanley Scott, *Governing California's Coast*. Berkeley: Institute of Governmental Studies, University of California, p. 203.

Croly, Herbert. 1909. *The Promise of American Life*. New York: Macmillan.

Cutler, M. Rupert. Jan. 26, 1978. Assistant Secretary for Conservation, Research and Education, U.S. Department of Agriculture, "Statement before the Subcommittee on National Parks and Insular Affairs, House of Representatives, Relating to H.R. 1771 and H.R. 1772."

Dales, J. H. 1968. *Pollution, Property and Prices*. Toronto: University of Toronto Press.

Davis, W. S. July 8, 1960. Chief, Division of Recreation (San Francisco), office memorandum to "Files."

———. July 11, 1960. Chief of Recreation (San Francisco), letter to Willy J. Schaeffler, Disney Ski Associates.

———. Dec. 8, 1964. Assistant regional forester, office memorandum to forest supervisor, Sequoia National Forest.

———. Feb. 5, 1965. Assistant regional forester, letter to Edward A. Hummel, regional director, Park Service (San Francisco).

———. Apr. 1, 1965. Assistant regional forester (San Francisco), letter to David D. Ward.

———. June 1, 1965. Assistant regional forester (San Francisco), letter to Peter and Carolyn Jensen.

———. Aug. 24, 1965. Assistant regional forester, office memorandum to Richard J. Costley, acting director, Recreation and Land Uses (Washington, D.C.).

———. Sept. 20, 1965. Assistant regional forester, letter to Mrs. C. E. Pennebaker.

———. Oct. 26, 1965. Assistant regional forester (San Francisco), letter to Mrs. W. V. Graham Matthews.

———. Nov. 21, 1972. Division of Recreation (San Francisco), letter to Nelson J. Tyberghein.

———. June 8, 1973. Division of Recreation (San Francisco), office memorandum to "File."

Day, Richard H., and Evan F. Koenig. 1975. "On Some Models of World Cataclysm." *Land Economics* 51 no. 1 (Feb.): 1–20.

Deinema, J. W. Mar. 22, 1968. Regional forester (San Francisco), letter to J. A. Legana, state highway engineer.

———. Aug. 15, 1969. Regional forester (San Francisco), letter to Phillip Berry, president, Sierra Club.

———. Oct., 1969. Regional forester (San Francisco), interview in Russ Leadabrand, "Mineral King: Go or No Go?" *American Forests* 75, no. 10: 35–49.

Delafons, John. 1969. *Land Use Controls in the United States*. Cambridge: MIT Press.

Dewey, John. 1927. *The Public and Its Problems*. New York: Henry Holt.

Doctor, Ronald D. Feb. 16, 1973. Rand Corporation, "Consequences of the Present Policy of Demand Association: A Statement before the California Assembly Subcommittee on State Electrical Energy Policy."

Dolgin, Erica L., and Thomas G. P. Guilbert (eds.). 1974. *Federal Environmental Law*. St. Paul: West Publishing Co.

Douglas, Peter. 1973. "Coastal Zone Management: A New Approach in California." *Coastal Zone Management Journal* 1, no. 1 (Fall): 1–25.

Doyle, W. K. 1939. *Independent Commissions in the Federal Government*. Chapel Hill: University of North Carolina Press.

Durick, Michael D. Dec. 26, 1973. San Diego Building Contractors Association, letter to Melvin B. Lane, California Coastal Zone Conservation Commission.

Durning, Marvin B. Mar. 25, 1970. Attorney for COHOE, letter to Bert L. Cole, Department of Natural Resources.

Economic Research Service. 1971. "Farm Real Estate Transfers: Average Value for an Acre by Potential Use after Sale, March 1, 1970."

Edel, Mathew, and Jerome Rothenberg (eds.). 1972. *Readings in Urban Economics*. New York: Macmillan.

Eder, Billie. July 29, 1971. Vice-chairman, Kitsap County Planning Commission, interview granted to Mitchell Moss.

EDF v. Corps of Engineers. 1972. 342F. Supp. 1211, 1217, 4ERC 1097, 1101 (E.D., Ark.).

Ehrlich, Paul R., and Anne H. Ehrlich. 1970. *Population, Resources and Environment*. San Francisco: W. H. Freeman.

Elazar, Daniel J. 1971. "Community Self-Government and the Crisis of American Politics." *Ethics* 81: 91–106.

_____. 1974. "Cursed by Bigness or toward a Post-Technocratic Federalism." In Daniel J. Elazar (ed.), *The Federal Polity*. New Brunswick, N.J.: Transaction Books, pp. 239–98.

Elliott, J. E. Nov. 13, 1945. Forest supervisor, office memorandum to E. B. Morse, assistant regional forester.

Elsner, G. H. 1972. *Application of Travel Research Techniques to Ski Area Planning*. Berkeley: USDA Forest Service Experiment Station.

Ferguson, Arthur B., Jr., and William P. Bryson. 1972. "Mineral King: A Case Study in Forest Service Decision Making." *Ecology Law Quarterly* 2, no. 3 (Summer): 493–531.

Fery, John B. May 18, 1970. Executive vice-president, Boise Cascade, "The Social Responsibilities of Business," address delivered before Yakima Chamber of Commerce, Yakima, Wash.

Fischer, Michael L. Nov. 9, 1979. Executive director, California coastal commission, memorandum on "Staff Recommendation on Radiological Discharge Monitoring and Conditions to be Added to Permit A 183–73 for the San Onofre Nuclear Power Plant," with appendices.

Fogarty, David J. Feb. 5, 1974. Vice-president, SCE, letter to Joseph E. Bodovitz, director, California Coastal Zone Conservation Commission.

Follett, M. P. 1924. *Creative Experience*. New York: Longmans, Green and Co.

Forbes 1973. SDG&E advertisement: "This is not just another pretty coupon because San Diego's more than just another pretty place." 112, no. 6 (Sept. 15): 19.

Forest Service n.d. *Forest Service Manual*.

_____. 1911. *The National Forest Manual*.

_____. Sept. 29, 1949. "Big Development Proposed for Mineral King Ski Area," news release.

_____. Dec., 1952. "Draft Prospectus for a Proposed Resort and Ski Development at Mineral King" (not issued).

_____. Feb., 1965. "Prospectus for a Proposed Recreational Development at Mineral King in the Sequoia National Forest."

_____. Jan. 27, 1969. "Mineral King Project Master Plan Approved," news release.

_____. Feb., 1969. "Mineral King: A Planned Recreation Development."

_____. Dec., 1974. *Draft Environmental Statement: Mineral King Recreation*

Development, USDA–FS–R5–DES (Adm)–75–02 (San Francisco).

———. Aug. 28, 1975. "For Immediate Release: Public Comments Lead to Revised Mineral King Development."

Fortune. 1971. "The Fortune Directory of the 500 Largest Industrial Corporations." 83, no. 5 (May).

Fox, G. K. Oct. 17, 1952. District ranger, Tule River, office memorandum to Sequoia forest supervisor.

Frautschy, Jeffrey D. Jan. 28, 1975. Member, San Diego Coast Regional Commission and California Coastal Zone Conservation Commission, interview granted to Ms. Pat Vance, research aide for author.

Freeman, Orville, Dec. 16, 1965. Secretary of Agriculture, letter to Roy O. Disney, president, Walt Disney Productions.

———. Aug. 30, 1967. Secretary of Agriculture, letter to Stewart L. Udall, Secretary of Interior.

Fresno Bee. July 30, 1953. "Mineral King Can Provide Parking for 2,000 Cars."

Friedmann, John, and John Miller. 1965. "The Urban Field." *Journal of the American Institute of Planners* 31, no. 4 (Nov.): 312–20.

Gamman, John K., Shavaun Towers, and Jens Sorensen. 1975. *State Involvement in the California Coastal Zone: A Topical Index to Agency Responsibility*. Sea Grant Publication No. 44. Berkeley: Institute of Urban and Regional Development. University of California.

Gardiner, Arthur P. Mar. 31, 1970. HCEC, letter to Kitsap County Planning Commission.

Gerth, H. H., and C. Wright Mills. (eds.). 1946. *From Max Weber: Essays in Sociology*. New York: Oxford University Press.

Gibson, James N. Oct. 1, 1945. Forester, office memorandum to C. B. Morse, assistant regional forester.

———. Aug. 29, 1949. Forest supervisor, letter to Lester Jay, publisher of *The Skier*.

Glaab, Charles N., and A. Theodore Brown. 1967. *A History of Urban America*. New York: Macmillan.

Golembiewski, Robert T. 1977. "A Critique of 'Democratic Administration' and Its Supporting Ideation." *American Political Science Review* 71, no. 4 (Dec.): 1488–1507.

Goodnow, Frank J. 1900. *Politics and Administration*. New York: Macmillan.

Gudde, Erwin G. 1969. *California Place Names*. Berkeley: University of California Press.

Gulick, Luther, and L. Urwick. (eds.). 1937. *Papers on the Science of Administration*. New York: Public Administration Institute.

Haefele, Edwin T. 1973. *Representative Government and Environmental Management*. Baltimore: Johns Hopkins University Press.

Hall, A. E., Jr. Jan. 6, 1967. Range and Wildlife Management (San Francisco), interoffice memorandum to Recreation.

Hamilton, Alexander, James Madison, and John Jay. 1961. *The Federalist Papers*. New York: New American Library.

Hanford, Chester. 1926. *Problems in Municipal Government*. Chicago: A. W. Shaw.

Hano, Arnold. 1969. "The Battle of Mineral King." *New York Times Magazine*, Aug. 17.

Hardin, Garrett, and John Baden. 1977. *Managing the Commons*. San Francisco: W. H. Freeman.

Harper, John L. Jan. 12, 1965. Kern-Kaweah Chapter, Sierra Club, letter to L. M. Whitfield, Sequoia National Forest.

Harstad and Associates. June, 1969. "Kitsap County Comprehensive Plan: Central Study Area."

Hart, Chet. Nov. 27, 1968. Department of Fish and Game, letter to B. K. Jones.

Hartesveldt, Richard J. Dec., 1966. "Study of the Possible Changes in the Ecology of Sequoia Groves in Sequoia National Park to Be Crossed by the New Mineral King Highway," commissioned by California Division of Highways.

Hartz, Louis. 1955. *The Liberal Tradition in America*. New York: Harcourt Brace.

Hasher, Ludvig J., and James N. Gibson. July, 1948. "Mineral King, Sequoia National Forest Winter Survey, 1947-1948," USDA Forest Service.

Haskell, Elizabeth H., and Victoria S. Price. 1973. *State Environmental Management*. New York: Praeger.

Hays, Samuel P. 1958. "The Mythology of Conservation." In Henry Jarrett (ed.), *Perspectives on Conservation*. Baltimore: Johns Hopkins University Press.

———. 1970. "Conservation and the Structure of American Politics: The Progressive Era." In Allan G. Bogue, Thomas D. Phillips, and James E. Wright (eds.), *The West of the American People*. New York: Peacock Publishers.

Healy, Robert G. 1976. *Land Use and the States*. Baltimore: Johns Hopkins University Press.

Heller, Alfred (ed.). 1971. *The California Tomorrow Plan*. Los Altos, Calif.: William Kaufman, Inc.

Heller, Walter W. Apr. 27, 1970. Professor, University of Minnesota, letter to Kitsap County Planning Commission.

Herring, Pendleton, 1940. *The Politics of Democracy*. New York: Rinehart.

Hicks, Robert B. June 18, 1966. Mineral King project manager, Walt Disney Productions, interoffice memorandum to "All Concerned."

———. Feb. 27, 1967. Disney project manager, letter to Peter Wychoff, forest supervisor, Sequoia National Forest.

———. 1969. "The Disney Position." *Natural History* 78 (Jan.): 68-72.

———. Apr. 26, 1969. Disney project manager, statement reported in *Fresno Bee*.

———. Aug. 17, 1969. Project manager, Walt Disney Productions, interview in Arnold Hano, "The Battle of Mineral King," *New York Times Magazine*, p. 56.

Hidy, Ralph W., Frank Ernest Hill, and Allan Nevins. 1963. *Timber and Men: The Weyerhaeuser Story*. New York: Macmillan.

Hill, Cortlandt T. Nov. 10, 1947. Letter and memorandum of master plan for Mineral King, to Paul Statham, forest supervisor, Sequoia National Forest.

Hillman, Donald M. Oct. 8, 1968. Tulare County Board of Supervisors, letter to James A. Moe, Department of Public Works, State of California.

Hofstadter, Richard. 1955. *The Age of Reform*. New York: Vintage Books.

Holum, Kenneth. Apr. 18, 1967. Acting Secretary of Interior, letter to Donald Tatum, Walt Disney Productions.

Hood Canal Environmental Council (HCEC). Summer, 1970. "Status Report."

———. Oct. 30, 1970. "Position Paper."

———. Feb., 1971. "Newsletter."

Hoover, Edgar M. 1948. *The Location of Economic Activity*. New York: McGraw-Hill.

Hope, Jack. 1968. "The King Besieged." *Natural History* 77 (Nov.): 52–82.

Horton, Jack K. Dec. 6, 1973. Chairman of the Board, SCE, letter to California Assemblyman Alan Sieroty.

Howard, Ebenezer. 1902. *Garden Cities of Tomorrow.* London: Faber and Faber.

Huey, James H. June 25, 1970. Central Kitsap School District, letter to Robert E. Mitchell.

Hughes, Phillip S. June 22, 1967. Deputy director, Bureau of the Budget, letter to Governor Ronald Reagan.

Hummel, Edward A. Mar. 3, 1965. Regional director, Park Service (San Francisco), letter to W. S. Davis, assistant regional forester.

———. Nov. 14, 1968. Associate director, Park Service, letter to Edward P. Cliff, chief, Forest Service.

Ise, John. 1920. *The United States Forest Policy.* New Haven, Conn.: Yale University Press.

Jacobs, Jane. 1961. *The Death and Life of Great American Cities.* New York: Random House.

Jefferson, Thomas. 1964. *Notes on the State of Virginia.* New York: Harper and Row.

Jensen, Albert C. 1970. "Thermal Pollution in the Marine Environment." *New York State Conservationist* 10, no. 4 (Oct.-Nov.): 13–22.

Kafoglis, Madelyn L. 1968. "Participatory Democracy in the Community Action Program." *Public Choice* 5 (Fall): 73–85.

Kartalia, David E. Nov. 13, 1975. Nuclear Regulatory Commission, "NRC Staff's Memorandum Evaluating the Applicants' Revised Exclusion Area," Docket Nos. 50–361, 50–362.

Kauffman, Donald E. Jan. 23, 1970. Department of Fisheries, letter to Jack Allison, environmentalist.

Kaufman, Herbert. 1967. *The Forest Ranger.* Baltimore: Johns Hopkins University Press.

Keen, Elmer. July, 1973. Member, San Diego Coast Regional Commission, quoted in Harold Keen, "Is the Coast Clear? No," *San Diego Magazine* 25, no. 9: 64.

———. Nov., 1974. Member, San Diego Coast Regional Commission, interview granted to Ms. Pat Vance, Research aide for author.

Kirby, L. 1973. "History of Mineral King." In Environmental Studies Group, *Mineral King.* Santa Barbara: University of California, Santa Barbara.

Kitsap County. June, 1969. "Zoning Ordinances for Kitsap County, Washington."

———. Sept. 30, 1969. "Planning Policies: Outline for the Future Growth of Kitsap County."

Kitsap County Commission. Sept. 9, 1970. "Public Hearing on Application from Boise Cascade Properties, Inc., for a Rezone and Planned Unit Development," Port Orchard, Wash.

———. Sept. 9, 1970. "Public Hearing on Application from Boise Cascade Properties, Inc., for a Rezone and Planned Unit Development," Port Orchard, Wash. (evening session).

———. Oct. 29, 1970. "Public Hearing on Application from Boise Cascade Properties, Inc., for a Rezone and Planned Unit Development," Port Orchard, Wash.

———. Oct. 29, 1970. "Public Hearing on Application from Boise Cascade Properties, Inc., for a Rezone and Planned Unit Development," Port Orchard, Wash. (evening session).

_____. Jan. 5, 1971. "Decision Regarding Boise Cascade Recreation Communities, Inc., Application," Port Orchard, Wash.

Kitsap County Planning Commission. Mar. 31, 1970. "Public Hearing on Boise Cascade's Nettleton Lakes on the Canal Planned Unit Development," Port Orchard, Wash.

_____. Apr. 28, 1970. "Public Hearing on Boise Cascade's Nettleton Lakes on the Canal Planned Unit Development," Port Orchard, Wash.

_____. July 28, 1970. "Minutes."

Kitsap County Planning Department. Feb. 15, 1972. Letter to J. C. Egman, research assistant.

Knight, T. F., Jr. Mar. 25, 1965. Executive vice-president, California Manufacturers Association, letter to David D. Ward, General Motors Corporation.

Krislov, Samuel. 1965. *The Supreme Court in the Political Process.* New York: Macmillan.

Kronberger, William, Jr. Mar. 13, 1974. General counsel for the San Diego Building Contractors Association, interview in "Coast Initiative: Tide of Opinion Still Out," *San Diego Evening Tribune.*

Lamb, Alan J. Feb. 2, 1976. Director, Recreation staff (San Francisco), letter to author.

Lane, Melvin B. Jan. 4, 1974. Chairman, California Coastal Zone Conservation Commission, letter to Clayton H. Brace, general manager, KGTV-10 (San Diego).

_____. May 15, 1974. Chairman, California Coastal Zone Conservation Commission, interview granted to Ms. Pat Vance, research aide for author.

Lane, Wallace. May 26, 1970. Director, state Department of Health, letter with multiple carbon copies to Kitsap County Planning Commission.

Latham, Earl. 1952. *The Groups Basis of Politics: A Study in Basing Point Legislation.* Ithaca, N.Y.: Cornell University Press.

Lawrence, F. G. Aug. 13, 1947. Chairman, Mineral King Committee, letter to M. M. Barnum, assistant regional forester (San Francisco).

Leisz, Douglas R. (Nov. 7, 1972. Regional forester (San Francisco), letter to Jerome R. Waldie.

Lewis, D. J. July 15, 1947. Acting forest supervisor, Sequoia National Forest, office memorandum to regional forester.

Lindblom, Charles E. 1965. *The Intelligence of Democracy.* New York: Free Press.

Lobe, Gene, Frank Randall, and Bill Mahan. July 6, 1971. Interview granted to Mitchell Moss.

London Times Literary Supplement. Sept. 14, 1973. "To Grow or Not to Grow?" no. 3, 732.

Los Angeles Times. Nov. 22, 1973. "Southland A-Plant Damaged, Closed," p. 1.

_____. Nov. 26, 1973. "No Excuse for San Onofre Coverup," pt. II.

_____. Dec. 7, 1973. "Compromise Sought on Expansion of A-Plant," pp. 3, 26.

_____. Jan. 10, 1974. "Coastal Commission to Reconsider A-Plant Expansion," p. 1.

_____. Feb. 21, 1974. "Coastline Board Approves Atom Plant Expansion," pt. I, p. 1.

_____. Mar. 13, 1974. Editorial cartoon.

_____. Mar. 14, 1974. "Edison Holding up on Power Plant Expansion," pt. I, p. 3.

———. Apr. 18, 1974. "Coast Panel Members' Private Talks Banned," pt. II, p. 4.

———. July 22, 1975. "Disney Focuses on Independence Lake," pt. II, pp. 1, 3.

Lowi, Theodore J. 1969. *The End of Liberalism*. New York: W. W. Norton.

Lundin, Rodney P. Mar. 18, 1970. Vice-president, Koebig & Koebig, letter to R. L. Healy, Boise Cascade Properties.

———. Mar. 30, 1970. Vice-president, Koebig & Koebig, letter to R. L. Healy, Boise Cascade Properties.

Luce, Charles F. July 13, 1967. Assistant Secretary of Interior, letter to Gilbert R. Swift, president, Tulare County Chamber of Commerce.

Madison, James. 1969. *Notes on the Debates of the Federal Convention of 1887*. New York: W. W. Norton.

Mandelker, Daniel R. 1971. *The Zoning Dilemma: A Legal Strategy for Urban Change*. Indianapolis: Bobbs-Merrill.

Marini, Frank (ed.). *Toward a New Public Administration: The Minowbrook Perspective*. Scranton, Pa.: Chandler Publishing.

Masley, Arpad. Aug. 3, 1971. Chairman, Hood Canal Advisory Council, interview granted to Mitchell Moss.

Maxey, Chester C. 1922. "The Political Integration of Metropolitan Communities." *National Municipal Review* 11 (Aug.): 229–53.

———. 1929. *Urban Democracy*. Boston: D. C. Heath.

Mayer, Marshall S. Mar. 20, 1970. California deputy attorney general, letter to Arpad L. Masley, Hood Canal Advisory Council.

McAllister, Donald (ed.). 1973. *Environment: A New Focus on Land Use Planning*. Washington, D.C.: NSF/Government Printing Office.

McArdle, Richard E. Jan. 19, 1953. Chief, Forest Service, office memorandum and position paper on alternative development options, to Region 5 (San Francisco).

McCloskey, Michael. Aug. 7, 1965. Sierra Club, letter to Edward Cliff, chief, Forest Service.

———. May 8, 1967. Sierra Club, "Why the Sierra Club Opposes Disney's Development of Mineral King."

———. Oct., 1969. Statement in "Mineral King: Go or No Go?" *American Forests* 75, no. 10: 44–46.

———. Mar. 31, 1975. Sierra Club, letter to Douglas R. Leisz, regional forester, Region 5.

McCloskey, Michael, and Albert Hill. Jan., 1971. "Mineral King: Mass Recreation versus Park Protection in the Sierra," Sierra Club reprint.

McCombs, C. E. 1924. "State Welfare Administration and Consolidated Government." *National Municipal Review*, Supplement, 13: 461–73.

McConnell, Grant. 1959. "The Multiple-Use Concept in Forest Service Policy." *Sierra Club Bulletin* 44, no. 7 (Oct.): 14–28.

———. 1966. *Private Power and American Democracy*. New York: Vintage Books.

———. Aug. 12, 1978. Professor of politics, University of California at Santa Cruz, private correspondence with author.

McConnell, R. E. Apr. 27, 1930. District engineer, U.S. Corps of Engineers, letter to Peter Pitell, COHOE.

McNutt, Jack J. Aug. 27, 1952. Forest supervisor, Sequoia National Forest, office memorandum to regional forester, San Francisco.

Meadows, Donella H., *et al.* 1972. *The Limits to Growth*. New York: Universe Books.

Merry, Kenneth J. June 24, 1970. State Department of Health, letter to Harstad and Associates.

Metzger, H. Peter. 1972. *The Atomic Establishment.* New York: Simon and Schuster.

Meyerson, Martin. 1954. "Research and City Planning." *Journal of the American Institute of Planners* 20, no. 4 (Aug.): 201–5.

Miller, Robert H., and Hugh W. Frank. Oct. 15, 1952. "Special Use Application," USDA Forest Service.

Mineral King Task Force. June, 1974. "Mineral King: Disney–Forest Service Proposal Background and Analysis."

Mitchell, Robert E. June 11, 1970. Kitsap County planning director, letter to Kitsap County Sheriff's Department.

———. June 15, 1970. Kitsap County planning director, letter to Dave Carey, Boise Cascade.

———. July 2, 1971. Kitsap County planning director, interview granted to Mitchell Moss.

Montgomery, C. P. Apr. 10, 1967. Director, Park Service, letter to Michael McCloskey, Sierra Club.

Morigeau, Gary. Mar. 31, 1970. Letter to Arpad L. Masley, chairman, Hood Canal Advisory Council.

Morken, Arthur N. June 26, 1970. Kitsap County sheriff, letter to Robert E. Mitchell, Kitsap County planning director.

Morrissey, Fred P. 1972. "Counterpoint." In SDG&E, *Annual Report,* pp. 19–20.

Morse, True D. Aug. 5, 1955. Acting Secretary of Agriculture, letter to chairman of Senate Committee on Agriculture and Forestry.

Multiple Use Act. June 12, 1960. Public Law 86–517, Sections 1 and 2, 74 Stat. 215. 16 U.S.C., Sections 528, 529.

National Commission on Urban Problems. 1968. *Building the American City* [Douglas Report]. Washington, D.C.: Government Printing Office.

Newsweek. Mar. 13, 1972. "Companies: Idaho's Cold Potato," pp. 80, 82.

New York Times. Feb. 2, 1969. "Editorial: Mineral King Folly."

Nienaber, Jeanne. 1972. "The Supreme Court and Mickey Mouse."*American Forests* (July): 29–43.

———. "Mineral King: Ideological Battleground for Land Use Disputes." Ph.D. dissertation, University of California, Berkeley.

Nisbet, Robert A. 1966. *The Sociological Tradition.* New York: Basic Books.

Norris, Norman L. Feb. 2, 1945. Forest supervisor, letter to Major Robert S. Wade.

———. May 8, 1965. Forest supervisor, Sequoia National Forest, letter to William R. Bergren.

Office of the Federal Register. 1969. *United States Government Organization Manual.* Washington, D.C.: Government Printing Office.

Olson, Mancur, Jr. 1968. *The Logic of Collective Action.* New York: Schocken Books.

Orleans, Peter. 1973. "Differential Cognition of Urban Residents." In Roger Downs and David Stea (eds.), *Image and Environment.* Chicago: Aldine Publishing.

Osenbaugh, Roger T. Apr. 6–7, 1976. Member, California Coastal Zone Conservation Commission, comments reported in state commission minutes.

Ostrom, Vincent. 1971. *The Political Theory of a Compound Republic.* Blacksburg, Va.: Public Choice, VPI, and SU.

———. 1973. *The Intellectual Crisis in American Public Administration.*

University: University of Alabama Press.

Ostrom, Vincent, Charles M. Tiebout, and Robert Warren. 1961. "The Organization of Government in Metropolitan Areas: A Theoretical Inquiry." *American Political Science Review*. 55, no. 4 (Dec.): 831–42.

Padover, Saul K. (ed.). 1953. *The Complete Madison, His Basic Writings*. New York: Harper & Bros.

Parkinson, Ariel. Dec. 29, 1970. HCEC, letter to William Mahan, Kitsap County Board of Commissioners.

Park Service, Nov. 21, 1966. "Official Report of Proceedings before the National Park Service: Proposed Establishment of Wilderness, Sequoia and Kings Canyon National Parks."

———. Jan., 1967. "The Mineral King Area as Related to Sequoia National Park," position paper.

———. 1971. "Sequoia and Kings Canyon National Parks, California, Communication from the President of the United States Transmitting Fourteen Proposals to Add to the National Wilderness System."

Paulson, Dennis R. May 4, 1970. Zoologist, University of Washington, letter to Mrs. Billie Eder, Kitsap County Planning Commission.

The People's Lobby v. SCE and SCG&E. May 2, 1973. "Reporter's Transcript before the Public Utilities Commission, Case No. 9291" (San Onofre Unit One), Los Angeles.

Pfiffner, J. M. 1935. *Public Administration*. New York: Ronald Press.

Pilkey, W. B. Sept., 1970. Washington State Research Council, "Kitsap County Tax Collections and Expenditures Resulting from the Nettleton Project: 1971–1990."

Pinchot, Gifford. 1910. *The Fight for Conservation*. New York: Doubleday Page.

———. 1947. *Breaking New Ground*. New York: Harcourt Brace Jovanovich.

Pitell, Peter. July 6, 1971. COHOE, interview granted to Mitchell Moss.

Porter, David O., and Eugene A. Olsen. 1976. "Some Critical Issues in Government Centralization and Decentralization." *Public Administration Review* 36, no. 1 (Jan.): 72–84.

Power Companies. 1973. Advertisement: "Radioactivity. It's been in the family for generations," reprinted in Environmental Alert Group, "The Clear and Present Danger: A Public Report on Nuclear Power Plants."

Prisbylla, Raymond A. 1977. *"The Impact of Organization Structure on Land Use Decisions."* Master's thesis, San Diego State University.

Puget Sound Task Force of Pacific Northwest River Basins Commission. Nov., 1968. *Pleasure Boating Study*. Olympia, Wash.: State Parks and Recreation Commission.

Radoumis, J. M. Feb. 11, 1953. Kern County Board of Trade, letter to R. E. McArdle, chief, Forest Service.

Rainwater, Harold G. Feb. 18, 1953. Tulare County Chamber of Commerce, letter to R. E. McArdle, chief, Forest Service.

Rawls, John. 1971. *A Theory of Justice*. Cambridge, Mass.: Harvard University Press.

Ray, Dixie Lee. Feb. 17, 1970. Letter to Bert Cole, Washington State Commissioner of Public Lands.

Reed, Henry E. 1921. "County Government in Oregon: A Growing Problem." *National Municipal Review* 10 (Feb.): 35–43.

Reilly, William K. (ed.). 1973. *The Use of Land: A Citizen's Policy Guide to Urban Growth*. New York: Thomas Y. Crowell.

Rettenmayer, John W. 1969. "Letter to the Editor on Mineral King." *Natural History* 78 (Jan.): 68.

Rosenberg, William S. Feb. 9, 1953. Three Rivers Chamber of Commerce, letter to R. E. McArdle, chief, Forest Service.

Rule, James B. 1978. *Insight and Social Betterment*. New York: Oxford University Press.

Rupp, Craig W. 1974. "Objectives and Goals." Paper presented at the Forest Service Environmental Quality Training Session, Denver, Colo., May 13.

Rutgers Law Review, Notes. 1970. "Mineral King Valley: Who Shall Watch the Watchmen?" 25, no. 1 (Fall): 103–44.

Rylander, Dick. Aug. 2, 1971. Chairman, Kitsap County Planning Commission, interview granted to Mitchell Moss.

Sabatier, Paul. 1975. "The Use of Technical Information in Land Development Review: California Coastal Zone Conservation Commissions." Paper delivered at American Political Science Association Annual Meeting, Sept. 2–5.

San Diego Coast Regional Commission. Aug. 10, 1973. "Reporter's Transcript of Public Hearing on Application No. 670" (San Onofre), at San Diego.

_____. Sept. 4, 1973. "Staff Recommendation," Control No. F0670 (San Onofre).

San Diego Gas and Electric (SDG&E). 1972. *Annual Report*.

_____. Dec. 4, 1973. "Prospectus: 2,000,000 Shares Common Stocks."

_____. 1974. *Annual Report*.

_____. N.d. "Nuclear Power Today and Tomorrow."

San Diego Tribune. Dec. 7, 1973. "Power-plant Rejection Draws AEC's Ire," p. B–1.

San Diego Union. Sept. 8, 1973. "More San Onofre A-Power Units OKd," p. B–1.

_____. Dec. 3, 1973. "Utility Plans San Onofre Fight," p. B–1.

_____. Dec. 4, 1973. "Nuclear Plant Is Essential."

_____. Dec. 5, 1973. "Stress Put on San Onofre Oil Savings."

_____. Dec. 6, 1973. "San Onofre Atom Plant Expansion Rejected by Coastline Commission," pp. B–1, 16.

_____. Dec. 20, 1973. "A-Plant Proposal Review Rejected."

_____. Jan. 23, 1974. "Nuclear Plant OK Predicted," p. B–2.

_____. Feb. 20, 1974. "Editorial: San Onofre Lesson," p. B–10.

_____. Feb. 21, 1974. "Nuclear Plant Expansion Authorized."

Schmidt, Stuart M., and Thomas A. Kochan. 1977. "Interorganizational Relationships: Patterns and Motivations." *Administrative Science Quarterly* 22: 220–34.

Scott, Mel. 1969. *American City Planning*. Berkeley: University of California Press.

Scott, Stanley. 1975. *Governing California's Coast*. Berkeley: Institute of Governmental Studies.

Scott, William G., and David K. Hart. 1979. *Organizational America*. Boston: Houghton Mifflin.

Selznick, Philip. 1949. *TVA and the Grass Roots*. Berkeley: University of California Press.

Sieker, John. Oct. 3, 1947. Chief, Division of Recreation and Lands (Washington, D.C.) office memorandum to Region 5 (San Francisco).

_____. Oct. 3, 1947. Chief, Division of Recreation and Lands (Washington, D.C.), office memorandum to Region 5 (San Francisco).

———. Jan. 8, 1948. Chief, Division of Recreation and Lands (Washington, D.C.), office memorandum to "the Record."

———. Mar. 31, 1959. Director of Recreation and Land Uses, letter to Hans R. Gramiger.

Sierra Club. 1969. "Mineral King at the Crossroads." *Outdoor Newsletter* 5, no. 1 (June).

———. May 3, 1972. "For Immediate Release: Sierra Club Will Still Oppose Mineral King Development."

———. Jan., 1974. "Newsletter."

Sierra Club Bulletin. 1974. "Southern California: Act Now for Mineral King." 59, no. 4 (Apr.).

Sierra Club v. Hickel. Aug. 4, 1969. "Memorandum of Decision," U.S. District Court (San Francisco), Case No. 24966 (unreported).

Sierra Club v. Morton, Apr. 19, 1972. No. 70–34, Supreme Court of the United States (ZELR 20192-20201).

Simon, Herbert. 1957. *Administrative Behavior.* 2d ed. New York: Macmillan.

Siri, William E. June 7, 1965. President, Sierra Club, letter to Charles Connaughton, regional forester, Forest Service.

Slavin, Richard H. May 20, 1970. Director, Washington State Planning and Community Affairs Agency, letter to Richard Rylander, Kitsap County Planning Commission.

———. Mar. 10, 1971. Director, Washington State Planning and Community Affairs Agency, letter to George Plescher, planning director, Bremerton.

Smith, D. H. 1930. *The Forest Service.* Washington, D.C.: Brookings Institution.

Smith, George A. Mar. 11, 1970. Planning director, Harstad and Associates, letter to Kitsap County Planning Commission.

———. July 6, 1971. Planning director, Harstad and Associates, interview granted to Mitchell Moss.

———. Feb. 23, 1972. Planning director, Harstad and Associates, interview granted to author.

Sorensen, Jens. 1978. *State-Local Collaborative Planning: A Growing Trend in Coastal Zone Management.* Washington, D.C.: Government Printing Office.

Southern California Edison (SCE). 1972. *Annual Report.*

———. Feb., 1972. "Power Crisis: Questions and Answers," pamphlet.

———. June, 1973. "To Help Meet Southern California Power Needs: San Onofre Nuclear Generating Station Units Two and Three," pamphlet.

Stark, Don. July 16, 1974. Environmental attorney, interview granted to Ms. Pat Vance, research aide for author.

Steffens, Lincoln. 1931. *The Autobiography of Lincoln Steffens.* New York: Literary Guild.

Sternberg, Richard W. Feb. 18, 1970. University of Washington, "Statement Concerning the Proposed Development of Anderson Cove," presented at DNR public hearing.

Stone, Christopher D. 1974. *Should Trees Have Standing.* Palo Alto, Calif.: William Kaufmann, Inc.

Tatum, Donn B. Mar. 16, 1967. Vice-president, Walt Disney Productions, letter to Stewart L. Udall, Secretary of Interior.

———. Oct. 9, 1968. Executive vice-president, Walt Disney Productions, letter to James A. Moe, California Transportation Agency.

Taylor, Peter B. Feb. 18, 1970. University of Washington, "Statement Concerning the Development of a Boat Marina in Anderson Cove," presented at DNR public hearing.

Taylor, Ron. 1970. "Subdividing the Wilderness," *McClatchy Newspapers,* Sacramento, Calif.

Teller, Edward. 1967. "Teller Voices Concern about Hazard of Breeder Reactors." *Scientist and Citizen* (June-July).

Thompson, James D. 1967. *Organizations in Action.* New York: McGraw-Hill.

Timms, Duncan. 1971. *The Urban Mosaic.* Cambridge: Cambridge University Press.

Tocqueville, Alexis de. 1956. *Democracy in America.* New York: New American Library.

Tollefson, Thor C. July 7, 1970. *State Department of Fisheries,* letter to Robert E. Mitchell, Kitsap County planning director.

Trackett, M. C. 1937. "The Committee as an Instrument of Coordination in the New Deal." *American Political Science Review* 31 (Apr.): 301–10.

Truman, David. 1951. *The Governmental Process.* New York: Alfred A. Knopf.

Turner, John T. 1970. "The Battle of Anderson Cove." *Seattle Magazine* 7, no. 74 (May).

Udall, Stewart L. Aug. 10, 1967. Secretary of Interior, letter to Orville L. Freeman, Secretary of Agriculture.

University of Washington Magazine. Winter, 1970. "Special Issue on the College of Forest Resources."

U.S. Bureau of the Census. June, 1969. "Second Houses in the United States," Current Housing Report Series H-121, no. 16. Washington, D.C.: Government Printing Office.

———. 1971. "Census of Housing, 1970, Housing Characteristics for States, Cities, and Counties," vol. 1, pt. 49, Washington. Washington, D.C.: Government Printing Office.

———. 1972. *1970 Census of Population: General Population Characteristics, Washington.* Washington, D.C.: Government Printing Office.

U.S. Department of Commerce. 1970. "Number of Inhabitants, U.S. Summary," PC (1)-Al, *U.S. Census of Population.* Washington, D.C.: Government Printing Office.

U.S. Department of Justice. Aug., 1971. "Brief for the Respondent," *Sierra Club v. Morton,* USSC, No. 70–34.

Veblen, Thorsten. 1899. *The Theory of the Leisure Class: An Economic Study of Institutions.* New York: Viking Press.

Vidich, Arthur J., and Joseph Bensman. 1968. *Small Town in Mass Society.* Princeton, N.J.: Princeton University Press.

Visalia Times-Delta. Jan. 11, 1947. "Ski Bowl World's Best," pp. 1, 3.

Von Haden, Lloyd. Oct. 26, 1973. San Onofre opposition member, letter to California Coastal Zone Conservation Commission (San Francisco).

Vose, Clement E. 1966. "Interest Groups, Judicial Review, and Local Government." *Western Political Quarterly* 19, no. 1 (Mar.): 85–100.

Wade, Robert S. Jan., 1945. letter to Norman L. Norris, forest supervisor.

Waldie, Jerome R. Oct. 31, 1972. U.S. congressman, letter to Norman Weeden, Forest Service.

Waldo, Dwight. 1948. *The Administrative State.* New York: Ronald Press.

———. (ed.). 1971. *Public Administration in a Time of Turbulence.* Scranton, Pa.: Chandler Publishing.

Wall Street Journal. Apr. 4, 1974. "Utility Executives Will Learn How to Take on Nuclear Power Plant Opponents," p. 1.

———. Feb. 3, 1975. "New Nuclear Regulating Agency to Face Hard Decisions on Atomic Power Buildup," p. 28.

———. June 7, 1976. "Fuel Shortage Forecast for U.S. Nuclear Plants within Decade or Two," p. 1.

Walsh, Raymond. Nov. 27, 1973. State Water Resources Control Board memorandum to Joseph Bodovitz, California Coastal Zone Conservation Commission.

Walt Disney Productions. 1965. "A Proposal for the Development of Mineral King."

———. 1967. "The Disney Plans for Mineral King."

———. Jan. 8, 1969. "Master Plan Presentation of Walt Disney Productions' Mineral King Project," submitted to Forest Service.

Walters, Emil. Aug. 7, 1947. Quoted in unknown newspaper attached to letter from M. M. Barnum, assistant regional forester, to Fay G. Lawrence.

Walters, Warren. 1974. "Land Use Planning in the National Forest System." Paper presented at Annual Conference of American Institute of Planners, Oct. 27–30.

Ward, J. Harris. Apr. 13, 1974. Director, Commonwealth Edison Co. as quoted in "Environmental Showdown," *New Republic,* p. 5.

Warren, Robert. 1970. "Federal-Local Development Planning: Scale Effects in Representation and Policy Making." *Public Administration Review* 30 (Nov.-Dec.): 584–95.

Warren, Robert, and Louis F. Weschler. 1972. "Governing Urban Space: Non-Territorial Politics." Paper delivered at Annual Meeting of American Political Science Association, Sept. 5–9.

Washington State Laws. Aug. 11, 1969. "Plats and Subdivisions," RCW 58.1, Laws of the First Extraordinary Session, Laws of 1969, Chapter 271.

Watts, Lyle F. Mar. 26, 1948. Chief, Forest Service, letter to Fay G. Lawrence.

———. July 8, 1948. Chief, Forest Service, office memorandum to Region 5 (San Francisco).

Webber, Melvin M. 1963. "Order in Diversity: Community without Propinquity." In Lowdon Wingo, Jr. (ed.), *Cities and Space: The Future of Use of Urban Land.* Baltimore: Johns Hopkins University Press.

Weigel, J. A. Apr. 24, 1970. Kitsap County Health Department, letter to Kitsap County Board of Commissioners.

Weinberg, Albert K. 1935. *Manifest Destiny.* Chicago: Quadrangle.

Wetzel, W. W. Feb. 12, 1953. Regional forester, office memorandum to Edward Cliff, assistant chief, Forest Service.

Whitfield, L. M. Jan. 20, 1965. Forest supervisor, Sequoia National Forest, interoffice memorandum to regional forester (San Francisco).

———. Feb. 15, 1965. Forest supervisor, Sequoia National Forest, letter to John L. Harper, Kern-Kaweah chapter, Sierra Club.

Wiebe, Robert H. 1967. *The Search for Order.* New York: Hill and Wang.

Wildavsky, Aaron. 1967. "The Political Economy of Efficiency." *Public Interest* 8 (Summer): 30–48.

Wilderness Society. Nov. 21, 1966. "Statement by the Wilderness Society in Support of the Establishment of Wilderness Areas within Sequoia and Kings Canyon National Park."

Willoughby, W. F. 1919. *The Government of Modern States.* New York: Appleton-Century.

Wilson, James. Feb. 1, 1905. Secretary of Agriculture, letter to Gifford Pinchot, chief, Forest Service.

Wilson, Woodrow. 1887 and 1941. "The Study of Public Administration." *Political Science Quarterly* 2 (June): 197–222, and 56 (Dec.): 481–506.

_____. 1956. *Congressional Government.* Cleveland: World Publishing.

Winters, John M. 1973. "Environmentally Sensitive Land Use Regulation in California." *San Diego Law Review* 10, no. 4 (June): 693–756.

Womack, J. C. Nov., 1968. California Division of Highways engineer, interview reported in "The King Besieged," *Natural History* 77: 75.

Wright, Joseph (ed.). 1925. *Selected Readings in Municipal Problems.* Boston: Ginn.

Wurster, Catherine Bauer. 1963. "The Form and Structure of the Future Urban Complex." In Lowdon Wingo, Jr. (ed.), *Cities and Space: The Future of Use of Urban Land.* Baltimore: Johns Hopkins University Press.

Wychoff, Peter J. Sept. 11, 1975. Recreation and Lands staff officer, Sequoia National Forest, letter to author.

Yale Law Journal, Comment. 1960. "Taxpayers' Suits: A Survey and a Summary." 69 (Apr.): 895–924.

Younger, Evelle J. Oct. 15, 1973. California attorney general, address before Urban Land Institute, San Francisco.

Zitlau, Walter. Mar. 1974. President, SDG&E, interview in Harold Keen, "Reddy Kilowatt's Finest Hour," *San Diego Magazine* 26, no. 5.

Index

Note on the Author

Herman L. Boschken was born in San Jose, California. He received his B.A. (1967) and M.A. (1968) from the University of California at Berkeley, and his Ph.D. (1972) from the University of Washington. He is presently a visiting professor in the School of Business at the University of California, Berkeley. His previous publications include several journal articles and a book, *Corporate Power and the Mismarketing of Urban Development* (Praeger, 1974).